# Work, Productivity, and Job Satisfaction

## An Evaluation of Policy-Related Research

by
Raymond A. Katzell and Daniel Yankelovich

with
Mitchell Fein, Oscar A. Ornati, and Abraham Nash

and assisted by
Jeffrey A. Berman, Robert A. Deliberto,
Ira J. Morrow and Howard M. Weiss

**THE PSYCHOLOGICAL CORPORATION**
a Subsidiary of
**Harcourt Brace Jovanovich, Inc.**

770033

FINAL REPORT: JANUARY 1975

Supported by a Grant from
Research Applied to National Needs,
Division of Social Systems and Human Resources
National Science Foundation
Washington, D.C. 20550
to
New York University

Grant No. SSH 73-07939 A01

Any opinions, findings, conclusions, or recommendations
expressed herein are those of the authors and do not
necessarily reflect the views of the National Science
Foundation.

ISBN: 0-15-003082-7

Library of Congress Catalog Card Number: 75-21726

# ABSTRACT

This report is a multi-disciplinary evaluation of research dealing with features of work which affect both the productivity and job satisfaction of employees. The emphasis is on recent research which meets relatively high standards of scientific validity.

Although it was found that such research falls short of what is required for firm conclusions, certain convergent findings suggest directions for future policies. These include:

1. Relatively limited programs, such as job enrichment, participation in decision-making, or incentive pay plans, seem unlikely by themselves to create large or enduring improvements in both productivity and job satisfaction; they are better regarded as possible ingredients in redesigned socio-technical systems of work.

2. Socio-technical systems which have the following features seem promising in their ability to improve both productivity and job satisfaction:

a. Financial compensation of workers must be linked to their performance.

b. Workers and work must be matched so as to create a work situation which workers will see as capable of meeting their needs and expectations, and where they will have the capabilities and resources to be successful.

c. For workers who desire it, their work should provide opportunity for full use of their abilities, making a meaningful contribution, having challenging and diversified duties, and being responsible for others.

d. Workers at all levels must have inputs to plans and decisions affecting their jobs and working lives.

e. Appropriate resources, including work methods and equipment, must be provided to facilitate workers' performance and minimize obstacles to carrying out their jobs.

f. Adequate "hygiene" conditions must exist, including competent supervision, fair pay, job security, good working conditions, and sound employee and labor relations.

Regarding implications for implementation:

1. Our survey indicates that managers and union officials alike regard improvements in both productivity and the quality of working life as desirable social goals.

2. Barriers to adoption of needed comprehensive programs along the above lines stem both from knowledge and political considerations.

3. What seems necessary is a coordinated drive by many agencies of society, including government, individual organizations, and research and consulting institutes.

# TABLE OF CONTENTS

**Chapter**                                                        **Page**

Foreword. . . . . . . . . . . . . . . . . . . . . . . . . . . . .     i

Preface . . . . . . . . . . . . . . . . . . . . . . . . . . . . .   viii

### PART ONE:  SUMMARY AND IMPLICATIONS

I      THE NATURE OF THE QUEST . . . . . . . . . . . . . . . . .     3

      Background of the Problem . . . . . . . . . . . . . .     3
      The Known and the Unknown . . . . . . . . . . . . . .     4
      Statement of the Study Objectives . . . . . . . . . .     7
      The Need . . . . . . . . . . . . . . . . . . . . . .     8
      Organization of the Report . . . . . . . . . . . . .    10

II     SUMMARY OF FINDINGS AND CONCLUSIONS. . . . . . . . . . .    11

      Summary of Policy-Makers' Assumptions . . . . . . . .    15
      Research Findings and Conclusions . . . . . . . . . .    23

III    IMPLEMENTATION. . . . . . . . . . . . . . . . . . . . . .    41

      The Need for a Coordinated Approach . . . . . . . . .    42
      The Role of Government. . . . . . . . . . . . . . . .    46
      The Individual Organization . . . . . . . . . . . . .    53
      Free-Standing Institutes. . . . . . . . . . . . . . .    64

### PART TWO:  RESEARCH FINDINGS

IV     MANAGEMENT AND UNION LEADER ASSUMPTIONS . . . . . . . . .    81

      Method. . . . . . . . . . . . . . . . . . . . . . . .    81
      Sample Description. . . . . . . . . . . . . . . . . .    83
      Table IV-1  Sample Description (Management) . . . . .    85
      Table IV-2  Sample Description (Unions) . . . . . . .    87
      Results . . . . . . . . . . . . . . . . . . . . . . .    88
      Conclusions . . . . . . . . . . . . . . . . . . . . .    99
      Table IV-3  Meaning of Productivity . . . . . . . . .   103
      Table IV-4  General Values and Beliefs . . . . . . .   104
      Table IV-5  Factors Influencing an Organization's
                   Productivity Considered to be "Very
                   Important". . . . . . . . . . . . . . . .   109

TABLE OF CONTENTS (cont.)

Chapter                                                          Page

IV.  (cont.)

     Table IV-6   Factors Influencing an Organization's
                  Productivity Considered to be Unimpor-
                  tant........................................ 111
     Table IV-7   Methods of Improving Employee Attitudes
                  and Motivation Considered to be "Very
                  Useful".................................... 113
     Table IV-8   Assumptions About the Relationship
                  Between Job Satisfaction, Worker
                  Motivation and Productivity............... 114
     Table IV-9   Management/Labor Relations as They
                  Bear on Productivity..................... 117

V.   CONCEPTS AND METHODS OF INQUIRY...................... 124

     Major Research Designs............................... 130
     Boundaries of the Sample of Studies................. 131

VI.  JOB DESIGN.......................................... 134

     Theory of Job Design................................ 134
     Studies of Job Design............................... 137
     General Conclusions on Job Design................... 177
     Table VI-1   Correlates and Consequences of Expanded
                  Jobs....................................... 179
     Table VI-2   Summary of Miscellaneous Case Reports.. 187

VII. PATTERNS OF CONTROL................................. 198

     Theory of Organizational Control.................... 200
     Management by Objectives............................ 209
     Work Group Control.................................. 221
     Table VII-1  Correlates and Consequences of
                  Greater Work Group Control............ 234
     Organizational Control Structure.................... 236
     Table VII-2  Correlates and Consequences of
                  Greater Organizational Control
                  by Workers............................... 258
     Table VII-3  AMA Survey of Labor-Management
                  Committees............................. 265
     Table VII-4  Comparison Among Three Swift
                  Plants................................... 278
     Discussion  and Conclusions Regarding Control
     Patterns........................................... 285

# TABLE OF CONTENTS (cont.)

Chapter | Page
--- | ---

VIII. PATTERNS OF COMPENSATION............................. 288

The Psychological Meaning of Money............... 291
Absolute Pay Levels.............................. 295
Relative Pay Levels.............................. 299
Table VIII-1  Laboratory Studies of Relative
              Pay Levels.......................... 304
Pay Increases.................................... 309
Conclusions on Amounts of Pay and Increments..... 313
Pay Plans........................................ 315
Conclusions About Compensation................... 332

IX.   SYSTEM-WIDE STUDIES................................. 335

Weldon Manufacturing Company..................... 336
Table IX-1  Indicators of Organization
            Effectiveness......................... 345
Corning Glass (Medfield, Mass. Plant)............ 350
Scanlon Plan..................................... 355
Conclusions from System-Wide Studies............. 366

References.............................................. 369

Additional Bibliography................................. 387

Glossary................................................ 414

Author Index............................................ 419

Subject Index........................................... 425

# FOREWORD

This evaluation of policy related research on relations among industrial organization, job satisfaction and productivity is one of 20 in a series of projects on the Evaluation of Policy Related Research in the Field of Human Resources, funded by the Division of Social Systems and Human Resources in the Research Applied to National Needs (RANN) Program of the National Science Foundation.

A large body of policy related research on human resources has been created over the last quarter century. However, its usefulness to decision-makers has been limited because it has not been evaluated comprehensively with respect to technical quality, usefulness to policy-makers, and potential for codification and wider diffusion. In addition, this research has been hard to locate and not easily accessible. Therefore, systematic and rigorous evaluations of this research are required to provide syntheses of evaluated information for use by public agencies at all levels of government and to aid in the planning and definition of research programs.

Recognizing these needs, the Division of Social Systems and Human Resources issued a Program Solicitation in January 1973 for proposals to evaluate policy related research in 21 categories in the field of human resources. This competition resulted in 20 awards in June 1973.

ii

Each of the projects was to: 1) Evaluate the internal
validity of each study by determining whether the research
used appropriate methods and data to deal with the questions
asked; 2) Evaluate the external validity of the research by
determining whether the results were credible in the light
of other valid policy related research; 3) Evaluate the
policy utility of specific studies or sets of studies bearing
on given policy instruments; 4) Provide decision-makers,
including research funders, with an assessed research base
for alternative policy actions in a format readily interpret-
able and useable by decision makers.

Each report was to include an analysis of the validity and
utility of research in the field selected, a synthesis of the
evidence, and a discussion of what, if any, additional research
is required.

The following is a list of the awards showing the research
area evaluated, the organization to which the award was made,
and the principal investigator.

(1)  An Evaluation of Policy Related Research on New Expanded
     Roles of Health Workers - Yale University, School of
     Medicine, New Haven, Connecticut  06520; Eva Cohen

(2)  An Evaluation of Policy Related Research on the Effective-
     ness of Alternative Allocation of Health Care Manpower -
     Interstudy, 123 East Grant St., Minneapolis, Minnesota
     55403; Aaron Lowin

(3)  An Evaluation of Policy Related Research on Effects of
     Health Care Regulation - Policy Center, Inc., Suite
     500, 789 Sherman, Denver, Colorado  80203; Patrick
     O'Donoghue

(4)  An Evaluation of Policy Related Research on Trade-
     Offs Between Preventive and Primary Health Care -
     Boston University Medical Center, Boston University
     School of Medicine, Boston, MA  02215; Paul Gertman

(5)  An Evaluation of Policy Related Research on Effective-
     ness of Alternative Programs for the Handicapped -
     Rutgers University, 165 College Avenue, New Brunswick,
     New Jersey 08901; Monroe Berkowitz

(6)  An Evaluation of Policy Related Research on Effects of
     Alternative Health Care Reimbursement Systems - Uni-
     versity of Southern California, Department of
     Economics, Los Angeles, Calif.  90007; Donal E. Yett

(7)  An Evaluation of Policy Related Research on Alternative
     Public and Private Programs for Mid-Life Redirection
     of Careers - Rand Corporation, 1700 Main Street, Santa
     Monica, Calif.  90406; Anthony H. Pascal

(8)  An Evaluation of Policy Related Research on Relations
     between Industrial Organization, Job Satisfaction and
     Productivity, Brandeis University, Florence G. Heller
     Graduate School for Advanced Studies in Social Welfare,
     Waltham, MA  02154; Michael J. Brower

(9)  An Evaluation of Policy Related Research on Relations
     between Industrial Organization, Job Satisfaction and
     Productivity - New York University, Department of
     Psychology, New York, New York 10003; Raymond A.
     Katzell

(10) An Evaluation of Policy Related Research on Productivity,
     Industrial Organization and Job Satisfaction - Case
     Western Reserve University, School of Management,
     Cleveland, Ohio  44106; Suresh Srivastva

(11) An Evaluation of Policy Related Research on Effective-
     ness of Alternative Methods to Reduce Occupational Ill-
     ness and Accidents - Westinghouse Behavioral Safety
     Center, Box 948, American City Bldg., Columbia, Md.
     21044; Michael Pfeifer

(12) An Evaluation of Policy Related Research on the Impact
of Unionization on Public Institutions - Contract
Research Corp., 25 Flanders Road, Belmont, Massachusetts;
Ralph Jones

(13) An Evaluation of Policy Related Research on Projection
of Manpower Requirements - Ohio State University, Center
for Human Resources Research, Columbus, Ohio 43210;
S.C. Kelley

(14) An Evaluation of Policy Related Research on Effectiveness of Alternative Pre-Trial Intervention Programs -
ABT Assoc., Inc., 55 Wheeler St., Cambridge, Massachusetts
02138; Joan Mullen

(15) An Evaluation of Policy Related Research on
the Effectiveness of Pre-Trial Release Programs, National
Center for State Courts, 1660 Lincoln St., Denver,
Colo. 80203; Barry Mahoney

(16) An Evaluation of Policy Related Research on Effective-
ness of Volunteer Programs in the Area of Courts and
Corrections - University of Illinois, Department of
Political Science, Chicago Circle, Box 4348, Chicago,
Ill. 60680; Thomas Cook

(17) An Evaluation of Policy Related Research on Effective-
ness of Juvenile Delinquency Prevention Program - George
Peabody College for Teachers, Department of Psychology,
Nasville, Tenn. 37203; Michael C. Dixon

(18) An Evaluation of Policy Related Research on Exercise
of Discretion by Law Enforcement Officials - College
of William and Mary Metropolitan Building, 147 Granby
St., Norfolk, Virginia 23510; W. Anthony Fitch

(19) An Evaluation of Policy Related Research on Exercise
of Police Discretion - National Council of Crime and
Delinquency Research Center, 209 2nd Street, Davis,
California 95616; M.C. Neithercutt

(20) An Evaluation of Policy Related Research on Post
Secondary Education for the Disadvantaged - Mercy
College of Detroit, Department of Sociology, Detroit,
Michigan 48219; Mary Janet Mulka

A complementary series of awards were made by the Division

of Social Systems and Human Resources to evaluate the policy

related research in the field of Municipal Systems, Operations, and Services. For the convenience of the reader, a listing of these awards appears below:

(1) Fire Protection - George Institute of Technology, Department of Industrial and Systems Engineering, Atlanta, Georgia 30332; D.E. Fyffe

(2) Fire Protection - New York Rand Institute, 545 Madison Avenue, New York, New York 10022; Arthur J. Swersey

(3) Emergency Medical Services - University of Tennessee, Bureau of Public Administration, Knoxville, Tenn. 37916; Hyrum Plaas

(4) Municipal Housing Services - Cogen Holt and Associates, 956 Chapel St., New Haven, Connecticut 06510; Harry Wexler

(5) Formalized Pre-Trial Diversion Programs in Municipal and Metropolitan Courts - American Bar Association, 1705 DeSales St., N.W., Washington, D.C. 20036; Roberta Rovner-Pieczenik

(6) Parks and Recreation - National Recreation and Park Association, 1601 North Kent St., Arlington, Va. 22209; The Urban Inst., 2100 M St., N.W., Washington, D.C. 20037; Peter J. Verhoven

(7) Police Protection - Mathematica, Inc., 4905 Del Ray Avenue, Bethesda, Md. 20014; Saul I. Gass

(8) Solid Waste Management - Massachusetts Institute of Technology, Department of Civil Engineering, Cambridge, Massachusetts, 02139; David Marks

(9) Citizen Participation Strategies - The Rand Corporation, 2100 M St., N.W., Washington, D.C. 20037; Robert Yin

(10) Citizen Participation: Municipal Subsystems - The University of Michigan, Program in Health Planning, Ann Arbor, Michigan 48104; Joseph L. Falkson

(11) Economic Development - Ernst & Ernst, 1225 Connecticut Avenue, N.W., Washington, D.C. 20036; Lawrence H. Revzan

(12) Goal of Economic Development - University of Texas-Austin, Center for Economic Development, Department of Economics, Austin, Texas 78712; Niles M. Hansen

(13) Franchising and Regulation - University of South
Dakota, Department of Economics, Vermillion, South
Dakota   57069; C.A. Kent

(14) Municipal Information Systems - University of California,
Public Policy Research Organization, Irvine, California
92664; Kenneth L. Kraemer

(15) Municipal Growth  Guidance Systems - University of
Minnesota, School of Public Affairs, Minneapolis,
Minnesota   55455; Michael E. Gleeson

(16) Land Use Controls - University of North Carolina,
Chapel Hill, Center for Urban and Regional Studies,
Chapel Hill, North Carolina   27514; Edward M. Bergman

(17) Land Use Controls - The Potomac Institute, Inc.,
1501 Eighteenth St., N.W., Washington, D.C. 20036;
Herbert M. Franklin

(18) Municipal Management Methods and Budgetary Processes -
The Urban Institute, 2100 M St., N.W, Washington, D.C.
20037; Wayne A. Kimmel

(19) Personnel Systems - Georgetown University, Public
Service Lab., Washington, D.C.  20037; Selma Mushkin

Copies of the above cited research evaluation reports for

both Municipal Systems and Human Resources may be obtained

directly from the principal investigator or from the

National Technical Information Service (NTIS) U.S. Dept. of

Commerce, 5285 Port Royal, Springfield, Virginia   22151

(Telephone 703/321-8517).

This research evaluation by Raymond A. Katzell, Principal

Investigator, and Daniel Yankelovich, Associate Principal

Investigator, of New York University, on relations among

industrial organization, job satisfaction and productivity,

was prepared with the support of the National Science

Foundation.  The opinions, findings, conclusions, or recom-

mendations are solely those of the authors.

It is a policy of the Division of Social Systems and
Human Resources to assess the relevance, utility, and
quality of the projects it supports.  Should any readers
of this report have comments in these or other regards,
we would be particularly grateful to receive them as they
become essential tools in the planning of future programs.


Lynn P. Dolins
Program Manager
Division of Social Systems
and Human Resources

# PREFACE

In terms of today's vernacular, our topic concerns what about work turns people "on" or "off". The reader must wonder why that ancient question warrants further inquiry.

Our reply, and that of our sponsors, is that its answer is still far from apparent. We thought we could help clear it up if we were to bring to bear on the voluminous literature on the subject the following emphases: (1)examining hard facts, in contrast to ambiguous findings or vague impressions; (2)weighing recent and contemporary studies, in the belief that the answer may change with the times; (3)seeking linkages between the satisfaction of workers and their economic performance, and with the hypothesis that circumstances can be discovered in which people really care about their work and their jobs; and (4)looking at this complex subject from a multi-disciplinary perspective, including management, labor, economics, psychology, sociology, and engineering, in the belief that to do less is likely to result in an incomplete or even biased picture.

We wish we could announce that our search had been completely successful, that it had clearly disclosed the secret of motivating people so that they are both satisfied with their work and productive in it. Unfortunately, as the reader will see, the facts are still too incomplete and equivocal to permit that. But we do think that we have learned much that can assist policy-makers in making plans and decisions for the future.

Naturally, the facts pertaining to so complex a topic, in which the state-of-the-art is still in flux, are susceptible to varying interpretations. Therefore, although the findings and conclusions of this report represent a rough consensus of the views of the project team, one or another member inevitably might see something in a different light than did others. What we found to be especially heartening was that representatives of different disciplines, approaching the subject from diverse conceptual and methodological standpoints, were able to agree as much as they did.

Accomplishment of the project depended on the time and talents of a number of other people in addition to those named on the title page. We wish first to acknowledge our gratitude to members of our Advisory Committee which included:

Irving Bluestone, United Automobile Workers
David Caplan, Concord Fabrics, Inc.
John W. Lawyer, TRW, Inc.
Lillian Roberts, Federation of State, County and
    Municipal Employees
Edward A. Robie, Equitable Life Assurance Society
Jerome M. Rosow, Exxon Corp.
Richard P. Shore, U.S. Department of Labor
John M. Stewart, McKinsey & Co., late of the National
    Commission on Productivity
Eric L. Trist, University of Pennsylvania.

The members of the Advisory Committee individually and collectively made numerous helpful suggestions. However, they

should not be held accountable for the contents of this
report, which does not necessarily represent their opinions.

Lynn P. Dolins, of RANN division of the National Science
Foundation, merits special mention not only for being a
participant-observer on the Advisory Committe, but especially
for her help while serving as NSF project officer throughout
the study.

The American Management Association furnished valuable
cooperation in conjunction with the opinion survey of managers
reported in Chapter IV; in particular, we are indebted to
Patricia F. Lewis and Dr. Mildred E. Katzell.

For the convenience of readers, we have organized the
report in two parts. Part One sets the stage, summarizes
the results and conclusions, and recommends strategies and
tactics of implementation. It therefore can serve as an
"Executive Summary" for policy-makers and others who may
wish to see the over-all picture without delving into the
details of the investigations. Part Two describes the methods
of our inquiry, our conceptual framework, and the findings
which emerged. A Glossary of technical terms is appended
for the general reader.

It is our hope that this report will be helpful to
those who are in a position to create conditions which will
improve the economic performance and human environment of

work organizations. We also hope that it may serve to
stimulate and guide future research on that important
subject.

New York              R.A.K.
January 15, 1975.     D.Y.

PART ONE:  SUMMARY AND IMPLICATIONS

# CHAPTER I
## THE NATURE OF THE QUEST

### Background of the Problem

This study is addressed to assessing the state of knowledge about how work affects the productivity and job satisfaction of workers. Those two subjects have long been of
interest to policy-makers in society. Interest in productivity
was crystallized during the Industrial Revolution, resurged at
the turn of the Twentieth Century in the forms of scientific
management and mass production, and revived still more recently
in the "Second Industrial Revolution" created by automation.
Concern with the satisfaction and quality of life of workers has
been expressed over the last century by various social planners
and reformers, and has been a formal objective of policy-makers
and social scientists during the past fifty years or so.

The last five years have witnessed a renewed quickening
of social concern with these topics. The issue of the quality
of working life has been caught up in the pervasive questioning
of the goals and meaning of life which burgeoned during the
1960's, epitomized by the student movement. That period of
self-doubt led to systematic studies of the topic, capped by
such federally-sponsored studies as the Survey of Working
Conditions (Survey Research Center, 1970) and Work in America
(U.S. Department of H.E.W., 1973).

The renewed concern for productivity is of even more recent origin, and has been sparked mainly by the shift in balance of international payments, escalating monetary inflation, and the threat of a depression, all of which have surfaced during the past two or three years. President Ford was a spokesman for that mounting concern when, in his pre-Labor Day address on August 30, 1974, he said, "Productivity must improve if we are to have a less inflationary economy.... It is essential in creating new jobs and increasing real wages. In a growing economy, everyone -- labor, management, and the consumer -- wins when productivity expands."

### The Known and the Unknown

We believe that strategies for increasing productivity are within the present competence of our nation and its policy-makers. The approaches exist at various levels and in various fields of knowledge, including macro-economic (e.g., redistribution of priorities for capital investment from consumption to production), micro-economic (e.g., increased outlays for more efficient plant technology), production engineering (e.g., more effective work methods), and personnel management (e.g., better training of workers).

Although not as well tested, strategies for improving the job satisfaction and quality of life of workers have also been developed. They include paying people more, giving them work which more completely utilizes their aptitudes and skills,

providing helpful and considerate supervision, composing
harmonious work groups, affording opportunities for upward
and lateral mobility, giving workers a voice in decisions
which affect them, and improving working conditions so as to
increase comfort, health and safety.

Indeed, those and similar avenues for improving productivity or job satisfaction are widely discussed in standard
textbooks on economics, industrial engineering, business
administration, personnel and labor relations, and industrial
psychology and sociology.

What, then, is the problem? It is that experience and
studies have taught how to improve either productivity or job
satisfaction irrespective of the other. What is not at all
clear is how both may be enhanced simultaneously. In fact, some
have argued that our best developed techniques for increasing
one do so at the expense of the other. For example, work
rationalization has often been accused of de-humanizing work,
and industrial democracy has been criticized by some as the
province of humanitarians who don't have to meet a payroll.
It is concern with this potential conflict of outcomes that
probably lies behind much of the resistance to exploring more
fully the existing knowledge about improving productivity or
job satisfaction independently of one another.

The focus of the present study is therefore to illuminate
this area of obscurity: how can productivity and job satisfaction be increased together? Put another way: how can the

economic performance of an organization be improved while at the same time increasing the satisfaction (rather than strain) of its workers? But even that focus is too diffuse, for its complete exploration would get us into a wide and diverse array of techniques having little conceptual or methodological coherence. These could be as disparate as equipment design, personnel selection, and plant layout, to name but three from among many relevant topics. Instead, we elected to limit our inquiry to three topics which are conceptually related, and which our knowledge of extant literature suggested have been extensively studied and have shown considerable promise for meeting the objectives of our study. The three are: design of jobs, distribution of control, and patterns of compensation. Their common core is that of organizational structure, i.e., ways in which the members of organizations are related, respectively, in terms of job responsibilities, influence, and financial incentives, or combinations of them. We gave some attention to the possibility of studying other dimensions of organization structure -- especially careers and status -- but found little in the way of factual information on how they affect both productivity and satisfaction. A fourth subject which we investigated involves experiments where such extensive changes were made in several aspects of organizational structure as to constitute revised operational or socio-technical systems.

Another important emphasis characterizing our study is its focus on trustworthy information. This has meant attending to objective and empirical facts generated by studies which are methodologically valid. We quickly discovered that our chosen topics have been the subject of endless opinions and advice, much of it inconsistent or ambiguous. Often the "facts" assembled to buttress opinions turned out to be imprecise or attributed to causes of questionable authenticity. In short, we concluded that we could learn more from a smaller number of studies of higher quality than from a larger number of more equivocal impressions.

Finally, it seemed to us that the policy-relevance of our findings would be enhanced if we could relate them to the assumptions and beliefs that policy-makers currently hold regarding productivity and job satisfaction. This led us to initiate a survey of opinions on those topics on the part of a sample of people who are associated with the American Management Association and a sample of labor union officials.

## Statement of the Study Objectives

In light of the foregoing, we are now able to set forth more specifically what we have attempted to do in this study:

To determine whether and how worker job satisfaction and productivity together may be enhanced by changing patterns of job responsibilities, control, and compensation; to do this by means of a critical review of relevant studies which have generated high-quality, factual information; and to relate the findings to prevalent beliefs on those topics held by policy-makers.

The study covers people who work for a wage or salary. For ease of a title, they are all called "workers" or "employees", ranging from presidents to the lowest skill levels, and including managers, professionals, salespeople, white-collar employees, blue-collar employees and all other employees in both the private and public sectors of our society. In certain sections of this report, job levels will be specified where the nature of the work affects the discussion.

## The Need

Because the renewed concerns with problems of job satisfaction and of productivity have been so widely publicized during the past few years, we have refrained here from commenting further on their extent and intensity. We should also take note that a number of analysts of the contemporary scene have elected not to jump on those bandwagons. For instance, the need for increased production has been challenged by some who believe that our culture has already tilted its priorities excessively toward material abundance. Those critics see our problems of inflation and unemployment as requiring a reordering of priorities with relatively more of our national capital and competence being addressed to increased human services, and _less_ to the production of goods -- particularly those in the domains of material consumption, military affairs, and the capital equipment serving those segments of the economy. Some analysts of that school also call for a shift in our work-oriented society toward greater emphasis on leisure and

personal self fulfillment. A related school of thought has
argued for increased emphasis on conservation of resources and
on environmental quality relative to concerns with production
and consumption. Others give little weight to improving productivity because of their concern that it could contribute to
increasing unemployment.

There are some who challenge the grounds for concern with
enhancing job satisfaction and the quality of working life.
They cite studies (e.g., Quinn, Staines & McCullogh, 1974)
indicating that the level of job satisfaction of Americans is
neither low nor declining, or they take the position that working for a living is inherently less attractive and satisfying
than play but must be done if our civilization is to be
maintained.

To evaluate the issues of whether we really need more
productivity and/or job satisfaction would in itself constitute
a massive inquiry. Moreover, in the last analysis its answer
would reflect value judgments, depending on the kind of society
one prefers. For those reasons, we have chosen not to become
embroiled with such questions. Rather, in the tradition of
science, we are endeavoring to provide valid guidelines to the
simultaneous improvement of job satisfaction and productivity
for the many who may see that as a desirable objective. Those
who do not are, of course, free to preserve the status quo or
to pursue separately the objectives of either increased productivity or job satisfaction, according to their lights.

## Organization of the Report

The results of our inquiry are reported in this document. In Chapter II, we will present a summary and discussion of the findings, with particular attention to their implications for policy-makers. Chapter III will consider implementation -- the strategies and tactics of taking action on the conclusions suggested by the research. Because Chapters I, II, and III are specially pertinent to the needs of the reader who is oriented more to policy issues than to details of methods and data, those chapters are grouped as Part One, Summary. The longer and more detailed Part Two, Research Report, contains chapters addressed to: a description of our method and framework; the survey of beliefs about productivity on the part of a sample of executives and a sample of labor union officials; three chapters reporting our findings regarding the effects of job design, control structures, and patterns of compensation; a chapter describing examples of system-wide changes; and finally, our references and bibliography. A glossary of technical terms is included.

The Table of Contents may be consulted for further information on the organization of the report, as well as page references to its various sections.

CHAPTER II

SUMMARY OF FINDINGS AND CONCLUSIONS

The purpose of this chapter and the one that follows is to present a summary and discussion of the vast body of recent research literature on factors affecting both the job satisfaction and productivity of workers. This task is complicated by the fact that the research findings are not entirely unambiguous or consistent. Part Two of this report explains those limitations in some detail. On the other hand, there is enough convergence of evidence to suggest certain directions for future policy, and it is on those implications which the present summary chapters will focus. But the reader should bear in mind that even these conclusions are not unequivocal, and that some might choose to interpret the picture somewhat differently from that presented below.

Perhaps the most general conclusion to be drawn from the research findings is that policy-makers must face up to a serious dilemma and find some way to resolve it. The dilemma is this: policy-makers would like to achieve two objectives for work organizations, on the one hand to enhance productivity and performance, and on the other to improve the quality of working life and job satisfaction for working Americans. Many policy-makers assume that the two goals are causally linked in a direct and overt manner such that if job satisfaction is enhanced, productivity will also be improved. But if

there is any one fact that stands out clearly from the massive
accumulation of data -- the hundreds of studies encompassed in
this report -- it is that worker job satisfaction and productivity do not necessarily follow parallel paths.

This does not mean that the two objectives are incompatible, for there is evidence that it may be possible
to achieve them together.  Nor does it mean that the two goals
are totally independent of one another.  Under certain conditions, improving productivity will enhance worker satisfaction
and improvements in job satisfaction will contribute to productivity.  What it does mean is that there is no automatic and
invariant relationship between the two.  Indeed, the two objectives are so loosely coupled, there are so many intervening
links between them, and the relationship is so indirect, that
efforts which aim primarily at improving worker satisfaction on
the assumption that productivity will thereby automatically
increase are more likely than not to leave productivity unchanged, or at best to improve it marginally, and may even
cause it to decline.

A careful analysis of the findings shows that such minimal
impact is the likely fate of the most popular, the most highly
publicized, and the most appealing, from a humanist point of
view, of current techniques being proposed to policy-makers on
the assumption that they will accomplish both ends.  These include such procedures as job enrichment, M.B.O., autonomous
work groups, participative management, etc.*

_____
*The Glossary may be consulted for definitions of these
and other terms which may not be familiar to the reader.

In other words, there exists a wide array of methods available for improving workers' job attitudes or performance, but each of them characteristically tackles some partial aspect of the workers' relationships to their jobs -- their financial incentives or their control over their work or their working conditions or their social relationships or their labor-management relations. No one of these, we have learned, is ordinarily enough to affect both productivity and satisfaction significantly, although in some instances improvements in one or the other objective may be realized. For reasons that will be discussed in a later section of this chapter, substantial and enduring improvements in performance as well as job satisfaction appear to require that an integrated combination of methods that relate the human to the economic concerns must be employed in order to bring about large-scale and enduring improvements in both domains simultaneously. Thus, there may be ways to achieve both goals, even though they are functionally independent, but not by means of any single-target program or standard formula that can be applied uniformly to any and all situations.

The central conclusion of this report, therefore, sounds both a negative note of warning about the dangers of holding unrealistic expectations for some of the currently fashionable but overly narrow approaches, as well as a positive note of hope that marked and enduring improvements can be achieved which will promote both objectives -- provided that due account is taken of the difficulty and complexity of the undertaking.

Making futher progress in both productivity and job satisfaction is complicated by two large obstacles -- inadequate knowledge and resistance to change. The knowledge obstacle derives from the aforementioned need for using a variety of methods rather than any single approach, and the requirement that these be adapted patiently and skillfully to each work setting. The multiple sources of resistance to change constitute a political obstacle in the broad sense of that term. Among the political barriers are the real or perceived adversary relations between management and other employees, or which the parties believe to be intrinsic. Managers may think that efforts to improve the quality of working life will compete with programs to improve economic performance; rank-and-file workers may see efforts to improve productivity as exploitation or as inimical to their job security.

Thus, a problem for the policy-maker is that to effect large-scale improvements in the productive and humane use of human resources, numerous and far reaching changes must be made before the desired effects become visible; but at the same time, political resistances require that the changes must be introduced cautiously, moving forward one step at a time. However, while it would be hard to exaggerate the difficulties of the task, that does not mean that they cannot be overcome in time, given a base of adequate knowledge and sufficient statesmanship on the parts of both management and labor.

We will return to political considerations in Chapter III, which addresses action implications for policy-makers of the research findings to be summarized in the remainder of the present chapter. Those findings will be presented in two sections: First, the results of our survey of beliefs and assumptions held by policy-makers pertaining to worker productivity and attitudes, and then a distillation of the research reports regarding job redesign, distribution of control, pay and compensation practices, and system-wide changes.

## Summary of Policy-Makers' Assumptions

One objective of the project was to analyze the assumptions policy-makers hold on the topics of worker productivity, job satisfaction, and their relationship. The purpose was to guide us in seeking literature that would bear most directly on these assumptions, and in framing our recommendations in relation to them. This section summarizes what we learned about prevailing policy assumptions. For further details, the reader is referred to Chapter IV in Part Two, where there is reported a statistical profile of the beliefs of two important groups of policy-makers -- managers of medium and large business enterprises, and union officials.

We wish to single out here as particularly relevant seven sets of assumptions currently held by management and union leadership. These are abstracted from a special survey conducted in connection with the project. There are methodological limitations to the survey as noted in Chapter IV, but for present purposes of providing a reference point for analysis, we believe the study is useful. The seven sets of assumptions or beliefs are these:

1. <u>Acceptance of Productivity as a Goal</u>. Both union leaders and managers generally assume that increasing productivity is an essential goal to insure a high standard of living for all Americans; however, this assumption is embraced more intensely by managers than by union officials, which suggests that union leaders may give lower priority to programs addressed to improving productivity unless tied to benefits and safeguards for workers.

2. <u>Improving Quality of Working Life</u>. Almost 9 out of 10 policy-makers in both groups say they accept the desirability of improving the quality of working life "even if it doesn't increase productivity." A large majority of both managers and union officials strongly reject the idea that "work is a necessary evil." Instead, they universally believe that work should be a rewarding part of life, not a form of drudgery. A majority also believe that workers should and do take pride in their work, however menial it may be, and that life's basic satisfactions should come from work as well as from home, family, and leisure activities. There is almost total rejection by both groups of the widely accepted idea that one should look to work solely for its economic benefits and to life outside of work for one's essential satisfaction.

3. <u>The Job Satisfaction/Productivity Link</u>. There is
general agreement on the assumption by both the management and
union representatives that "if workers were more satisfied with
their jobs, there would be greater productivity." But, whereas
the majority of managers feel that the "nation's productivity
is suffering because the traditional work ethic has eroded,"
only about one-third of union officials hold that view. Nevertheless, both sets of policy-makers feel that higher job satisfaction and greater concern on the part of employers with
workers' welfare would lead to higher levels of productivity.
Both groups also reject the idea that "employee motivation has
little or no bearing on productivity." In short, the joint
improvement of productivity <u>and</u> job satisfaction would appear
to constitute a goal which attracts both management and labor.

4. <u>Worker Dissatisfaction a Reality</u>. Both groups state
their belief that worker dissatisfaction is a real problem and
not "an invention of professors, journalists, and the 'left'."
But some unclarity and disagreement exist about how widespread
the dissatisfaction is. Both groups of policy-makers typically
assume that "union members want more interesting work than they
did a decade ago," and that a younger, better-educated work
force is demanding more participation in decision-making than
was characteristic of the older, less well-educated work force
of the past. They also agree, however, that "making work more
interesting doesn't offset a desire for increased pay"; both
groups reject the idea that "the paycheck isn't as important to

people as it used to be."

5. <u>How to Improve Productivity and Motivation</u>. There is
general agreement among both policy-making groups that the most
important factors in improving productivity are essentially
managerial techniques:  better planning for productivity, more
effective management, improved job procedures, better communication, and more effective manpower and personnel policies.  In
addition, a three out of four majority feel that "job enrichment is a promising strategy for improving productivity."  More
than 8 out of 10 state that workers' ideas are a good source for
methods of improving productivity.  But union officials, more
than managers, believe that various improvements in the quality
of working life are valuable in improving productivity.  For
example, the union officials see more value in human relations
as an aid to productivity (52% to 36%); improving work conditions (41% to 16%), and creating more democracy in the organization (22% to 6%).  Union leaders also place more stress than
do managers on the usefulness of improving employee attitudes
and motivation by such methods as giving employees greater job
security (54% to 11%); higher pay (51% to 17%); improved working conditions (45% to 17%); improved grievance procedures (48%
to 18%); and better treatment by supervisors (46% to 27%);
these traditional key "bread-and-butter" issues are therefore
likely to be laid on the bargaining table when any programs are
proposed.  Generally speaking, managers even more than union
officials exhibit skepticism that various worker-centered

techniques and programs are likely to be "very useful" in improving either attitudes or productivity; this may suggest an important obstacle to the development of such programs.

6. Union/Management Relations. There is strong consensus among both groups that "it is possible for the union and management to cooperate on specific programs that will improve productivity." However, by a 10 to 1 ratio managers more often hold that unions impose an unnecessary adversary relationship on efforts to improve productivity, and both groups are in general agreement that unions tend to be suspicious of management-sponsored programs for increasing productivity. Some degree of mistrust of each other's intentions is clearly evident in such findings, but many more union leaders than management (49% to 21%) assume that the interests of the two are essentially and inherently opposed.

7. Meaning of Productivity. Neither leadership group follows the economist's definition of productivity as meaningful solely in terms of total industries or sectors of the economy and as confined to quantitative measures of output in relation to input. By productivity, management and union policymakers refer essentially to the overall effectiveness and performance of individual organizations. In addition to quantity of output of goods and services, they take into account various less tangible features such as the absence of disruption, trouble, sabotage, "shrinkage," and other indications of unrest in the organization, as well as low rates of absenteeism and

turnover, and even customer satisfaction. Given that broad
conception of productivity, it is understandable that policy-
makers see a link between worker satisfaction and productivity.
However, union leaders are somewhat more prone to emphasize the
tangible outputs, which helps to explain why they are suspicious
of productivity improvement efforts as benefitting management
but not workers.

It should be pointed out that the term "productivity" is
not even used clearly or consistently in the professional literature. Sometimes it is used in its broad, all-inclusive sense
to mean overall performance and sometimes in its narrower sense
of output per unit of time or cost. To help establish a clearer
link between our findings and the concerns of policy-makers,
we also will be using the term "productivity" in this report in
the broad sense of effective performance.

Parenthetically, it may be noted that the terms "quality
of working life" and "job satisfaction" suffer from even less
standardization than "productivity". We will defer a discussion
of them until later, but may note now that most studies have been
addressed to job satisfaction rather than the fuller, more
complex concept of work quality.

It will be seen from the enumeration above that the areas
of agreement between management and unions, at least as suggested by this study, are large and substantial, although there
are some areas of disagreement, at least in emphasis. By and
large both groups say they would like to achieve the dual objectives of improving satisfaction and productivity, and also

say they are ready to cooperate on specific programs, although cautiously and with some mistrust. What appears to be lacking is the specific agreement and knowledge, both theoretical and practical, of how to achieve the desired goals. The costs of changing -- in terms of time, effort, and money -- are also undoubtedly an implicit barrier.

It should be noted that in answering questions in the survey, the respondents sometimes appeared to contradict themselves or expressed views that are not consistent with what is actually happening in the workplace today. For example, at one point 87% of the managers stated their belief that greater work satisfaction will lead to greater productivity, but when asked to identify the factors that contribute most to improving productivity in their organization, improving the quality of working life was cited by only 16% as an important factor -- nearly at the bottom of the list. Apart from such internal inconsistencies -- and there are a number of them -- there are also beliefs expressed which are not carried out in action. Thus almost nine out of ten policy-makers in both groups say that they are committed to improving the quality of working life for its own sake even if it doesn't increase productivity. Yet, even the most casual familiarity with the reality of what takes place in many organizations arouses one's skepticism about this response.

Are these policy-makers hiding or distorting their true beliefs? Are they merely giving lip service to socially approved viewpoints that are meaningless in predicting their future action and their receptivity to change? It is not possible to answer these questions definitively, but there are some well-established principles that help us to make reasonable interpretations of what such inconsistencies may mean. In all domains of attitudes, one finds disparities between social norms and actual behavior. But changing norms often anticipate changes in behavior. Whenever one finds a norm that endorses a course of action, it often signals receptivity to future social change in behavior patterns. It is as if the person were saying, "This is what I would like to do -- if the obstacles were not too great." Between the ideal and the action there is a world of resistance, compounded of lack of knowledge, lack of familiarity with how to deal with obstacles, lethargy, and the preoccupation with day-to-day problems that inevitably stand in the way of launching programs that are expensive, time consuming, and demanding of energy and commitment. That, in brief, is how we interpret the meaning of the assumptions survey; namely, that it expresses more than lip service, but less than commitment. Perhaps the word "receptivity" is the most apt one. That is, admittedly, an interpretation, and alternative interpretations are reasonable. But this one is consistent with what we know about attitudes in general, and also what we know about policy-maker beliefs about the work place from sources other than the current survey.

## Research Findings and Conclusions

The research literature on this subject is less helpful to policy-makers than one would wish it to be. Policy-makers confront a vast and uneven body of research on worker productivity and job satisfaction whose scientific status is largely problematic, and whose results are often inconclusive, ridden with jargon, and irrelevant to the policy-maker's concerns. In spite of the scope of the literature, valid and pertinent studies are too few to permit definitive answers to most questions.

Nonetheless, it is possible to draw from the wide variety of experiments, surveys, and case histories reviewed in this report a number of conclusions which, although they do not have the status of incontrovertible fact, appear to be reasonably valid on the basis of the weight of the evidence. Where it is meaningful to do so, in summarizing the principles we will relate them to the policy-makers' assumptions described in the preceding section.

1. <u>Job Satisfaction and Productivity</u>. Over the years, a body of knowledge has been built up through behavioral science research on how to improve job attitudes and worker satisfaction. Much less is known about how simultaneously to improve job attitudes and productivity. The little that is known suggests (a) achieving this dual objective is therefore far more diffi-cult and complex than improving job attitudes alone without

respect to productivity or _vice versa_; (b) the two outcomes can
be successfully linked only if a number of conditions are met;
and (c) just as policy-makers believe, the task of effecting
those outcomes is primarily managerial in character, more particularly the management of human resources. This last point
should not be interpreted to mean that capital investment, new
technology, and marketing strategy may not be equally or more
important in determining levels of productivity; rather, it
means that the specific task of mobilizing human resources to
maximize quality of working life and economic performance at
the same time is largely a matter of sound managerial practices,
many of which lie within the current state of the art, if employed correctly. Of course, this does not mean that management should be solely involved in planning and devising improved programs; for example, union cooperation should be sought,
government should provide incentives, scientists should pursue
new information, etc. But it does imply that management must
take the initiative and responsibility.

    2. The "Critical Mass" Principle. Perhaps the best way
to think about the requirements for improving productivity together with job satisfaction is by rough analogy with the
physicist's notion of "critical mass." The organizational
changes required to achieve the critical mass must be sufficiently deep and far-reaching: superficial or narrow efforts
tend to be transitory in their effects, and as often reported in
the research literature, hardly even noticed by workers. This

does not mean that the necessary changes must be made all at once; but it does suggest that marked improvements in both satisfaction and performance will generally not show up until at least several major steps are taken, which in combination create a qualitatively new and better socio-technical system.

3. The "Motivation" Principle. Of course, programs will not achieve the dual objective just by being comprehensive; the elements must be integrated in terms of some general principle which runs through those which attain the desired results and is absent from those which do not. That integrating principle can best be understood by reference to the important distinction between work satisfaction and motivation. Many people are satisfied with their jobs because their work is undemanding and requires only the minimal effort on their part. Others are dissatisfied because they are highly motivated to do a good job but frustrated by obstacles in the work situation which prevent them from doing so. Thus, one can find workers who fall into any of four possible categories:

(1) satisfied and highly motivated;

(2) satisfied and weakly motivated;

(3) dissatisfied and highly motivated;

(4) dissatisfied and weakly motivated.

Forging the link between work satisfaction and productivity depends critically on increasing the size of the first of the four groups -- people who are both satisfied and highly motivated. The other three groups fail to contribute to achieving one or both of the dual objectives.

Of all of the factors which help create highly motivated/ highly satisfied workers, the principal one appears to be that effective performance be recognized and rewarded -- in whatever terms are meaningful to the individual, be it financial or psychological or both. This means that programs, in order to enhance both productivity and job satisfaction, must function so that workers find effective performance to be rewarding and that doing what one finds rewarding results in effective performance. Conversely, performing ineffectively should not result in rewards, nor should doing rewarding things result in poor performance. Needless to add, we use the term "reward" to refer to any of a number of gratifying consequences, including recognition, financial gain, and the satisfaction that comes from the successful use of one's full capabilities.

This principle adds up to the simple, but nonetheless valid, precept that the key to having workers who are both satisfied and productive is motivation, i.e., arousing and maintaining the desire and will to work effectively -- having workers who are productive not because they are coerced but because they are committed.

4. Shared Benefits. An extension of the previous principle is that workers at all levels must see that the program will be beneficial to them in terms that are important to them. For example, a productivity improvement program involving job changes, in a mass production plant with a large number of

unskilled and semiskilled workers, would probably have little interest to those workers if they do not receive additional pay for the increased productivity. Not that pay alone will positively affect their attitudes, for there are also other factors. The point is that those workers must perceive the program as benefitting them. Similarly, workers at managerial levels cannot be expected to support programs which they see as unrelated to their own interests.

It follows that successful programs will be characterized by wide sharing of financial and other benefits throughout the organization.

5. <u>Job Design</u>. The preceding points can be exemplified by reference to the research literature on job enrichment and redesign, which is one of the major strategies currently proposed for enhancing worker motivation. Before summarizing that research, it is important to avoid a common misunderstanding which arises from ambiguity in the use of the terms "job enlargement," "job enrichment," and "job redesign." Sometimes those terms are used in a broad, all-encompassing sense to cover not only the refashioning of the job itself but also greater worker autonomy, more democracy in the work place, and even productivity-sharing incentive plans. At other times, the terms are used in a more narrow and specific sense, confined to modification in the character of the work task -- the activities and responsibilities that constitute the "job." It is in this latter sense that we are using these terms here. (See

the Glossary for further information.)

Our analysis of the literature on this topic indicates that job redesign programs are by no means a sure-fire road to improving both job satisfaction and productivity. As will be specified in Chapter VI of this report, examples were found in which job redesign improved workers' attitudes but not productivity, both attitudes and productivity, and neither attitudes nor productivity.

There are too few well-controlled studies to permit us to explain those inconsistencies with certainty, but it would seem that job redesign had clearly beneficial effects on both job attitudes and productivity only when the preceding general principles of effective programs were implemented. Where job redesign had negligible results, one or more of those principles had been violated. We are referring here to the aforementioned principles of critical mass, rewarding performance, and shared benefits. More specifically:

a. The critical mass principle operates here in two ways. Job redesign is likely to improve both attitudes and performance only when:

> (1) The changes in job content are sufficiently non-trivial to be perceptible to the workers, typically in terms of greater self-regulation, diversity, meaningfulness, challenge, and social responsibility (however, as will be noted below, what is non-trivial to some workers may be quite

trivial to others);

(2)   the changes in job content are part of a more
pervasive program of improved working policies
and practices, which include also as elements
adequate pay and job security, proper resources
and working conditions, increased mutual influence by people at all levels, and constructive
labor-management relations.

b.  Not all workers are seeking greater challenge or
responsibility, and hence not all will find enriched jobs to
be more rewarding.  Furthermore, to some workers working may be
more of a means to other ends, such as increased income or
socializing, and such workers would be less affected by changes
in job content alone.

In short, rewards must be tailored to who is being rewarded, thereby illustrating the principle of "rewarding
work".  Expanding the content of jobs is more likely to be
rewarding to workers whose "bread-and-butter" needs have been
reasonably satisfied and who are now seeking opportunities
for self-expression and growth, i.e., particularly better-
educated, younger workers, and those in higher-level, white-
collar jobs.

c.  The principle of shared benefits is not as manifest
in the controlled experiments as it is in case studies and the
experience of practitioners.  Job changes which threaten job
security, which disrupt wage scales  that  have been accepted as

fair, or which result in inequities in the distribution of resulting financial benefits, seem likely to fail in their intent. This is prone to occur when workers believe that increased responsibility will not be matched by increased earnings, or where managers anticipate that costs will exceed benefits. Job redesign is likely to work best when everyone involved stands to share equitably in resulting financial benefits.

d. In addition to the above ways in which the basic principles of program design need to be observed, the studies reveal that there may be other obstacles or problems that must be overcome in implementing programs of job redesign; among these are:

(1) some work systems are less amenable to the efficient restructuring of jobs than others; that is especially the case where jobs are closely interdependent on one another and/or tied to a complex machine technology; job redesign may simply be a less suitable strategy in such situations;

(2) enlargement of the jobs of some workers may entail reduction of the jobs of others, e.g., expanding the self-regulation of workers may diminish the number and scope of supervisory jobs; inadequate absorption of the latter workers somewhere in the revised organizational set-up can generate a destructive force.

The purpose of enumerating the foregoing conditions on which the effects of job design depend is to emphasize several points:

- Failure to meet one or more of the necessary conditions may account for why programs of job redesign can have negligible results.

- Where those conditions can be accommodated successfully, programs involving job redesign can serve as a useful way of helping improve job satisfaction and productivity.

- The conditions are sufficiently numerous and restrictive as to require considerable commitment to pervasive change on the part of the typical long-established organization; this means that programs should not be undertaken casually if they are to succeed.

- It is because the pre-conditions are so numerous and basic that a critical mass of integrated changes is more likely to deal with them successfully than is a single-target program, such as job enlargement alone.

These points apply to the other single-target programs to be discussed below as much as to job redesign.

6. Patterns of Control. The redistribution of influence and control in organizations has been proposed as a road to improving worker motivation for an even longer time than has job redesign. Programs for redistributing control have ranged from a focus on greater self-regulation by the worker over his own job, to greater autonomy for work groups, increased mutual influence throughout organizations via participative management,

and formal modes of labor-management cooperation such as
through co-determination or collective bargaining.  All of
those approaches may serve to give workers a feeling of greater
influence; their effects on job satisfaction and performance
will be summarized below.

   We have already seen that increased self-regulation is an
element in job enrichment, the effects of which depend partly
on whether the workers in question have needs for greater
responsibility and autonomy.  The same consideration also plays
a part in the effects of programs for increasing control by
workers.  On the other hand, as detailed in Chapter VII,
research has identified beneficial consequences of greater
influence on the part of workers in a variety of jobs at various skill and organizational levels.  Undoubtedly there are
personal and cultural influences on the appropriateness of
different patterns of control, but they cannot be reduced simply
to any single factor, and therefore have to be assessed in
each situation.

   Although such considerations may produce different results
in specific work situations, it is still possible to discern
some general trends in the impact of various programs for
shaping control patterns.  These will first be discussed in
general terms, and then in terms of three foci of control:  the
individual job, the work group, and the organization as a whole.

a.   General Trends.

 (1)   Workers who see themselves as having more in-
        fluence over what goes on in their jobs, their
        work groups and their organizations generally
        have more favorable attitudes about their jobs
        than do those who believe they are less influ-
        ential.

 (2)   Workers having more influence are also less
        prone to leave their jobs.

 (3)   The effects of control patterns on productivity
        are not as clear or as strong.   However, the
        following statements may be offered tentatively:

       (a)   Equalization of control among hierarchical
              levels does not appear in itself to affect
              productivity very much.

       (b)   However, greater over-all influence among
              members of an organization or group does
              seem to be conducive to better productivity.

       (c)   Greater voice in defining work goals, methods,
              and compensation at both the individual and
              group levels may be particularly relevant to
              the improvement of productivity.

b.   In the Individual Job.

 (1)   As already noted, increased autonomy or self-
        regulation on the job is an element in job en-
        richment which may, given the right workers and

the appropriate conditions, help enhance job
satisfaction and productivity.

(2) Management by Objectives (MBO) programs, which
feature an increased role for the worker in setting goals for his or her own job, represent one
approach to increasing self-control relative to
control by others. Based on a small number of
studies using managerial and exempt employees,
our review suggests that MBO programs serve to
increase those employees' motivation to attain
the goals set for their work, and also to improve
their job satisfaction (especially regarding the
evaluation system and supervisors). Effects on
actual job performance are not clear, but there
are indications that they too may be positive.
The utility of this approach with rank-and-file
workers has yet to be demonstrated.

c. In Work Groups.

(1) Giving workers more "say" over what goes on in
their groups usually has favorable effects on
job satisfaction, work motivation, and turnover.

(2) Effects on productivity are more clearly favorable when the scope of influence includes goal-
setting, work methods, and the method of compensation.

(3) Beneficial consequences are more likely to occur
if workers' personalities and values are congenial

to self-determination, e.g., those who tend to
be independent and non-authoritarian in outlook.

d. In the Organization as a Whole.

    (1) Organizations in which members at all levels
exercise greater control over what goes on in
the organization are typically more productive
and have more highly motivated, better satisfied
personnel than those where the total amount of
control is relatively low; however, it is not
clear whether high organizational control is the
cause or the effect of having high motivation.

    (2) Those organizations where control is more equal-
ly shared by various echelons of the work force
usually have better-satisfied workers, but are
not consistently more productive; this may be
due to the difficulty of equalizing control
throughout large or complex organizations, and/or
to the importance of situational factors such as
the personalities of members, task requirements,
and amount of commitment to organizational goals.

    (3) The effects on job performance and satisfaction
of formal mechanisms of participation, including
labor-management committees and collective bargaining with unions, have received little attention in the scientific literature; they appear
from the rather scattered available data to

constitute useful ways of increasing worker participation and possibly also work motivation, but such positive results depend upon a host of preconditions, chief among them being mutual trust between management and labor.

7. <u>Patterns of Compensation</u>.

a. Workers who are more highly paid generally like their pay and their jobs better and, if so, are less likely to quit or be absent.

b. Workers in a given job who are paid more are also likely to have higher motivation and productivity, but only if their pay level is linked to their performance.

c. Workers whose compensation is out of line with their standards of equity are less satisfied with their pay and jobs than those who are paid equitably; a related point is that satisfaction with pay is greater when it is clearly tied to performance than when it is not.

d. The potentially favorable results of improved compensation patterns are cancelled out if they have an adverse impact on other worker rewards, such as job security and social relations.

8. <u>System-Wide Changes</u>. We have summarized above our conclusions regarding the effects of three structural programs which have been widely discussed as ways of raising employees' motivation and therefore their job satisfaction and performance: job redesign, increased participation by employees, and reward-for-

performance. None of them, considered separately, has yielded unequivocal results in terms of <u>both</u> job satisfaction and productivity. Moreover, when the results were positive, they tended often to be disappointingly small. Finally, positive results were likely to happen only when the programs "fit" other conditions in the situation.

This set of conclusions suggests that greater effects might result from more extensive changes which include more than any one of the foregoing programs to create what amounts to new work systems. There exist in the literature perhaps a dozen reasonably well-documented experiments of this sort, from which we have reached the following conclusions:

a. Changes of the nature and magnitude of those represented in those system-wide studies can have major effects in raising the productivity and improving the economic performance of manufacturing plants. (They have not generally been tested in service organizations.)

b. Those kinds of changes also appear to have some favorable effect on the overall job satisfaction of the workers, although that finding is not as well documented nor does its magnitude seem to be as great as are the effects on productivity and other aspects of performance.

c. There is some evidence that people do work harder and that their job involvement and commitment may be increased, although again this impression is not solidly documented. The weight of the evidence suggests that the beneficial effects of

those systems on employee productivity are probably mediated
more by improvements in work methods and production capability
than by increased worker motivation.

    9.  <u>Critical Ingredients of Effective Systems</u>.  The
totality of the findings reviewed above may be summarized by
the following list of critical ingredients of systems which may
attain the desired dual objectives of higher productivity and
job satisfaction.  Such systems, we believe, have potential to be
<u>efficient</u> -- in Barnard's use of the term -- that is, not only
productively effective but also serving to satisfy the needs
and desires of their members.  It is probably not essential
that every system contain all of the ingredients in order to be
efficient.  Indeed, some may be inappropriate where the nature
of the technology or the needs of the work force call for different treatments.  But it seems unlikely that much progress
can be made if most are absent.

      a.  Financial compensation of workers must be
          linked to their performance and to productivity
          gains.

      b.  Workers and work must be matched so as to create
          a work situation which workers will see as capable
          of meeting their needs and expectations, and
          where they will have the capabilities and re-
          sources to be successful.

      c.  For workers who desire it, their work should pro-
          vide opportunity for full use of their abilities,

making a meaningful contribution, having challenging and diversified duties, and being
responsible for others.

d.  Workers at all levels must have inputs to plans
and decisions affecting their jobs and working
lives.

e.  Appropriate resources, including work methods and
equipment, must be provided to facilitate workers'
performance and minimize obstacles to carrying
out their jobs.

f.  Adequate "hygiene" conditions must exist, including competent and considerate supervision,
fair pay and fringe benefits, job security, good
working conditions, and sound employee relations.

10.  Incompleteness of List.  The foregoing list of six
ingredients is not necessarily complete.  There are other
elements which theory and practice suggest as being of possible
importance, but which suffer from insufficient attention in the
research literature.  As a consequence, their role in improving
both job satisfaction and performance has not yet been sufficiently well established to include them.  Examples of such
additional possible elements include:

- career structures which afford favorable future
  prospects for promotion, personal growth, and
  greater rewards.

- revised use of time for work and leisure, such as

the four-day week, the sabbatical leave, the educational leave, split schedules for couples, and
early and partial retirement plans.

- cooperative patterns of labor-management relations,
such as by new roles for unions or through works
councils.

11. Toward Implementation. We hope we have made clear
that the principles and conclusions discussed above are by no
means unequivocal even in our own thinking. As we have already
noted, and as the reader of Part Two will see, the research on
which they are based is not always sufficiently convincing,
either in terms of quality or quantity, to permit firm conclusions. On the other hand, it does point in certain direction
which we believe can serve as guidelines for policy and practice, and these we have set forth above.

We therefore suggest that the uncertain state of the art
does not call for immobility on this important front. Nor does
it imply that policy-makers are reduced to blind trial-and-
error if they wish to move ahead. Rather, we believe that the
research does illuminate the way to go, albeit somewhat dimly,
and that the best course is one of cautious movement in the
directions indicated with frequent soundings along the way.

In Chapter III, we will consider strategies and tactics
of initiating and implementing programs which incorporate the
positive elements discussed above.

# CHAPTER III
## IMPLEMENTATION

In the preceding chapter we summarized the findings of the study and discussed the nature of the problem. We now move to the all-important matter of strategies and tactics of putting that information to use.

The heart of the problem of implementation is this:

> To advance the dual objective of enhancing quality of working life and economic performance simultaneously, large scale changes have to be introduced into the work-place before results become visible, measurable, and demonstrably worth the effort. Yet, due to a combination of inadequate knowledge, resistance to change, suspicion of motives and weakness of commitment, changes must be introduced slowly and cautiously. But if the changes are too slow and too cautious, there is a real danger that the objective may never be reached.

A sound and practical strategy for breaking out of this bind    is only partly implied by the research we have reviewed, since most of it is addressed to the issue of inadequate knowledge and not to the practical/political obstacles.

In formulating our recommendations, some of the labor and management representatives on the project's Advisory

Committee urged that we take into account the full complexity
of the problem, including the political as well as the knowledge aspects -- on the grounds that to fail to do so would
lessen the usefulness of the report to policy-makers.  They
pointed out that while it is possible to separate the several
components analytically, in practice they are inseparable.
We have accepted this suggestion.  In what follows, therefore,
we go beyond the technical scope of the project in the interest
of providing guidance for effective action.

## The Need for a Coordinated Approach

To break out of the dilemma described above, the main
obstacles  to be overcome are the absence of consensus, lack
of knowledge, weakness of commitment to change, and overcoming
a heritage of mistrustful adversary relationships between
employees and management.

These obstacles surface in the form of skeptical questions raised by both management and labor.  Here, for example,
are the kinds of questions, fears, and doubts expressed by
managers:

- "How do I know it will work?"
- "How can I convince my Board of Directors and
  stockholders to stay with it long enough to
  prove it out?"
- "'hy should I get involved in something long
  range that may not show results until after I
  retire?"

- "Should I be putting so much time, effort and
  money into something as vague and intangible as
  worker satisfaction?"
- "Why should I preside over an activity that may
  well succeed in undermining management's pre-
  rogatives?"
- "Why can't I achieve the same results through
  actions I am more familiar and comfortable with --
  automation, for example?"
- "Why should I waste so much of the company's time
  and money on something that may be less important
  to our economic performance than new product
  development, more aggressive marketing, or
  better technology?"
- "Is the reward for success worth the risk of
  failure?"

Here are some of the questions and concerns which are
likely to bother labor officials:

- "How do I know that it is not just another more
  insidious form of speed-up?"
- "How do I know that the results will not be used
  to jeopardize job security?"
- "Why should I cooperate when the results may
  undermine the authority of this union just to
  play management's game?"
- "How do I know that this is what workers really
  want?"

- "Will this kind of effort deflect attention away from the bread-and-butter issues of better pay, more economic security and improved work conditions?"

The sources of indecision among both groups relate to whether the ratio of benefits to costs -- in terms of their respective values, interests and priorities -- are worth the effort.

Our analysis suggests a number of actions that must be taken if the benefit/cost ratio is to tilt in favor of innovative programs to improve worker motivation, productivity, and satisfaction along the lines suggested in the previous chapters. Among the more urgent are:

Goal-setting and leadership

Accelerating national consensus on goals

Removing disincentives to change

Furnishing new incentives

Protecting workers from unwanted consequences

Improving worker qualifications

Developing new tools and techniques

Performing basic and applied research

Performing and evaluating demonstration projects

Training new types of specialists

Communication of information

Clearly, no one agency of society can be solely responsible for initiatives along all these lines, not individual employers, nor labor unions, nor government. All must be involved, plus the other social institutions which have a part in cultural change and development, including philanthropic foundations, mass media, educational institutions, professional societies, and research and consulting organizations. Some of the functions listed above will fall mainly in the province of one or two of these institutions rather than the others. For example, removing disincentives and creating new incentives to change are primarily a responsibility of government, with its vast legislative, taxing, and regulatory powers. By contrast, communication and dissemination of information regarding the nature and results of new programs is a function that all institutions can and should perform. Several, but not all, would share responsibility for performing research. And so on regarding the various other functions.

It is neither appropriate nor desirable for us to attempt here to fix responsibilities for all these functions. However, we will suggest what would be most useful if done by two of the major existing institutions: government and employing organizations. We will also describe certain functions that could usefully be performed by a type of institution which as yet does not exist in this field, the free-standing institute devoted to advancing knowledge and methods of improving worker motivation, productivity, and satisfaction.

## The Role of Government

The main functions of government in relation to this emerging national objective are three: setting directions, funding, and legislation.

1. <u>Setting Directions and Goals</u>. The question of the proper role of government in firming up a sense of commitment in the private sector is a troublesome one, raising fundamental questions of values and political philosophy. This is because there are two distinctly different rationales at issue. One is the economic rationale. Put bluntly, the economic rationale here would be that under specified conditions, enhancing the worker's quality of working life is a more cost-effective means for increasing productivity than alternative uses of the same amount of money and effort. Undoubtedly, many employers -- and employees too -- would support such efforts if this proposition could be demonstrated unequivocally and beyond a reasonable doubt. Unfortunately, the research findings on this point are, as we have seen, far from unequivocal. They say neither yes or no, but maybe -- and only under conditions which are vaguely suggested by the research but by no means fully specified.

This economic rationale draws mixed support from leaders in the labor movement, and from many citizens as well. It is not that they oppose the idea of improving productivity, but they are skeptical about the benefits to workers, and also they place equal or greater emphasis on pursuing the goal of enhancing work satisfaction as a good in itself, apart from its economic benefits. They are willing to try to reconcile the two goals in the interests of accomplishing two worthy objectives at the same time, but they are not content with an exclusive emphasis on economic performance as a rationale for introducing massive changes and dislocations in the workplace.

What is the role of government under such ambiguous conditions? We believe that government actions which embody fundamental values should, in a democracy, reflect an emerging consensus among all citizens, or at least a majority sentiment. Our interpretation of current survey data is that such a consensus is, in fact, slowly emerging. It is a consensus not unlike that which has emerged over the past few years with respect to preservation of the environment even when this entails some economic sacrifices. This growing consensus has not yet articulated itself clearly, and may not for several more years, but the basis for it is present. An important action step for the government should be to articulate this social goal even though it may take many years to achieve. This could take many forms, including hearings, conferences, publications, demonstration projects, research, and legislation. The model for the last is the Full Employment Act of 1946. The goal of full employment is yet to be achieved and the Act has yet to be fully implemented. Between 1947 and 1960, the Act helped forge a broad socio-political consensus around the idea of full employment, and led many agencies to take steps all aiming at the same broad goal. Some of that consensus was later dissipated, yet the Act still stands on the books as a reminder of unfinished business the society agrees must be carried out.

In a similar spirit, we would recommend that the goal of achieving a better quality of working life for all Americans should be a clear and inherent part of any federally chartered new organization established to pursue the goals at issue in this study. It would also be appropriate in our judgment to have such an objective clearly enumerated in any revisions made in the Full Employment Act of 1946 and other related legislation.

2. Funding. In order to fund activities like those described above, consideration might be given to creating a federally chartered National Endowment as a funding apparatus. Alternatively, or in conjunction with the above, consideration should be given to enlarging the scope and budget of the National Commission on Productivity and the Quality of Work, and/or the Division of Advanced Productivity Research and Technology of NSF/RANN, giving them greater permanence and continuity in recognition of the long-term character of the problem and the need to attract good people. In their agenda, emphasis should be placed on encouraging the development of professional "know-how" in addition to theoretical knowledge, since the task of applying knowledge that has already been gained and adapting it to the special conditions of each individual workplace is an important aspect of the current problem

Their special mission should not be basic research as an end in itself, though such research will be involved, but the development of practical, demonstrable, transferable applications.

Funding will also be needed for the additional research and development that must be performed in order to generate and test new or more refined knowledge about how jointly to elevate worker productivity and the quality of working life. As we have reiterated at numerous points in this report, the state of the art is still rather primitive. Additional R&D efforts are needed to upgrade it while cautious applications of the lessons already learned are being tested. Although it is to be hoped that some of this essential research will, to an appreciable extent, be subsidized by others, federal planning and funding will also be needed if it is to be done on the scope required by the complexity of the problem. Responsibility for this funding might be vested in the agency or agencies proposed above, or shared with various other relevant federal agencies, including the Departments of Labor, Commerce, and HEW.

An important aspect of funding is related to the creation of new free-standing institutes to carry out a great deal of the training, research, communications and development of programs that are needed. The major functions of such institutes are described later in this chapter. The important points to be made here are, first, that they be jointly funded from the outset by management, labor, and the foundations as well as by government; this will help ensure their independence and sensitivity to the needs of the major participants.  Secondly, the funding should be of a sufficiently large scale to guarantee enduring impact.

    3.  Legislation.  The opportunities for creative legislation in this area are virtually boundless.  Such legislation should concern itself both with the human and the economic benefits and costs of change to help reduce economic dislocations and to insure that workers are not victimized by the changes envisaged but have the opportunity to benefit from them.  Only then will the full cooperation of the work force be forthcoming.  For purposes of illustration, some possible legislative targets are described below:

    a.  Economic Security.  It is unlikely that the piecemeal process of collective bargaining will help to insure a sufficient level of economic security for the work force so as to free workers from the fear that they may be undermining their own job security by encouraging substantial increases in the economic efficiency of their organizations.  This is perhaps the most important of all possible legislative targets.

    b.  Undoing Current Disincentives.  There are many anomalies in legislation now on the books that operate as disincentives to the productive use of human resources.  Welfare legislation is a notorious example. Another is Social Security rules that do not permit people on Social Security to earn money beyond a bare minimum until they have reached the age of seventy-two. Public interest law firms which are concerned with identifying and rooting out such anomalies should be strengthened by permitting and encouraging a more equitable fee structure. (The American Bar Association is considering support for such a program at this time.)

c. Unemployment Insurance. This area requires thorough review, not only to make provisions for taking inflation into account, but also to provide a more effective mechanism for mitigating the economic consequences of unemployment.

d. Retraining for Workers. Legislation is almost undoubtedly required to insure more effective programs of retraining. One possibility is to create a National Manpower Training Fund to which employers contribute, and from which they receive refunds up to the amount of their contribution upon successful implementation of retraining programs.

e. Post-Secondary School Education. There is an urgent need to do something about the approximately three out of four young people in the country who do not receive a four-year college education but who have strong aspirations to equip themselves better for jobs and careers. We require many new institutions and programs to give young people opportunities for continuing training and education relevant to their jobs and potential new careers.

f. Incentives to Employers. As noted earlier, one of the barriers to movement is the financial cost of experimentation and change. There may be employers in industry or local government who would be interested in moving in the directions indicated here, but who are not in a position to incur the expense which may be entailed. The federal government can play a role here similar to one it performed in connection with manpower training via MDTA, namely, making available funds which will absorb such incremental costs and share the economic risks, for the sake of the anticipated social benefits.

Clearly, there is no dearth of opportunities for a creative and constructive role by government, particularly if Public Manpower Policy is conceived as a partnership between government and the private sector. Those mentioned above are illustrations of these major objectives for legislation: (a) reducing the fear of economic insecurity; (b) removing

current disincentives; (c) furnishing positive incentives;
(d) doing more about the education, training and career opportunities for the average worker; and (e) making provisions to
counter economic dislocations.

## The Individual Organization

The employing organization -- private or public -- is, in
the last analysis, the fulcrum for action in implementing programs aimed at improving productivity and the quality of working life. It is here that programs will be proposed or ignored,
adopted or rejected, succeed or fail.

We propose that programs of action by individual organizations be planned to proceed through four stages of development:

Stage I:    Firming up Commitment

Stage II:   Preparing the Groundwork

Stage III:  Identifying the Initial Action Steps

Stage IV:   Managing Change and Progress

We estimate that the first three stages, essentially planning steps, should take at least six to twelve months under
optimum conditions. Because of the complexity of the task and
the long term commitment it implies, future success depends on
how skillfully and thoroughly these initial steps are carried
out. Consequently, the discussion that follows focuses mainly
on the three planning stages.

## Stage I:  Firming up the Commitment

Any organization would be foolish to launch an ambitious
human resources program of the kind described in this report
without thinking through in advance its willingness and readiness to make a long term and lasting commitment.  Unfortunately,
the organization cannot count on quick results to help persuade
skeptics and doubters and to dispel the kinds of fears cited
earlier in this chapter.  Also, the various parties involved
must face up to conflicting interests early in the planning
process; otherwise these will emerge later to disrupt and
possibly destroy the program.

There is no doubt that joint productivity/quality of working life programs face formidable obstacles.  At the same time,
it is also clear that for certain organizations, the rewards
are well worth the effort to overcome them.  It is therefore
necessary for each organization to determine for itself whether
the rewards are sufficiently great to merit such an undertaking.

How can this be done?  We propose that each organization
interested in determining whether or not it is ready to make
a major commitment to overhauling its human resources management along the lines outlined in this report undertake a special study to answer the following eight questions.  These can
serve as an effective checklist to enable each organization to
determine whether this type of approach is right for them, in
light of the conditions noted in Chapter II as prerequisites to
its success.  If any one of the eight questions cannot be
answered positively, at least in part, then the likelihood of

success is greatly reduced. If all can be answered positively, then the likelihood of success of such programs is great, and the organization can feel confidence in making a commitment that will pay off both in terms of enhanced economic performance and a dynamic, vigorous and highly motivated work force.

The eight-question checklist is as follows:

1. <u>Does the organization's performance depend substantially on the efforts of its human resources</u>? We are using performance here in its broad sense, including intangible and qualitative aspects, such as customer service and quality of workmanship, as well as efficiency of production. Those organizations in which worker care and effort play a major part in performance, so that management places high priority on such factors, are more open to change programs. Service organizations are particularly dependent upon their workers' performance. However, the roster of eligibles undoubtedly includes many manufacturing, sales, and financial institutions as well.

2. <u>Is the organization's background of employee and labor relations such that an expression of desire to enter upon cooperative ventures will be viewed by employees with some credibility</u>? Success depends upon the existence of at least a moderate amount of good will and confidence among employees and management, enough that the various parties are willing to give a new approach a try without undermining it in advance out of cynicism and mistrust.

3. <u>Does the organization have a fairly high standing on "hygiene" factors</u>? If there is fear of job insecurity through-out the organization, or if working conditions are substandard

and a source of widespread complaint, or if pay levels are felt to be unjustly low, then the climate for launching new cooperative programs may not be right.

4. Does the technology with which the organization is identified leave room for flexibility and change in the organization of work? There are variations among organizations in the extent to which their proven production system is amenable to the kinds of changes which may be needed to implement these programs. In some instances, experimentation may be more costly -- in terms of investment and risk of failure -- than in others. It is not easy for the outsider to make the right judgment. Some high-technology  highly structured industries which might seem the least likely candidates (e.g., a petroleum refinery) may turn out on closer inspection to have a surprisingly great potential for enhancing both productivity and worker quality of life.

5. Is there a genuine interest at the policy-making levels of the organization in giving equal emphasis to the dual objectives? Some organizations are not serious about improving their economic performance; others are intensely interested in productivity but have little concern for employees beyond serving as a means to this end. Unless agreement among policy makers exists that both goals are vitally important, it probably makes little sense to launch an ambitious human resources/productivity program.

6. Is there willingness at the policy-maker level to share with workers at all levels the economic benefits of improved productivity? If not, employees will soon lose interest. The program might even backfire if it became understood as only another

device for generating greater profits for management with no
benefit to workers.

7. <u>Is there willingness at the policy-maker level to let
go of some power and authority in the interest of enhancing
and enlarging the overall authority and power of the organization?</u>
Beyond a doubt, a cooperative venture will mean sharing decision-
making among a larger group of people. If the key policy-makers
in the organization are unwilling to face such a prospect, the
program is likely to bog down in the early stages.

8. <u>Is the work force predominantly young, fairly well
educated and possessing actual or potential high levels of
technical skills which are needed in the organization?</u> A well-
educated, young work force -- high school graduates and above --
has different needs and responds to different motivations than
one that is old, set in its ways, and lacking in potential for
learning. There is an almost universal desire among young
people today to make full use of their potential skills. Better
educated, higher skill workers are also generally more interested in seeing changes along the lines proposed here than are
those at lower educational and job levels.

These eight questions are not easy to answer, but they all
are answerable. We strongly urge any organization considering a
program of the type described here to make the effort to
answer them as thoroughly and formally as possible before
making a major commitment. This effort would be assisted if
there were available a systematic assessment procedure, resulting
in a "Program Readiness Profile". Development of such
a procedure should be a major undertaking of the free-standing

institutes to be discussed later.

At this point the policy-maker may ask, "Why bother? Why go through so much trouble, effort, and expense to link together two objectives that have been pursued in the past separately? Productivity is best enhanced through intelligent applications of technology and capital, while worker satisfaction is best achieved by improving their standard of living. Why should we now abandon these successful and proven methods in favor of new approaches that are relatively unproven, difficult to apply and obviously fraught with hazards?"

If this were twenty years ago, or even ten, such questions would be difficult to counter. Even today, for certain organizations who cannot answer these questions positively, it is likely that the approaches outlined here may not be appropriate. Such organizations would do better to pursue separately the objectives of productivity and increased job satisfaction. Overall, however, our interpretation of current trends suggests that an increasing number of organizations no longer have that as a viable alternative open to them -- if they are to improve their health and effectiveness.

There are many signs that work motivation is changing and becoming unresponsive to carrot-and-stick incentives exclusively. In the current gloomy economic climate the average person's assumption that he can look forward to an ever-increasing standard of living is being swiftly undermined. Also, in many organizations, especially the growing number of service organi-

zations, the tendency to rely mainly on capital, technology
and formal organization methods for their efficiency with a
comparative neglect of human resources has reached a point
of diminishing returns; in such organizations, effectiveness
means effective (i.e., motivated) employees.

It goes beyond the scope of this study to document these
points, and some readers may take issue with them.  They are
cited here not for the purpose of arguing a case but simply
to underscore the point that, however long and difficult the
journey, many organizations will find it worth making -- because they do not have any alternative.  We expect that each
year will find more and more organizations asking themselves
these eight questions.

## Stage II:  Preparing the Groundwork for Action

It is essential that employee representation, including
union participation if there is a union, be built-in from the
very outset.  Otherwise, a joint effort -- a necessary pre-
condition for lasting success -- will be jeopardized.  There
are many organizational formats for carrying this out; the one
selected should, of course, be the one that makes most sense
in each particular situation.

The study of organizations shows that three approaches
to work organization are possible.  The most prevalent is the
authoritarian approach whereby direction is imposed from the
top, aided by expert advice.  The drawbacks here are that
knowledge that resides elsewhere in the organization is not

productively channeled into the decision-making and implementing process. Also, this format characteristically generates the greatest amount of covert but nonetheless effective resistance.

A second approach features a "grass roots" format, as exemplified in extreme forms of participation. The great danger here is the converse of the authoritarian model: there may be a less than optimum contribution from the top, as well as subtle but effective patterns of resistance from management.

The third approach is that of management-union (or if there is not a union, management-employee) cooperation, with experts brought in as resources when needed. This is the least familiar model because of the tradition of maintaining a fairly rigid distinction between "the management" and "the workers."

It is, therefore, necessary to prepare the ground for a cooperative effort, if one is unfamiliar to the organization, by creating an atmosphere of trust and confidence. This means no hidden agendas, a willingness to clarify goals in mutual cooperation with the union or other worker representatives, and a willingness to place as much emphasis on the quality of working life goals as on the productivity goals.

In various experiments in job redesign, compensation, participation, as well as in other areas, participants have found helpful an approach that is known as "action research." The action research approach proceeds through the following steps: first, there is an attempt to unfreeze the <u>status quo</u>

by formulating plans jointly and taking some initial action that seems to make sense; the action step is accompanied by evaluation, the results of which are fed back to improve the action; the next step is further action, evaluation, and feedback in a dynamic process that continues until a new and more desirable status quo is reached which is then frozen into policy once again.

Securing management/worker cooperation within an action research format is not only a good way to establish a working relationship, it achieves by itself one of the objectives of the program, namely, increasing the level of mutual influence all up and down the line.

## Stage III: Identifying Initial Steps for Action

Each organization can select from a wide array of available tactics those most suitable to its own situation. Systematic review and evaluation should be made of each available plan from the point of view of its "fit" with the history and culture of the organization, and the type of people employed.

There exist a variety of ways in which any one of the six critical elements outlined in Chapter II can be engineered into a system. For example, the ingredient specifying increased worker influence can be achieved by job redesign, MBO, autonomous work groups, organizational "flattening," or adoption of a Scanlon Plan. Ingenuity may suggest still additional techniques. This choice of means to a given end is manifestly an advantage, since it increases the opportunity to adopt techniques which fit the requirements or traditions of a given situation or organization.

The crucially important decisions of who is to do what and where to begin should be left up to the joint management/union work group. The process of diagnosing organization strengths and weaknesses and deciding on an initial point of entry, with outside help available on a resource basis, should be a key part of their mission. This can be done by any of the time-tested approaches to problem identification such as by a special task force, setting up a Works Council or Committee, surveying staff opinions, etc. But whatever technique is used, it should be under the aegis of the cooperating parties.

In many instances, it may be useful to focus on some problem that has been a longstanding source of irritation and where a solution lies readily at hand. Such a starting point is a good one: it attacks a point of low resistance, and yields a success story which generates the confidence and good-will needed to fuel the attack on more unyielding problems. Thus, for both psychological as well as practical reasons it is unwise to decide the most strategic point of entry in advance. This must be the initial prerogative of the newly cooperating parties.

## Stage IV: Managing Change and Progress

We suggest that general responsibility for the success of such efforts be placed at the highest level of the organization. This high level is required because of the breadth of the task, extending across all functions, and also because of the policy issues that will be made explicit when the organization is confronted with problems of a basic value, such as programs that enhance quality of life without a clear-cut and swift productivity benefit.

Because of the experimental and continuing character of the program and the commitment, it is important that some measurement system be instituted to evaluate progress and to help give the program focus and direction. There should be two types of measurements, corresponding to the dual objectives of the program -- a method for measuring productivity gains in the broadest sense of the word, and a method for measuring improvement in worker satisfaction, motivation and quality of working life.

We suggested earlier that each organization formally define the components of productivity and performance that are important to it. Some organizations will stress quality of product and customer/client satisfaction; others will place greater emphasis on more conventional measures of quantity of output per manhour of cost. To still others, stability of the work force may be vital.

Once the components of performance that are important to the organization have been identified, an effort should be made to quantify what each element is worth and how to measure it. Brogden & Taylor (1950), Flamholtz (1972), Likert (1973), and Macy & Mervis (1974) are among those who have suggested approaches to obtain such measures.

Measuring improvements in the quality of working life is a less familiar undertaking, although partial starts have been made in the form of attitude surveys. It is, we believe, desirable that the basic groundwork and key indicators of quality of working life be developed by an appropriate national organization, as described in the next section, although individual organizations or researchers are to be encouraged to contribute to such an effort as well. Once standard measures are developed and national norms set by type of industry, age, sex, level of education and type of work, each individual organization will be able to take measurements of its own work force relative to national and other appropriate norms.

Research and development work on such new measurement tools should be one of the main tasks addressed by the type of free-standing institutes described in the next section.

## Free-standing Institutes

We recommend the establishment of one or more free-standing and independent institutes, both national and specialized by region or sector of the economy. Their function will be to perform tasks of training, communications, research and evaluation that cannot be done with optimum cost-effectiveness at the level of the individual organization or by government directly; in addition, they could assist individual organizations in planning and carrying out their programs. Such institutes should be jointly supported by management, labor, government and private sources, in order to help assure representation of the interests of the several segments of the public.

An imposing list of needs and functions for such institutes is suggested by our analysis. We would like to emphasize the following six:

1. accelerating the process of consensus;

2. developing new measurement tools;

3. serving as a clearing-house of information;

4. performing applications research;

5. performing demonstration projects; and

6. offering expertise as a resource.

There are other necessary and desirable functions these institutes can perform, such as serving as a clearing-house for all of the work being done worldwide on this issue, and the all-important function of training people to carry out the new programs. The six we are choosing to emphasize were selected because they may warrant more explanation. We also wish to repeat the point made earlier that we are not recommending that performing any of these needed functions be the sole responsibility of this or any other agency of society.

1. <u>Accelerating Consensus</u>. This step is logically first, and is a prerequisite for the success of the others. Much needs to be done to find the common ground of agreement among participants who now may see their interests as divergent. In

particular, both labor and management need to confront their own assumptions and to realize -- if the findings of our Assumptions Survey hold up -- that there may be a larger common area of agreement among them than they suppose. Also, finding common ground presupposes a certain amount of conceptual clarification. As we have seen, much confusion exists about the meaning of productivity and the relationship between job satisfaction and job motivation. As a result of misunderstandings of these concepts, labor, management, and economists often find themselves speaking at cross purposes with one another. There is also a deep-rooted predisposition to grasp at gimmicks and single target programs -- and then to be disillusioned when these do not work. Finally, the presence of so many inarticulate fears tends to undermine the commitment to engage in long term programs until these fears are brought out into the open where they can be confronted directly.

Various organs of society can play invaluable roles in accelerating the process of education, clarification and consensus-seeking. One avenue especially suitable to the free-standing institutes would be the organization of carefully staffed conferences, not less than three days in duration, to give participants the opportunity to "work through" their doubts, reservations and questions and to assimilate the considerable amount of information and clarification they need.

2. Developing New Measurement Tools. Organizations need to place new long term programs on a firm foundation of fact,

and they need new information to enable them to assess their own unique economic and human incentives, to set reasonable objectives, to measure progress, and to adapt and change programs in the light of feedback about how they are progressing. As we have noted above, to carry out the tasks, major new measurement devices need to be developed. Although some organizations may have the staff capability to do the necessary R&D work themselves, most will probably turn for assistance to external sources such as the new institutes.

a. Program Readiness Profile. We mentioned earlier, in connection with Stage I of the agenda confronting the individual organization, the necessity of sizing up its readiness to make a long-term commitment to achieving the dual objectives of improving productivity in relation to the quality of working life. To this end, we noted the necessity of answering eight key questions. Answers to those questions cannot and should not be given glibly; often, they will require digging for relevant facts. We believe that the institutes can furnish a useful service procedure whereby an organization can assess its situation in those regards, resulting in a "Program Readiness Profile."

For example, the very first of those questions asks how important to organizational per-

formance is the behavior of workers. This requires an analysis of organizational goals and
the extent to which each depends on employee performance. Where those goals have financial implications (e.g., obtaining repeat business or
producing defective items), then the human contributions can be estimated in dollar terms
through the approaches of cost accounting and
human resource accounting. In short, this calls
for the use of productivity measures along the
lines suggested as being needed for monitoring the
consequences of changes, except that here such
measures would be applied for another purpose.

The institutes could similarly be helpful in
devising ways whereby individual organizations
could assess their suitability for program adoption
in terms of the remaining seven issues discussed
in Stage I: characteristics of the work force,
state of labor relations, standing on "hygiene"
factors, flexibility of technology, commitment to
dual goals, openness to increasing level of mutual
influence, and willingness to share with workers
the economic benefits of improved performance. To
be sure, some of these assessments would be more
judgmental than factual in their basis, but even
there, assistance could be furnished in obtaining

more systematic and reliable judgments.

The institutes could also be helpful by compiling the Profiles resulting from application of the procedure in a number of different organizations, and analyzing the composite picture broken down by types of organization, size, industry, etc. This would furnish background for organizations to compare and interpret their own profiles in making assessments of readiness.

b.   Work Motivation/Quality of Life Indicators. This comprises another needed measurement system. This system needs to be distinguished from the familiar job satisfaction or morale surveys.

As suggested in an earlier section, the latter types of polls typically fail to take into account the critical difference between job satisfaction and work motivation. The former relates to how well people like their jobs, whereas the latter is concerned with how important it is for them to do their work and do it well. Our technology for measuring the former is far more advanced than the latter. Yet it is the level of work motivation, not just satisfaction, which appears to be the common denominator of productivity and the quality of working life.

For purposes of this report we will define

quality of working life as the aggregate of the worker's job satisfaction, plus his motivation, plus the balance with other aspects of his life. A worker can be said to enjoy a high quality of working life when he (i) has positive feelings towards his job and its future prospects, (ii) is motivated to stay on the job and perform well, and (iii) feels his working life fits well with his private life to afford him a balance between the two in terms of his personal values. This definition is all too brief and is undoubtedly controversial since it raises thorny issues of values. But it does have the virtue of permitting workers to define quality of working life in terms that are most meaningful to them; it avoids the problem of the expert imposing his own value judgments (i.e., the intellectual who assumes that the assembly-line worker cannot enjoy a high quality of working life), and it leads to a practical method of measuring these vitally important "intangibles." As noted earlier, nowhere do we have today even the crudest estimate of the number of workers in the country who are both satisfied <u>and</u> highly motivated.

We recommend the design and execution of a set of work motivation/quality of working life indicators to fill the vacuum of information that now exists. These should be measured annually among a cross-section of working Americans, to serve as a set of national, regional and industry norms against which individual organizations can compare themselves. They should include measures of (i) job satisfaction, (ii) job involvement, (iii) behavior on the job (estimates of absenteeism, plans for changing jobs, etc.), (iv) the character of the work ethic, and (v) the nature of worker values and expectations. It should seek to define empirically and specifically what quality of working life means to various groups in the work population. Some types of people thrive under greater responsibility, others do not. For some, job enlargement means personal fulfillment, for others it means an added burden that diminishes their quality of working life.

If they have to make critically important decisions without such information, decision-makers will necessarily fall back on the inadequate data they are most familiar with, with the consequent risk of wrong judgments.

3. Serving as an Information Clearing-house. It is important that program-planners have available a descriptive catalog of the various kinds of techniques and methods being used

in one place or another to implement or improve programs of work motivation. Evaluative findings, where available, should also be reported.

There are, for example, innumerable forms of compensation plans and productivity-sharing programs, many of which have been tried and then abandoned. Some have been discarded because they are unworkable, others because they have been misapplied or applied under the wrong set of conditions. If organizations are not to "reinvent the wheel," they should have access to a practical, systematic, continuously updated inventory of alternative tactics for achieving specific objectives.

The institutes can provide a useful role by inventorying and disseminating such information. The inventory should not only describe each technique, but also should specify (a) the preconditions needed to make it most effective, (b) the pitfalls to look out for, (c) the magnitude and nature of results, (d) time and money requirements, and (e) alternative means of achieving the same goals.

4. Applications Research. In addition to cataloging the current state of the art, there is a massive need to advance it through large scale programs of applications research, particularly in areas somewhat underdeveloped in the current literature. As illustrations, we cite the following:

> a. Longitudinal case studies going beyond before-and-after measurements. There should be continuous

moving trend-line measurements, plus qualitative observations by participant observers who maintain a daily diary of changes relevant to understanding what is happening.

b.  Cost-benefit studies of productivity and economic performance in a wide variety of work settings, taking into full account the intangible aspects of economic performance such as product quality and customer/client service, as well as output per man hour. Such studies can serve as input for the productivity cost-benefit profile outlined above.

c.  Studies on how to motivate policy makers to undertake long-term programs (e.g., post-retirement awards in money and recognition for programs that come to fruition after the executive has retired.)

d.  Organization studies on how to overcome psychological and social resistance to change.

e.  Studies on how to upgrade the personnel function in organizations, including special training programs to recruit and attract broad-gauged people into this line of work.

f.  Case studies that are not proprietary in nature. Many interesting experiments never see the light of day because of the sponsoring organization's reluctance to give away "trade secrets." This resistance can probably be overcome through advance provisions and by a _quid pro quo_ wherein the institute offers skills and even partial funding in exchange for freedom to publish results that do not violate the organization's privacy rights.

g. Studies on how to expedite technology transfer in this field. Many organizations have found it easier to transfer machine technology from one location to another than to transfer skills in utilizing human resources. Studies are needed to show how to transfer "best practice" more swiftly and faithfully in this domain.

5. _Demonstration Projects._ Closely related to the above is the need for demonstration projects that aim at testing the effectiveness of the kinds of programs we have been discussing. It should be emphasized that the purpose here is as much psychological as it is a search for objective knowledge. If policy makers can see demonstrable proof that the pursuit of these dual objectives achieves tangible and measurable results, both in the sense of an economic payoff and also in the sense of a net increase in human well-being, their willingness to act will be immensely advanced. Consequently, with this purpose in mind, it would be self-defeating to rush prematurely into the performance of large-scale demonstration projects before all of the development work needed to evolve effective strategies has been completed. In science, the so-called crucial experiment

is preceded by a series of lesser experiments conducted to gain
the knowledge needed to put an important hypothesis to a critical test. Similarly, in the current situation, the design of
crucial demonstrations are at least a few years away, awaiting
the completion and refinement of multi-target programs sufficiently well-designed to insure the likelihood of large-scale
positive results.

6. Expertise as a Resource. It is to be anticipated
that, as commitment grows and as organizations are increasingly
willing to go forward with new programs but are somewhat unsure
about how to proceed, there will be increased need for expert
advice to assist in that process. In addition to the usual
sources of such expertise, the know-how developed in the free-
standing institutes needs to be made available for that purpose.

Although the consulting process will eventually cover a
wide variety of activities, we would place initial emphasis on
consulting with organizations about the very first step in the
process of change. We envisage this first step as one in
which management and labor come together to settle on the
strategically-best point of departure for their particular
organization, given its past history and current problems.
Often, there will be some one trouble spot which, if it can be
remedied, will give all parties a sense of accomplishment and
enhance the feeling that the other side is approaching the
problem in good faith. It will give the program momentum.
Given the prevailing climate of mistrust, it would be a mistake
for either party to enter such a process with a plan for pro-

ceeding that had been worked out in advance, requiring the manipulation of the other side rather than a true cooperative effort. Here is where a specially trained consultant can be an invaluable asset. If he can help the organization get off to a good start, the chances of continuing along productive lines are greatly enhanced. Institutes of the type envisaged should give priority attention to recruiting and training men and women who can carry out this function with confidence and skill. There are many potential candidates for these positions, but they require extensive training and experience.

Summary

We have examined hundreds of studies and have found only relatively few which clearly point to a sound approach to increasing job performance and the quality of work life as a related process. The literature is slim but its very existence indicates that there are possibilities for success. It has demonstrated that when the appropriate variables are combined under the proper conditions, significant improvements may occur in both job performance and quality of work life. By bringing the attention of policy-makers to the empirical studies which illuminate new methods or refine old concepts, needless blind alleys and time-consuming detours may be avoided and greater encouragement provided for more effective experiments or efforts. As Robert Merton (1962) has observed,

> "In the world laboratory of the sociologist, as in
> the more secluded laboratories of the physicist
> and chemist, it is the successful experiment

which is decisive and not the thousand-and-one
failures which preceded it. More is learned
from the single success than from the multiple
failures. A single success proves it can be
done. Thereafter, it is necessary only to
learn what made it work. This, at least, is
what I take to be the sense of those revealing
words of Thomas Love Peacock, 'Whatever is,
is possible.'" (p. 436).

PART TWO:  RESEARCH FINDINGS

CHAPTER IV

MANAGEMENT AND UNION LEADER ASSUMPTIONS

One of this study's objectives is to compare the research findings on job satisfaction and productivity with the
policy assumptions that underlie current policies, practices
and beliefs. A well-tested method for insuring that policy
makers understand the relevance of research findings to their
concerns is to permit them to check their own beliefs against
facts that confirm or deny them. In Chapter II, we summarized
which assumptions appear to be sound and which are cast in
doubt by the findings.

Method

The method of gathering and analyzing the policy assumptions described in this chapter proceeded through two stages.
The first was a content analysis of speeches and articles by
business leaders, labor leaders, economists, psychologists
and the general public. This effort led to the preparation
of individual position papers which were then consolidated
into an Inventory of Policy Assumptions. The Inventory was
then reviewed by the full staff and by the Advisory Committee,
raising the following two issues: (1) The possibility that the
speeches and articles in which management and union views were
put forward might not be truly representative of the viewpoints
of these two groups; and (2) The possibility that the personal

preconceptions of the staff in selecting the assumptions could bias the analyses.

To obviate these difficulties and help insure equal standards of objectivity and factuality on this lesser but nonetheless critical component of the research, the study was amplified by two questionnaires with 563 respondents from businessmen -- gathered through the AMA -- and 69 union leaders who completed the same questionnaire.

Before describing the results of the two surveys it is important to enter several qualifications on their scientific status. Although the survey findings are decidedly more representative and informative than the results obtained by the preliminary content analysis, they should not be treated as anything more than a pilot study. One reason relates to the limitations of mail surveys. The rate of return on both samples is approximately 20 percent, a rate of return that raises the possibility of bias, i.e., those who respond may be self-selective and have a different point of view than those who do not respond. Also, mail surveys are not as penetrating as, for example, personal interviews. It is not possible in a mail survey to probe for the context of meaning and qualifications that would more accurately reflect a manager's or union leader's thinking. A third qualification relates to the characteristics of the list from which the sample was drawn. The list consists of all AMA members augmented by resources from attendees at AMA conferences. While the list undoubtedly represents a large and significant managerial group, the extent to which it is representative of all managers is unknown.

The above qualifications do not invalidate the results. But they do imply that they should be regarded as hypotheses rather than confirmed findings. In spite of such limitations, the surveys do provide us with more information, in a more quantitative and objective form, than we had originally anticipated or been committed to in the study; and they provide a frame of reference and a practical device for insuring their use for policy purposes. Since, however, these hypotheses possess interest and value in their own right, we believed it was important that their scientific status be appropriately qualified.

## Sample Description

The "management" returns come from questionnaires sent out to two separate subsamples. One is a subsample of the AMA list of 117,000 chief executive offices, the other of the AMA list of 8,900 industrial relations offices. Approximately 2,450 questionnaires were mailed to chief executive offices -- a one-in-forty rate; and 950 questionnaires were mailed to industrial relations offices, a one-in-eight rate. The overall rate of return was 16.6 percent.

The union leadership sample was drawn from a comprehensive list of national unions and employee associations

enumerated in the Directory of National Unions and Employee
Associations, 1971 (BLS, 1972). Questionnaires were sent
out to both the chief officers of the unions and the research director or education director. The union rate of
return was 19.8 percent. Virtually all those responding
expressed an interest in learning the results of the study.
Tables IV-1 and IV-2 below describe the characteristics of
the management and union leadership samples.

Analysis of the samples shows that the management
respondents appear not atypical of national manufacturing
managers as a group -- they are in the middle forties, from
a medium to large size firm in terms of sales, from a
medium to small size firm in terms of employment. In terms
of functional specialization respondents are heavily
weighted with managers with expertise in the human resources area.

The union respondents are, on the whole, older than
the managers; and include more chief executive officers.
Union respondents come from a broader spectrum of unions
than the managers that seemed to be representing manufacturing employment. In terms of membership size, the union
respondents are very much in line with the union membership
as a whole.

Table IV-1

Sample Description (Management)

Total Respondents:  563

|  | Percent |
|---|---|
| Rate of Response | 16.6 |
| Age of Respondents | |
| Under 40 years | 27 |
| 40-49 years | 34 |
| 50-59 years | 29 |
| 60 & over | 10 |
| Area of Employment | |
| General Management | 46 |
| Personnel and/or Industrial Relations | 46 |
| Other | 8 |
| Principal Activity of Respondent's Organization | |
| Manufacturing | 52 |
| Service | 16 |
| Wholesale/Retail | 12 |
| All Other | 20 |
| Annual Sales/Budget of Respondent's Organization | |
| Under 1 Million | 7 |
| 1 to 5.9 Million | 20 |
| 6 to 25.9 Million | 19 |
| 26 to 50.9 Million | 12 |
| 51 to 100.9 Million | 13 |
| 101 Million to 1 Billion | 18 |
| Over 1 Billion | 8 |

Table IV-1 - Cont'd.

| Number of Employees - Per Organization | Percent |
|---|---|
| Under 50 employees | 13 |
| 50-250 employees | 25 |
| 251-750 employees | 14 |
| 751-2000 employees | 17 |
| 2001 to 10,000 employees | 19 |
| Over 10,000 employees | 12 |
| Geographic Area of Organization | |
| Northeast - New York Area | 32 |
| Midwest - Chicago Area | 29 |
| South - Atlanta/Dallas Area | 2 |
| West - San Francisco/Los Angeles Area | 1 |

Table IV-2

Sample Description (Unions)

Total Respondents:  69

| | Percent |
|---|---|
| Rate of Response | 19.8 |
| Age of Respondents | |
|     Under 40 years | 19 |
|     40 - 49 years | 25 |
|     50 - 59 years | 42 |
|     60 and over | 14 |
| Respondent's Functional Area | |
|     Union or Association Officer | 61 |
|     Research Director and/or Education Director | 39 |
| Respondent's Union Represents Workers Principally Engaged in | |
|     Manufacturing | 35 |
|     Government | 25 |
|     Service | 16 |
|     Crafts | 10 |
|     All Other | 14 |
| No. of Members Respondent's Union Represents | |
|     Under 100,000 | 55 |
|     100,000 - 299,999 | 26 |
|     Over 300,000 | 19 |
| No. of Employees Employed by Union | |
|     Under 100 | 57 |
|     100 - 249 | 30 |
|     250 & Over | 13 |

## Results

The major results of the two surveys are reported in tabular form at the end of this chapter. In comparing the responses of managers and union leaders, differences of less than about 8 percent should be discounted as too likely to be due to chance fluctuations, i.e., as being "statistically insignificant." Immediately below, we briefly describe the highlights of the findings.

1.  The Meaning of Productivity

Analysis of Table IV-3 shows sharply and clearly that a large majority of both managers (78%) and union leaders (70%) do not employ the economist's definition of productivity as relating solely to a total industry or its section of the economy, rather than an individual organization. Instead, most (a) relate productivity to the individual organization, and (b) include a much broader and more qualitative conception than the economist's narrow and essentially quantitative definition. By productivity managers mean: (1) the overall efficiency and effectiveness of the operation (88%); (2) intangibles such as disruptions, "shrinkage," sabotage and other indicators of trouble in the organization (73%); (3) rates of absenteeism and turnover, as well as measures of output (70%); (4) measures of customer or client satisfactions (64%); and (5) intangibles such as employee loyalty, morale, job satisfaction (55%). Union leadership, by and large, has a similar conception of productivity except that they are less likely to include indicators of trouble in the organization or measures of customer or client satisfaction. (See Table IV-3.)

We consider this finding a significant one worth calling to the attention of policy-makers. Indeed, the broader meaning given to the term productivity by unions and management goes a long way in explaining the limited support economists have traditionally given to job restructuring, personnel manipulation, incentive systems, etc. To the extent that economists have spoken out on this topic in what appeared to be in contradiction to management and labor, their opposition can now be viewed more as a failure of communication than as a difference of substance.

2. General Values and Beliefs

Table IV-4 consists of 15 sub-tables, each of which describes the extent and intensity of agreement or disagreement with a number of general values and beliefs that relate to the desirability of productivity, the nature of work, and the picture leadership holds of current work attitudes and worker satisfaction. Inspection of these tables reveals the following highlights:

a. There is complete and general agreement among both union and management leaders that "work should be a rewarding part of life not a form of drudgery." (See Table IV-4B.)

There is virtual unanimity of agreement among
both union leaders and management with respect to
certain characteristics of today's work force.
At least four out of five union leaders and
management people hold the views (a) that workers
demand more from their jobs today because they are
better educated, (b) that younger workers in particular are more interested than older workers in
participating in decision-making, but that,
(c) nothing that has been done to make work more
interesting offsets the worker's desire for
increased pay. (See Tables IV-4D, 4E, 4F and 4J.)
A majority of both union and management leaders
believe that workers take pride in their jobs
even when the work is routine. They strongly reject the idea that "workers do not care what they
produce or how they produce it -- as long as they
are well paid." And they are virtually unanimous
in rejecting the notion, "that the average unskilled worker is interested in doing as little as
possible," or that "work is a necessary evil;
people avoid it if they can." In other words,
both groups believe that work is important and that
pride of work continues to be a strong force in the
country even when dull routine jobs are held. (See
Tables IV-4K, 4L, 4M, and 4N.)

d. Interestingly, there is also a high level of
agreement by a majority of both groups that people
derive much of their satisfaction in life from
work, that worker dissatisfaction is real today and
not just "an invention of professors, journalists,
and 'the left'," and that workers' dissatisfaction
comes not from their jobs not from the problems of the
society as a whole. There is, however, some disagreement about the extent of work dissatisfaction
that now prevails: A 55 percent majority of
management believe that "most workers are satisfied
with their work," compared to a 45 percent minority
of union leaders who hold this view. (See Tables
IV-4G, 4H, 4I and 40.)

e. Management far more than union leadership holds the
view that "increasing productivity is essential to
insure a high standard of living for all Americans."
This view is held in an intense form by a 61 percent
majority of management in contrast to only 30 percent
of union leadership. (See Table IV-4A.)

f. A 79 percent majority of management believe that,
"the nation's productivity is suffering because the traditional American work ethic has eroded," in contrast to only one out of three (35%) of union leaders
who hold this perception. This is one of the largest
discrepancies in points of view revealed by the
research. (See Table IV-4C.)

Thus, except for the matter of the degree of attachment to the traditional American work ethic and the related importance of productivity -- both loosely defined ideas -- there is very little difference in the general values of managers and union leaders. When their responses in this survey are compared with broader surveys of general public opinion, both management and union representatives appear almost indistinguishable from the typical American, be he soldier, sailor, tinker, tailor...economist or industrial psychologist.

Points on which there is considerable disagreement between the two groups include:

3. Factors Influencing Productivity

As shown in Table IV-5, among management respondents, the factors considered "very important" in influencing an organization's productivity are, in rank order: better planning (66%), more effective management (65%), improved job procedures (49%), improved communications (48%), giving more recognition to employees for their achievements (45%), and better training of employees (45%). Factors considered least important by management (Table IV-6) include: providing better transportation to work, increasing competition among companies, creating more democracy in the organization, providing more worker incentive programs, and encouraging greater participation by workers in decision-making.

The rank order of union views are not strikingly dissimilar to those of management but there are some glaring disparities in emphasis. Thus, almost three times as many union leaders as managers (43% to 16%) cite improving the quality of working life and improving working conditions (41% to 16%) as "very important" to an organization's productivity. By a 52 percent to a 36 percent margin union leaders also give greater emphasis to improving human relations as a spur to productivity. They also place greater emphasis on such factors as: improved communications, participation by workers in decision-making, creating more democracy in the organization, and work incentive programs. Union leaders minimize to a greater extent than managers the importance of such factors as increasing market demands as a spur to productivity, harder work by employees, capital investment and stimulating more employee loyalty. (See Tables IV-5 and IV-6.)

Such disparities in emphasis stem in part from functional specialization: indeed, managers deal also with non-employee problems while union leaders are concerned primarily with workers. They know -- through experience -- that they can deal more easily with the rank and file when communications between workers and managers are improved. Also, having operated all their life in a political environment, union leaders are perhaps more sensitive to the importance of participation in decision-making and of democratic organizational structure.

4. Relationships Among Job Satisfaction, Motivation and

   Productivity

   There is a surprising degree of consensus on the relationship between job satisfaction, worker motivation, and productivity, as shown in Table IV-8. More than nine out of ten
union leaders and managers agree that job dissatisfaction leads
to "high turnover, tardiness, loafing on the job, disruptions,
poor workmanship, and indifference to customers and clients,"
-- all factors which are part of their conception of productivity. Almost nine out of ten (87%) agree that job satisfaction leads to greater productivity, and almost equal numbers
feel that a manager's concern for the welfare of his employees
improves productivity. Both groups strongly reject the idea
that workers are not capable of suggesting improved production
methods, and union leaders to an even greater extent than
managers believe that if work were enriched with higher skills,
workers would be more highly motivated (73% to 61%). There
is virtual unanimity among both groups in rejecting the idea
that "employee motivation has little or no bearing on productivity (94% among management, 91% among union leaders). There
is less agreement on the view that "workers believe that productivity is management's responsibility not theirs"; sixty-
five percent of management holds this view compared to 52 percent of union leaders. Interestingly, a majority of both
groups disagree with the idea that the best way to increase
output is by performance incentives. (See Tables IV-8A thru
8I.)

5. Management/Labor Relations As They Bear on Productivity

On the important subject of management/labor relations with respect to productivity (Table IV-9), there are many areas of agreement between the two groups and also many areas of dramatic disagreement. Among the areas of agreement are the following:

a. Almost nine out of ten union leaders and management agree that "improving the quality of work life is a desirable management goal even if it doesn't increase productivity." More union leaders than managers hold this view at a high level of intensity.

b. More than seven out of ten in both groups agree that "unions are suspicious of job enrichment but they will support it once they are confident that it isn't a productivity gimmick."

c. Almost all union leaders (97%) and managers (92%) agree that it is "possible for the union and management to cooperate on specific programs which will improve productivity."

d. A large majority of both groups agree that "one must be careful about introducing new equipment and procedures that may mean elimination of jobs."

e. Approximately three out of four in each group hold the view that "workers who have experienced job enrichment almost invariably indicate greater satisfaction with their work."

f.  There is also agreement by more than six out of ten
    of each group that "unions are always suspicious of
    management sponsored programs for increasing
    productivity."

Among the most dramatic areas of disagreement are the following:

g.  Seven out of ten managers (68%) as compared to only
    seven percent of union leaders (7%) hold the view
    that "management and employees share a community of
    interests in improving productivity but the unions
    impose an unnecessary adversary relationship."

h.  By a greater than two to one margin over management
    (49% to 21%) union leaders agree that "the interests
    of management and workers are, by and large, in
    conflict."

i.  By an even greater margin (49% to 13%) management
    assumes that "unions are opposed to productivity
    improvements."

j.  Three times as many union leaders as managers (64%
    to 22%) make the assumption that "few managers and
    supervisors are genuinely concerned about workers
    and their jobs."

k.  Three times as many managers as union leaders (53%
    to 17%) assume that "workers would support produc-
    tivity improvement if their unions did not oppose
    them."

1. By a similarly wide margin (36% to 14%) union
   leaders hold the assumption that "since jobs are
   scarce a greater emphasis on productivity may
   jeopardize jobs." (See Table IV-9A through 9T.)

When the high degree of agreement between union leaders
and managers on the relationship between job satisfaction,
motivation (the mediating variables) and productivity (the
independent variable) is juxtaposed with the findings that
bear on manager/labor relations as they bear on productivity,
the value to the policy-makers of this assumptions analysis
becomes more obvious.

Managers and union leaders appear to agree on the behavioral dynamics of the work setting -- job dissatisfaction
leading to tardiness -- and on the immediate manner in which
change must be introduced -- jointly and without job dis-
placement. The disagreement centers around matters of
"ideology" and the social/institutional dynamics with managers
perceiving the problem to be the union as an institution,
rather than the union leaders' specific actions or the
workers' attachment to the union. Similarly, union leaders
appear to be more wary of management as an institution than of
its specific restructuring programs.

6. Methods for Improving Employees' Attitudes

Table IV-7 shows how managers and union leaders respond to
a wide range of proposals for improving employee attitudes.
Equal numbers of union leaders and management (55%) stress

better communication from management as a key change needed to improve employee attitudes. On most other items, there is some degree of disagreement and difference in emphasis by the two groups. Management stresses better feedback to employees on how well they are doing (45% to 38%). Union leaders, on the other hand, put far greater emphasis on giving employees greater job security (54% to 11%), higher pay (51% to 17%), improving working conditions (45% to 17%), protecting workers from arbitrary and unfair treatment (48% to 18%), better treatment by supervisors (46% to 27%), and providing employees with greater opportunities for advancement (42% to 31%). Fewer than one out of ten managers emphasize such factors as giving workers more autonomy on the job, providing better fringe benefits, shorter hours, work that is socially useful, and giving workers more opportunity to socialize with each other. But, union leaders emphasize all but the latter proposal to a far greater extent, at the rate of three, four, or five times that of management endorsement. In general, Table IV-7 shows that union leaders, more than managers, are inclined to see more ways of improving worker attitudes and motivation.

All in all, the above findings show that while there is agreement on many substantive issues and on the idea that management and labor can get together on specific programs, there remain significant areas of disagreement when assumptions are made about ideological matters and the historic adversary relationship between management and labor.

In general, historical and ideological differences as
to value assumptions -- to the extent that these matters are
sufficiently probed by the questions and the responses of
this survey -- do not seem to be a barrier to the introduction
of management initiatives meant to increase job satisfaction,
motivation and productivity.  If the relationship between
mediating and dependent variables truly exists -- and nine
out of ten of the respondents believe that it does -- and if
there is agreement on substantive issues, then a great variety
of programs could be launched in the organized as well as in
the non-organized sector of our society.  The difficulty rests
in the fact that -- as this report makes clear -- implementation
is a complex matter, requiring large-scale change, careful
monitoring and feedback, and a commitment that goes far beyond
lip service.

## Conclusions

Our survey of limited samples of managers and union officials indicates that:

1.  Most of them conceive of productivity in its broad
rather than technical sense, i.e., as embracing various aspects
of organizational effectiveness and performance.

2.  Most believe that increasing productivity, in the
above sense of the term, is an important goal.  Although union
officials generally subscribe to this view, they espouse it as
a group less strongly than do managers.  This suggests that

union leadership will probably need to be more strongly con-
vinced of the potential benefits to their members before they
give active support to a program aimed at productivity
improvement.

3. The overwhelming majority embrace the goal of improving the quality of working life even if economic benefits
are not thereby increased. In part, this is because they also
believe that work is and should be a salient part of a worker's
life, and a major source of his satisfactions.

4. Most also assume that if workers were more satisfied
with their jobs there would be greater productivity. Since
they also believe that productivity depends on worker motivation, it is possible that they are confusing the two concepts.
As we shall see later, the empirical literature does not
confirm a close tie between job satisfaction and productivity.
It is important that such groups of policy-makers understand
that not all programs for improving job satisfaction will improve productivity and _vice versa_ -- only those which have the
quality also of increasing work motivation.

5. Most believe that job dissatisfaction is a real
problem and that workers increasingly desire more interesting
work and more participation in decisions. However, they do not
assume that these desires are diminishing the importance
of the paycheck. In these respects, their assumptions are
supported by our research findings, which show that all three
are factors in job satisfaction.

6. As to ways to improve productivity, the majority
endorse the usefulness of standard managerial practices such
as better planning, efficient work methods, more communication, and sound personnel policies.

Although certain more worker-centered approaches, such
as job enrichment and worker participation, are regarded as
promising, the majority do not regard human factors as important as managerial techniques in improving organizational
productivity. Union officials are inclined to give more
weight to various human factors in productivity than are
managers, but apparently neither group sees them as very
important in improving productivity. Here may lie a major
reason why programs for improved worker motivation are not
pursued more vigorously.

7. More union leaders than managers believe that a
variety of methods exist which are "very useful" in improving
employee attitudes and motivation, especially higher pay,
greater job security, and more opportunity for advancement.
Such newer approaches as increasing worker autonomy or the
challenge of work are not seen as very useful in this respect
by either group, especially by managers. Again, these results
suggest why there is often less than enthusiasm in pursuing
programs aimed at improving work attitudes and motivation.
The skepticism of managers in this respect is particularly
noteworthy.

8. There is strong consensus that it is possible for

unions and managements to cooperate on productivity improvement programs. However, there is also evidence of fairly widespread although not universal mutual mistrust between the two groups. Such mistrust, where it exists, would manifestly need to be neutralized, or at least suspended, before cooperative programs of productivity improvement could be undertaken. On the other hand, the aforementioned agreement by most managers and union leaders on the importance of improving both productivity and the quality of working life points to a potential springboard for joint action.

Table IV-3

Meaning of Productivity

"Please tell us what you yourself mean by 'productivity' by indicating whether you AGREE or DISAGREE with each of the following statements."

| | % Agreeing | |
|---|---|---|
| | Unions<br>% | Management<br>% |
| Productivity means quality of output as well as quantity. | 80 | 95 |
| Productivity refers to the output per man hour in any one company or organization. | 77 | 90 |
| Productivity means the overall efficiency and effectiveness of the operation. | 84 | 88 |
| Productivity includes such intangibles as disruptions, "shrinkage," sabotage, and other indicators of trouble in the organization, even when their impact on output cannot be measured easily. | 55 | 73 |
| Productivity includes such factors as rate of absenteeism and turnover as well as measures of output. | 70 | 70 |
| Productivity includes measures of customer or client satisfaction | 46 | 64 |
| Productivity includes such intangibles as employee loyalty, morale and job satisfaction. | 57 | 55 |
| Productivity refers to the ratio of output to input by industry or section of the economy, not by individual organization. | 30 | 22 |

Table IV-4

General Values and Beliefs

IV-4A. "Increasing productivity is essential to insure a high standard of living for all Americans."

|  | Unions % | Management % |
|---|---|---|
| Strongly Agree | 30 | 61 |
| Agree | 39 } 69 | 32 } 93 |
| Disagree/Strongly Disagree | 28 | 7 |

IV-4B. "Work should be a rewarding part of life, not a form of drudgery."

|  | Unions % | Management % |
|---|---|---|
| Strongly Agree | 41 | 45 |
| Agree | 55 } 96 | 53 } 98 |
| Disagree/Strongly Disagree | 0 | 1 |

IV-4C. "The nation's productivity is suffering because the traditional American work ethic has eroded."

|  | Unions % | Management % |
|---|---|---|
| Strongly Agree | 3 | 28 |
| Agree | 32 } 35 | 51 } 79 |
| Disagree/Strongly Disagree | 61 | 20 |

Table IV-4 - Cont'd.

IV-4D. "Younger workers insist more on participating in decision-making than older workers."

|                        | Unions % |     | Management % |     |
|------------------------|----------|-----|--------------|-----|
| Strongly Agree         | 23       | 87  | 13           | 80  |
| Agree                  | 64       |     | 67           |     |
| Disagree/Strongly Disagree | 9    |     | 19           |     |

IV-4E. "Workers are better educated today and therefore demand more from their job."

|                        | Unions % |     | Management % |     |
|------------------------|----------|-----|--------------|-----|
| Strongly Agree         | 20       | 85  | 12           | 86  |
| Agree                  | 65       |     | 74           |     |
| Disagree/Strongly Disagree | 12   |     | 12           |     |

IV-4F. "Making work more interesting doesn't offset a desire for increased pay.

|                        | Unions % |     | Management % |     |
|------------------------|----------|-----|--------------|-----|
| Strongly Agree         | 23       | 90  | 12           | 86  |
| Agree                  | 67       |     | 74           |     |
| Disagree/Strongly Disagree | 6    |     | 13           |     |

Table IV-4 - Cont'd.

IV-4G. "Workers' dissatisfaction does not come from their jobs but from the problems of society as a whole."

|  | Unions % | Management % |
|---|---|---|
| Strongly Agree | 1 | 6 |
| Agree | 29 ⟩ 30 | 37 ⟩ 43 |
| Disagree/Strongly Disagree | 64 | 54 |

IV-4H. "Most people get their real satisfaction from their home life and their leisure, not their work."

|  | Unions % | Management % |
|---|---|---|
| Strongly Agree | 7 | 4 |
| Agree | 39 ⟩ 46 | 32 ⟩ 36 |
| Disagree/Strongly Disagree | 51 | 62 |

IV-4I. "The hue and cry about mounting job dissatisfaction is an invention of professors, journalists, and the 'left'."

|  | Unions % | Management % |
|---|---|---|
| Strongly Agree | 1 | 4 |
| Agree | 14 ⟩ 15 | 21 ⟩ 25 |
| Disagree/Strongly Disagree | 80 | 71 |

Table IV-4 - Cont'd.

IV-4J. "The paycheck isn't as important to people today as it used to be."

|  | Unions<br>% | Management<br>% |
|---|---|---|
| Strongly Agree | 6 | 4 |
| Agree | 9 $\Big\rangle$ 15 | 17 $\Big\rangle$ 21 |
| Disagree/Strongly<br>Disagree | 82 | 79 |

IV-4K. "Workers don't care what they produce or how they produce it --
as long as they are well paid."

|  | Unions<br>% | Management<br>% |
|---|---|---|
| Strongly Agree | 1 | 4 |
| Agree | 10 $\Big\rangle$ 11 | 19 $\Big\rangle$ 23 |
| Disagree/Strongly<br>Disagree | 86 | 74 |

IV-4L. "Most workers take real pride in their jobs -- even if their
work is simple and routine."

|  | Unions<br>% | Management<br>% |
|---|---|---|
| Strongly Agree | 10 | 4 |
| Agree | 51 $\Big\rangle$ 61 | 51 $\Big\rangle$ 55 |
| Disagree/Strongly<br>Disagree | 36 | 43 |

Table IV-4 - Cont'd.

IV-4M.  "The average unskilled worker is interested in doing as little as possible."

|  | Unions<br>% | Management<br>% |
|---|---|---|
| Strongly Agree | 1 ⟩ 10 | 3 ⟩ 22 |
| Agree | 9 | 19 |
| Disagree/Strongly Disagree | 87 | 77 |

IV-4N.  "Work is a necessary evil; people avoid it if they can."

|  | Unions<br>% | Management<br>% |
|---|---|---|
| Strongly Agree | 1 ⟩ 14 | 1 ⟩ 16 |
| Agree | 13 | 15 |
| Disagree/Strongly Disagree | 82 | 83 |

IV-40.  "Most workers are satisfied with their work."

|  | Unions<br>% | Management<br>% |
|---|---|---|
| Strongly Agree | 0 ⟩ 45 | 1 ⟩ 55 |
| Agree | 45 | 54 |
| Disagree/Strongly Disagree | 52 | 43 |

Table IV-5

Factors Influencing an Organization's Productivity Considered

To Be "Very Important"

"In your opinion, what is the importance of each of the following in improving productivity in your organization?"

|  | Unions % | Management % |
|---|---|---|
| Better planning | 61 | 66 |
| More effective management | 59 | 65 |
| Improved job procedures | 49 | 49 |
| Improved communications | 57 | 48 |
| More recognition for achievement | 49 | 45 |
| Better training of employees | 48 | 45 |
| More management attention to productivity | 23 | 39 |
| Better human relations | 52 | 36 |
| Improved technology | 36 | 35 |
| New ways to motivate workers | 33 | 34 |
| Increase market demand | 28 | 31 |
| Changes in government regulations | 30 | 30 |
| Greater capital investment | 20 | 27 |
| Harder work by employees | 14 | 25 |
| More employee loyalty | 22 | 23 |
| Greater union cooperation | 26 | 22 |
| More opportunities for advancement | 28 | 18 |
| Improving the quality of working life | 43 | 16 |
| Improved working conditions | 41 | 16 |
| Job redesign and enlargement | 13 | 12 |

Table IV-5 - Cont'd.

| | Unions % | Management % |
|---|---|---|
| Greater participation by workers in decision-making | 23 | 10 |
| More worker incentive programs | 19 | 10 |
| More democracy in the organization | 22 | 6 |
| More competition among companies | 7 | 6 |
| Better transportation to work | 14 | 4 |

Table IV-6

Factors Influencing an Organization's Productivity Considered

To Be Unimportant ("Not Very Important" and Not At All

Important" Combined)

"In your opinion, what is the importance of each of the following in improving productivity in your organization?"

|  | Unions % | Management % |
|---|---|---|
| Better transportation to work | 62 | 83 |
| More competition among companies | 64 | 67 |
| More democracy in the organization | 34 | 64 |
| More worker incentive programs | 50 | 52 |
| Greater participation by workers in decision-making | 20 | 49 |
| Job redesign and enlargement | 37 | 44 |
| Greater union cooperation | 35 | 42 |
| Changes in governmental regulations | 44 | 38 |
| Improved working conditions | 16 | 34 |
| Increased market demand | 52 | 32 |
| Improving the quality of working life | 10 | 27 |
| More opportunities for advancement | 21 | 25 |
| More employee loyalty | 38 | 24 |
| Greater capital investment | 39 | 23 |
| Improved technology | 26 | 23 |
| Harder work by employees | 37 | 20 |
| New ways to motivate workers | 30 | 17 |
| Better human relations | 17 | 13 |

Table IV-6 - Cont'd.

|  | Unions % | Management % |
|---|---|---|
| More management attention to productivity | 22 | 11 |
| More recognition for achievement | 9 | 10 |
| Improved communications | 8 | 9 |
| Better training of employees | 10 | 8 |
| Improved job procedures | 8 | 7 |
| More effective management | 4 | 4 |
| Better planning | 2 | 2 |

Table IV-7

Methods of Improving Employee Attitudes and Motivation

Considered To Be "Very Useful"

"In your organization at this time, how useful would each of the following be in improving employee attitudes and motivation?"

| | Unions % | Management % |
|---|---|---|
| Better communication from management | 55 | 55 |
| More feedback to employees on how well they are doing | 38 | 45 |
| More opportunities for advancement | 42 | 31 |
| Better training/education programs | 33 | 29 |
| Building loyalty to the organization | 26 | 28 |
| Better treatment by supervisors | 46 | 27 |
| Sharing of profits or productivity gains | 39 | 25 |
| More interesting and challenging work | 32 | 23 |
| Greater employee participation | 38 | 21 |
| More opportunities for employees to use their minds | 29 | 19 |
| Better provisions to protect workers from arbitrary and unfair treatment | 48 | 18 |
| Improved work conditions | 45 | 17 |
| Higher pay | 51 | 17 |
| Job redesign, enrichment, and enlargement | 23 | 16 |
| Giving employees greater job security | 54 | 11 |
| Giving workers more autonomy on the job | 22 | 7 |
| More fringe benefits | 26 | 6 |
| Shorter hours | 26 | 5 |
| Providing work that is socially useful | 22 | 5 |
| More opportunities for employees to socialize with each other | 7 | 2 |

Table IV-8

Assumptions About the Relationship Between Job Satisfaction,

Worker Motivation and Productivity

IV-8A. "Job dissatisfaction leads to high turnover, tardiness, loafing on
the job, disruptions, poor workmanship, and indifference to
customers or clients."

|  | Unions % | Management % |
|---|---|---|
| Strongly Agree | 36 | 40 |
| Agree | 57 ⟩ 93 | 54 ⟩ 94 |
| Disagree/Strongly Disagree | 4 | 5 |

IV-8B. "If workers were more satisfied with their jobs, there would be
greater productivity."

|  | Unions % | Management % |
|---|---|---|
| Strongly Agree | 25 | 17 |
| Agree | 62 ⟩ 87 | 70 ⟩ 87 |
| Disagree/Strongly Disagree | 10 | 12 |

IV-8C. "Managers' concern for the welfare of their employees improves
productivity."

|  | Unions % | Management % |
|---|---|---|
| Strongly Agree | 22 | 15 |
| Agree | 64 ⟩ 86 | 67 ⟩ 82 |
| Disagree/Strongly Disagree | 12 | 17 |

Table IV-8 - Cont'd.

IV-8D.  "Job enrichment is a promising strategy for improving productivity."

|  | Unions % | | Management % | |
|---|---|---|---|---|
| Strongly Agree | 14 | | 11 | |
|  | | > 78 | | > 75 |
| Agree | 64 | | 64 | |
| Disagree/Strongly Disagree | 18 | | 22 | |


IV-8E.  "Workers believe productivity is management's responsibility, not theirs."

|  | Unions % | | Management % | |
|---|---|---|---|---|
| Strongly Agree | 6 | | 10 | |
|  | | > 52 | | > 65 |
| Agree | 46 | | 55 | |
| Disagree/Strongly Disagree | 45 | | 33 | |


IV-8F.  "The best way to increase output is by performance incentives."

|  | Unions % | | Management % | |
|---|---|---|---|---|
| Strongly Agree | 6 | | 4 | |
|  | | > 39 | | > 42 |
| Agree | 33 | | 38 | |
| Disagree/Strongly Disagree | 58 | | 55 | |

Table IV-8 - Cont'd.

IV-8G. "If work were enriched with higher skills, workers would be more highly motivated."

|                              | Unions<br>% | Management<br>% |
|------------------------------|:-----------:|:---------------:|
| Strongly Agree               | 9           | 4               |
| Agree                        | 64          | 57              |
| Disagree/Strongly<br>Disagree | 21         | 35              |

Unions: 73 (Strongly Agree/Agree)
Management: 61 (Strongly Agree/Agree)

IV-8H. "Employee motivation has little or no bearing on productivity."

|                              | Unions<br>% | Management<br>% |
|------------------------------|:-----------:|:---------------:|
| Strongly Agree               | 1           | 2               |
| Agree                        | 4           | 3               |
| Disagree/Strongly<br>Disagree | 91         | 94              |

Unions: 5 (Strongly Agree/Agree)
Management: 5 (Strongly Agree/Agree)

IV-8I. "Most workers are not capable of suggesting improved production methods."

|                              | Unions<br>% | Management<br>% |
|------------------------------|:-----------:|:---------------:|
| Strongly Agree               | 6           | 2               |
| Agree                        | 4           | 13              |
| Disagree/Strongly<br>Disagree | 87         | 84              |

Unions: 10 (Strongly Agree/Agree)
Management: 15 (Strongly Agree/Agree)

## Table IV-9

## Management/Labor Relations As They Bear On Productivity

IV-9A. "To produce more with the same amount of human effort is a sound economic and social objective."

|  | Unions % | Management % |
|---|---|---|
| Strongly Agree | 30 | 46 |
| Agree | 52 ⟩ 82 | 50 ⟩ 96 |
| Disagree/Strongly Disagree | 13 | 3 |

IV-9B. "It is possible for the union and management to cooperate on specific programs which will improve productivity."

|  | Unions % | Management % |
|---|---|---|
| Strongly Agree | 33 | 20 |
| Agree | 64 ⟩ 97 | 72 ⟩ 92 |
| Disagree/Strongly Disagree | 1 | 6 |

IV-9C. "One must be careful about introducing new equipment and procedures that may mean elimination of jobs."

|  | Unions % | Management % |
|---|---|---|
| Strongly Agree | 23 | 16 |
| Agree | 55 ⟩ 78 | 56 ⟩ 72 |
| Disagree/Strongly Disagree | 18 | 24 |

Table IV-9 - Cont'd.

IV-9D.  "Improving the quality of work life is a desirable management goal even if it doesn't increase productivity."

|  | Unions<br>% | Management<br>% |
|---|---|---|
| Strongly Agree | 32 | 16 |
| Agree | 55 ⟩ 87 | 73 ⟩ 89 |
| Disagree/Strongly Disagree | 12 | 10 |

IV-9E.  "Workers who have experienced job enrichment almost invariably indicate greater satisfaction with their work."

|  | Unions<br>% | Management<br>% |
|---|---|---|
| Strongly Agree | 20 | 15 |
| Agree | 54 ⟩ 74 | 58 ⟩ 73 |
| Disagree/Strongly Disagree | 13 | 23 |

IV-9F.  "Management and employees share a community of interests in improving productivity, but the unions impose an unnecessary adversary relationship."

|  | Unions<br>% | Management<br>% |
|---|---|---|
| Strongly Agree | 0 | 13 |
| Agree | 7 ⟩ 7 | 53 ⟩ 68 |
| Disagree/Strongly Disagree | 91 | 30 |

Table IV-9 - Cont'd.

IV-9G.  "Union members today want more interesting work than they did ten
        uears ago."

|                             | Unions<br>% | Management<br>% |
|-----------------------------|-------------|-----------------|
| Strongly Agree              | 32          | 12              |
| Agree                       | 52 ⟩ 84     | 61 ⟩ 73         |
| Disagree/Strongly<br>Disagree | 14        | 24              |

IV-9H.  "The adversary relations between workers and management seriously
        impede productivity improvement."

|                             | Unions<br>% | Management<br>% |
|-----------------------------|-------------|-----------------|
| Strongly Agree              | 4           | 11              |
| Agree                       | 38 ⟩ 42     | 46 ⟩ 57         |
| Disagree/Strongly<br>Disagree | 55        | 38              |

IV-9I.  "Unions are always suspicious of management-sponsored programs for
        increasing productivity."

|                             | Unions<br>% | Management<br>% |
|-----------------------------|-------------|-----------------|
| Strongly Agree              | 4           | 11              |
| Agree                       | 59 ⟩ 63     | 54 ⟩ 65         |
| Disagree/Strongly<br>Disagree | 35        | 32              |

Table IV-9 - Cont'd.

IV-9J. "Relations between workers and management would improve if the benefits of productivity improvement were shared with workers."

| | Unions % | Management % |
|---|---|---|
| Strongly Agree | 41 | 10 |
| Agree | 54 | 65 |
| Disagree/Strongly Disagree | 2 | 21 |

Unions: 41/54 > 95
Management: 10/65 > 75

IV-9K. "Most unions are opposed to productivity improvements."

| | Unions % | Management % |
|---|---|---|
| Strongly Agree | 1 | 8 |
| Agree | 12 | 41 |
| Disagree/Strongly Disagree | 84 | 47 |

Unions: 1/12 > 13
Management: 8/41 > 49

IV-9L. "Workers feel more loyalty to their unions than to the companies they work for."

| | Unions % | Management % |
|---|---|---|
| Strongly Agree | 6 | 7 |
| Agree | 49 | 42 |
| Disagree/Strongly Disagree | 41 | 46 |

Unions: 6/49 > 55
Management: 7/42 > 49

Table IV-9 - Cont'd.

IV-9M. "Efficiency is not the responsibility of the worker, but of management."

|  | Unions<br>% | | Management<br>% | |
|---|---|---|---|---|
| Strongly Agree | 9 | > 34 | 6 | > 30 |
| Agree | 25 | | 24 | |
| Disagree/Strongly Disagree | 64 | | 69 | |

IV-9N. "Workers view profit sharing as productivity sharing."

|  | Unions<br>% | | Management<br>% | |
|---|---|---|---|---|
| Strongly Agree | 12 | > 69 | 4 | > 57 |
| Agree | 57 | | 53 | |
| Disagree/Strongly Disagree | 27 | | 35 | |

IV-9O. "The interests of management and workers are, by and large, in conflict."

|  | Unions<br>% | | Management<br>% | |
|---|---|---|---|---|
| Strongly Agree | 14 | > 49 | 3 | > 21 |
| Agree | 35 | | 18 | |
| Disagree/Strongly Disagree | 48 | | 77 | |

Table IV-9 - Cont'd.

IV-9P. "Workers would support productivity improvements if their unions didn't oppose them."

|  | Unions<br>% | Management<br>% |
|---|---|---|
| Strongly Agree | 1 | 3 |
| Agree | 16 ⟩ 17 | 50 ⟩ 53 |
| Disagree/Strongly Disagree | 80 | 38 |

IV-9Q. "Few managers and supervisors are genuinely concerned about workers and their jobs."

|  | Unions<br>% | Management<br>% |
|---|---|---|
| Strongly Agree | 12 | 3 |
| Agree | 52 ⟩ 64 | 19 ⟩ 22 |
| Disagree/Strongly Disagree | 35 | 77 |

IV-9R. "Unions are suspicious of job enrichment, but they will support it once they are confident it isn't a productivity gimmick."

|  | Unions<br>% | Management<br>% |
|---|---|---|
| Strongly Agree | 7 | 2 |
| Agree | 67 ⟩ 74 | 70 ⟩ 72 |
| Disagree/Strongly Disagree | 20 | 22 |

Table IV-9 - Cont'd.

IV-9S. "The 'human relations' approach is a device for undermining the union."

|  | Unions<br>% | Management<br>% |
|---|---|---|
| Strongly Agree | 3 | 1 |
| Agree | 20 | 7 |
| | > 23 | > 8 |
| Disagree/Strongly Disagree | 73 | 89 |

IV-9T. "Since jobs are scarce, a greater emphasis on productivity may jeopardize jobs."

|  | Unions<br>% | Management<br>% |
|---|---|---|
| Strongly Agree | 6 | 1 |
| Agree | 30 | 13 |
| | > 36 | > 14 |
| Disagree/Strongly Disagree | 59 | 85 |

CHAPTER V

CONCEPTS AND METHODS OF INQUIRY

As noted in Part One, the main focus of our review is to
see whether we can identify the conditions which lead to improving both the job satisfaction and performance of workers.
Were either of those factors to be the principal cause of the
other, the problem would be relatively simple.  It would be
necessary only to induce improvements in the causal one to improve also the other.  This, in fact, was a hope that buoyed the
efforts of the early theorists.  The scientific management
school expected that by raising productivity, the "economic man"
would be better satisfied, whereas the human relationists hoped
that more satisfied workers would be more productive.

However, the conclusion of numerous investigations over
the past three decades is that the degree of relationship between job satisfaction and job performance is so tenuous and
variable that, if there is a causal connection, it must either
be intrinsically weak or conditioned by other circumstances in
the work situation.  There exists a number of thorough reviews
of the literature pointing to that conclusion, including
Brayfield & Crockett (1955); Herzberg et al. (1957); March &
Simon (1958); Katzell (1964); Vroom (1964); Robinson, Athanasiou
& Head (1969); Schwab & Cummings (1970); Quinn, Staines &
McCullogh (1974).  At least one of those reviews concluded that

the relationships between job satisfaction and performance are so convoluted that it would be advisable for the present simply to deal with each separately (Schwab & Cummings, 1970).

However, the research evidence does, on the whole, depict a positive, albeit weak, connection between the two. This coincides with the experience of knowledgeable people, as witnessed by the opinions cited in the preceding chapter. We therefore believe that it is not idle to hypothesize that there are certain conditions under which job satisfaction and job performance are linked, and other conditions under which they are not, and therefore to seek clarification of what those conditions are.

Logic and theory suggest that job satisfaction and job performance may be associated because of any of the following mechanisms:

1. the two are the result of the same factor (such as better supervision or reducing disruptive labor-management relations); or

2. better performance leads or is expected to lead to greater rewards (such as when producing more is more remunerative than producing less, or when clients praise good service); or

3. doing what is more rewarding results in better performance (such as when doing tasks that one likes better leads to performing them more carefully or when one stays on a job that one enjoys but quits a job that fails to furnish enough rewards).

Conditions necessary for the operation of any of those three mechanisms include:

1. workers who are motivated, that is, who are attracted by and find satisfying the rewards available in that work situation, and

2. performance essentially under the control of the workers, e.g., not governed largely by limitations of ability or by technology or by the labor market.

To the extent that either of the two conditions is not fulfilled, the relationship between job satisfaction and performance would be weakened. In short, when rewards are insufficient or inappropriate or when job performance is not under the control of workers, their level of job satisfaction can have little bearing on their job performance even if one or more of the three basic mechanisms is present.

The common thread which relates productivity to satisfaction is therefore basically motivation resulting from the association of rewards with productive behavior. In short, when attainment of rewards is based on productive behavior, higher productivity as well as satisfaction will result (all other things being equal).

The parenthetical phrase at the end of the last sentence may create problems, since a major parameter of the equality is the efficiency of the worker-task system. Thus, any modifications of work which change efficiency can change productivity for better or for worse, irrespective of motivation. Failure to take account of effects on efficiency may create spurious associations or contradictions between productivity and satisfaction -- a potential booby-trap in evaluating experience in the field of work organization.

To discover under what conditions both job satisfaction and performance may be enhanced therefore entails more than comparing the two of them. Rather, the work situation must be considered as a system having labor productivity and worker satisfaction as separate outputs or results. Our task, thus viewed, is to trace the system characteristics which led to improvements (or relatively high levels) of both. To do so, it is ultimately necessary to relate the following panels of systems characteristics:

1. Independent Variables, comprising the policies and practices under investigation -- in this study, consisting of different patterns of work assignment, control, and/or compensation. We wish to repeat here the points made in Chapter I that:

a. those particular independent variables were selected for inquiry because they happen to be those structural characteristics of work organizations concerning which there is the largest amount of relatively good information, and

b. in addition to structural changes in work, another valid strategy for improving productivity and job satisfaction is to better fit workers for their work by means of improved selection,

training, counseling, and personnel development; however, the present study is not endeavoring to evaluate the impact of the independent variables of personnel management which
focus on attributes of persons rather than jobs.

2. Take (or Impact) Variables -- measures of whether differences in the above patterns are in fact perceived or experienced differently.

3. Mediating (or Intervening) Variables -- consisting of
the processes which link the foregoing to the dependent or output variables listed below; there are basically two sets of
mediating variables:

   a. Capability, or the extent to which workers have
      the psychological and material resources with
      which to produce; and

   b. Motivation, or the extent to which they have the
      desire to produce.

4. Job Satisfaction is one of the two main categories of
dependent variables, and consists of workers' evaluation of
their jobs and/or various aspects thereof.

5. Job Performance is the other major type of dependent
variable, of which there are three main sub-groups:

   a. Productivity, or, more precisely, labor produc-
      tivity, by which is meant the ratio of output
      (expressed in quantity and quality of the goods
      and services produced) to labor input (man-hours

or costs); in practice, few studies furnish precise measures of labor productivity, so that ap-
proximations in terms of levels of output are
more typically available; and

b. Withdrawal (or avoidance), consisting of measures
of disengagement from work including quitting
(turnover) and absenteeism; and

c. Miscellaneous, which covers a variety of less
commonly studied results of work motivation, such
as accidents, health, or strikes.

6. Moderator (or Situational) Variables comprise aspects
of the internal and external environment in which the above
variables exist, with which they are in interaction, and which
may therefore affect the relationships among them; examples
include characteristics of the workers, of the technology, and
of the socio-politico-economic milieu.

By way of summary, our conceptual framework considers work
organizations as open systems (Katz & Kahn, 1966), certain
structural properties of which we are examining as independent
variables, namely patterns of work responsibilities, of control,
and of compensation. We are tracing the "take" or impact of
those variables on the perceptions of organization members, and
seeing also how they affect the members' work motivation and
capability. In turn, the latter effects should enable us to
identify conditions leading to improvement in both job satisfaction and one or more aspects of job performance. Recognizing that those conditions may vary in different situations,

contextual moderators will also be taken into account when possible.

In reviewing each study, we categorized the variables measured in terms of the rubrics outlined above. Results were summarized in terms of the relationships found within and between variables in the various categories.

Having said these things, we must note now that not a single study approximated the ideal of furnishing data on all of the foregoing categories of variables. Hence, in order to fulfill the agenda, we found it necessary to piece together a mosaic out of bits and pieces formed by various studies. The compromise requirements we imposed on the studies used for that purpose will be described in the section on our sample.

## Major Research Designs

Before turning to that section, it should be noted that there are three fundamental methodologies or strategies of investigation which have been employed in studying these phenomena.

1. Laboratory experiments, in which conditions and methods of work are represented under simplified and more controllable circumstances than exists in "real-life" organizations; in such experiments changes are made in one or more independent variables, and the effects measured on one or more dependent variables.

2. Field experiments, in which interventions are made in work organizations to change one or more conditions or

practices (independent variables), and the effects measured on one or more dependent variables.

3.  Surveys or correlational studies, also conducted in the field but where variations in the independent variable(s) are measured as they happen to occur rather than being induced by intervention; those variations are then compared or correlated with variations in one or more dependent variables.  As compared to field experiments, correlational studies are easier to conduct and therefore often have more extensive sampling of cases; however, the cases being compared often differ in various respects in addition to the independent variable, so that the cause-and-effect relationships are obscured, a problem which is further compounded by the fact that the independent and dependent variables are usually measured concurrently, thus raising the question of which is cause and which is effect.

As will be mentioned below, we have relied primarily on field investigations in our assessment of the state of the art.

## Boundaries of the Sample of Studies

As we got into the literature, we quickly were impressed with its inconclusiveness, due to gaps and flaws in the reports. On recommendation of our Advisory Committee, we therefore decided not to be encyclopedic in our coverage, but rather to focus on studies of reasonably high quality and clarity -- what we called "prototypes."

By prototypes, we meant investigations which attained

reasonably high standards of validity or credibility. As Campbell (1957) has pointed out, there are two main aspects of validity. <u>Internal validity</u> refers to the certainty with which we can conclude that a given result is attributable to the conditions which were investigated. Circumstances detracting from internal validity include absent or faulty control conditions, imprecise measurements, samples of insufficient size, and inadequate analysis of results. <u>External validity</u> pertains to the extent to which the results are generally true or whether they are peculiar to the situation under investigation; the main detractors from external validity are peculiarities of sampling and/or of circumstances under which the data were collected.

The following standards were set for "prototypes":

1. Field studies, but not laboratory studies, in an attempt to maximize external validity and generalizability.

2. Studies which report data from at least three of the following four sets of variables, as described in the preceding section:

    a. Independent or Take;

    b. Intervening (Motivation or Capability);

    c. Job Satisfaction;

    d. Job Performance.

(This stipulation represents an effort to maximize the interpretability of each study, i.e., our ability to "explain" the results.)

3.  Studies meeting at least modest standards of internal
    validity (precision of measures, exercise of controls,
    etc.).

4.  Studies performed in the U.S.A., thereby increasing
    the external validity of our findings as applicable
    in this country.

We did not disregard other studies, but rather employed
them mainly to supplement or to check the findings drawn from
the prototypes.*

Another parameter of the sample was its emphasis on recent studies, i.e., those published in the 7-year period of
1967-1973. This was done in the expectation that recent
studies, by building on earlier ones, would yield information
that was not only more contemporary but more valid. However,
a number of key or classic studies which remain pertinent  were
also covered. In addition, our boundaries were extended to
include a few 1974 publications that seemed particularly important, but no attempt was made to survey systematically the
literature appearing after 1973.

---

* Early in our search, we attempted to increase the number of "prototypes" by seeking additional information about
studies which, from published reports, seemed potentially useful but which lacked certain data needed in order to meet our
prototype standards. It turned out that the necessary supplementary information was either not in existence, or that it
would need to be compiled and analyzed by us from company
records. Our time and resources prevented us from pursuing the
latter course. Also, previous efforts by Mitchell Fein to ex-
tract such data indicated that they are not very fruitful.

CHAPTER VI

JOB DESIGN

In this chapter, we shall first summarize those aspects of organizational theory which lead to hypotheses concerning the cogency of job design factors in affecting both worker satisfaction and performance. This will be followed by a review of empirical studies which bear on those issues. The final section will present the inferences and conclusions which we draw from our findings. At the end, Table VI-2 will summarize a number of widely cited case studies where jobs have been re-designed.

## Theory of Job Design

In Chapter IV, we sketched a theoretical framework for integrating knowledge about how various structural aspects of work affect worker job satisfaction and performance. We indicated our position that crucial to the concerns of policy-makers was the discovery of the circumstances which are conducive to high levels of both job satisfaction and performance, or stated somewhat differently, the policies and practices under which job satisfaction and performance are positively correlated.

To accomplish that objective, our theory suggested that we seek to discover those conditions which enhance motivation without adversely affecting capability to perform.

One domain in which capability and motivation considerations may be expected to intersect has to do with the division of labor among workers. If the job roles and responsibilities prescribed for workers are inconsistent with their personalities (especially role preferences or motivations), we may expect that either (a) in order to maintain their personal satisfactions, they will not perform their roles adequately, or (b) they will conform to role expectations and consequently be dissatisfied. In either instance, worker performance and satisfaction would be out of phase with each other. Also, jobs which may be so constituted as to be satisfying to workers may nevertheless not be amenable to effective performance because they fail to utilize or they actually obstruct worker capabilities; conversely, in jobs which are engineered so that workers have little control over performance, high productivity may occur in tandem with low satisfaction.

Work rationalization and methods study are two terms which have been applied to the analysis of how the structuring of jobs affects the capacity of workers to perform them effectively. As Davis (1957) points out, there are really three aspects of that question: (1) which tasks or activities are specified; (2) how they are done; and (3) how they are distributed among jobs. Davis notes that quite a lot has been learned about principles of work rationalization so as to improve workers' capability to produce; only relatively recently

has much attention been given to how the content of jobs
affects workers' motivation to produce.

The attempt to design jobs so as to increase worker
motivation has been called job enrichment or enlargement. The
two most explicitly articulated theories bearing on relations
of job design to motivation are those of Herzberg (1966) and
of Hackman & Lawler (1971).

Herzberg's view is essentially that jobs are motivating
to the extent to which they are "vertically loaded," i.e.,
afford opportunities for greater responsibility, challenge,
and self-fulfillment. He does not regard the "horizontal loading" of jobs, such as by increasing diversity or social relations, as particularly relevant to motivation. The same is
said of other "hygiene" factors such as adequate pay or working conditions: their absence may generate dissatisfaction
and withdrawal, but their presence does not create satisfaction
and motivation to perform the job well.

Hackman & Lawler (1971) postulate four "core dimensions"
to jobs, all of which they believe must be present at some
critical level in order for workers to be maximally motivated
and satisfied: (1) autonomy or self-direction; (2) diversity
or variety; (3) wholeness or identity; and (4) feedback or
knowledge of results. The theoretical explanation is that
"...when jobs are high on the four core dimensions, employees
have the opportunity to find out (feedback) that they personally
(autonomy) have accomplished something meaningful and worthwhile

(<u>variety</u> and <u>task identity</u>) when they perform well."

## Studies of Job Design

In Chapter IV, it was noted that either of two basic strategies is likely to be  employed in studying behavior in work organizations:  (a) experimentation or intervention, as when a change in some organizational policy (X) is made and its effects on people are studied in terms of (Y), and (b) correlational, as when a number of persons is sampled, and existing differences which occur among them with respect to X are compared with differences that exist with respect to Y. Our survey shows that these two strategies have been employed in the study of job design, as well.

Also noted in that chapter was the salience of issues of validity, which are applicable irrespective of which of these two strategies is employed.  <u>Internal validity</u> pertains to whether the findings are trustworthy for the situation which was studied, i.e., was there really an effect on Y (mainly issues of observational measurement) and, if so, to what extent can we be sure it is due to X (mainly issues of research design).  <u>External validity</u> is concerned mainly with the extent to which findings, even if trustworthy in one situation, may be representative of other situations as well.

Also noted in that chapter was the need to know, in addition to X and Y (the independent and dependent variables), how the two were linked via take and mediating variables, and what parameters might affect that linkage.

When we apply the foregoing methodological considerations to a study of the effects of job design, we need to ask:

1) In what respects did the jobs being compared differ from one another in design (independent variables)?

2) In what ways were they experienced or perceived as different by their incumbents and/or observers (take variables)?

3) Is there evidence that the different designs made a difference in motivation and/or capability of workers (mediating variables)?

4) Is there evidence that the different designs made a difference in workers' job satisfactions (dependent variables)?

5) Is there evidence that the different designs made a difference in workers' performance of their jobs (dependent variables)?

6) Are any of the above results affected by situational characteristics, such as attributes of the workers or the work settings (moderator variables)?

7) Can we be confident that the results noted were true, and not due to errors of measurement or chance, or to the effects of factors other than those under investigation (internal validity)?

8) Can we be confident that the results are generalizable to other situations, and are not limited by peculiarities of the situation under study (external validity)?

As we already noted in Chapter IV, none of the investigations which we discovered provided unequivocally positive answers to all of those questions. This circumstance requires that our assessment of knowledge be based on converging evidence from a number of studies, each in itself incomplete and/or fallible. In doing so, it is apparent that greater weight should be given to studies which provide information bearing on more of those issues than to those which deal with fewer, and on those which furnish more valid information. Moreover, studies most relevant to the objectives of the review should bear on the relations of job design to <u>both</u> job satisfaction and job performance; if only one of these outcomes is actually measured, there needs to be at least some assessment of the effects also on work motivation.

Accordingly, we will in our review below focus on those studies which, at minimum, offer information pertinent to at least three of the first five issues, including at least two of the three issues bearing on work motivation, job performance and job satisfaction. We will also feature those studies which give evidence of being reasonably valid.

When the foregoing criteria were applied to the dozens of studies of job design which we have reviewed, only fourteen were found to approximate even the compromise standards which we adopted. In our analysis, we will therefore focus initially and primarily on those "prototypes." Studies which fail to meet enough of the criteria noted above, but which are nevertheless cited in influential sources, will be considered

separately in Table VI-2.  Studies which may offer useful
but incomplete findings will be mentioned when they supplement the information yielded by the prototypes.

In discussing the studies of job design, we will divide
them between the two main methodological approaches mentioned
earlier.  First, we will consider five major correlational
studies, and later turn to nine interventions.

## 1.  Correlational Studies

a.  Herzberg, Mausner, & Snyderman (1959) reported a study
which may be regarded as one of the landmarks in this area in
the sense that it helped re-open the question of how jobs
should be designed from the standpoint of worker motivation.
They compiled retrospective reports from some 300 middle-
management workers concerning incidents in which they had
felt especially good or bad about their jobs.  These reports
were then analyzed for concurrences among job factors, worker
attitudes, and performance.  Herzberg and his associates reported that the incidents characterized by positive attitudes
most frequently entailed job factors intrinsic to the actual
job, including achievement, work content, and advancement.
Factors which were concerned mainly with the context of the
job (such as working conditions, interpersonal relations, and
supervision) were infrequently mentioned as causing high attitudes, but instead were usually cited in connection with unfavorable or negative attitudes.  Moreover, positive attitudes
more often than not were associated with reports of high or

improved job performance, whereas the incidents involving negative attitudes were often associated with actual or desired leaving the organization.

These findings led Herzberg and his associates to conclude that factors affecting workers' attitudes were of two sorts: satisfiers (growing out of the work itself) and dissatisfiers (derived from the work context), and that proper treatments of the former were conducive to high job performance (i.e., were "motivators"), whereas the latter could be regarded as "hygiene" factors in that their proper utilization could be expected to forestall withdrawal and avoidance behavior but not improve productivity.

Herzberg (1966) later summarized a number of additional studies performed by his associates and others which furnished partial or complete confirmation of the findings of the original study. There have also been some studies providing support for the "Two-Factor" theory using methods of investigation other than the critical-incident approach featured by Herzberg (e.g., Friedlander, 1963, 1964, and 1965; Friedlander & Walton, 1964). However, still other investigations have not confirmed the satisfier-dissatisfier dichotomy (e.g., Burke, 1966; Dunnette, Campbell & Hakel, 1967; Ewen, 1964; Ewen et al., 1966; Hinrichs & Mischkind, 1967; Hulin & Smith, 1967; Wernimont, 1966), which has led to the belief that the two-factor results may be largely an artifact of the "critical-incident" method of investigation employed. The original study, and most of the confirmations, also are limited by their focus on occupants of jobs which are both high-level and white-collar in nature. Another limitation of the original study is that the data on job conditions, satisfaction, and performance all came from the same subjective reports of the workers involved.

In their original report, Herzberg and associates espoused the potential advantages of proper job design, and this inspired much of the subsequent attention to the subject.

b. Turner & Lawrence (1965) performed an intensive correlational study of job attributes in relation to job satisfaction and absenteeism. They obtained their data from 470 male, blue-collar workers occupying 47 jobs in 11 companies. The job design characteristics were rated by observers in terms of each job's Variety, Control, Interaction, Learning Time, and Responsibility; these ratings were also summed into an index of overall job scope. Several associated task attributes, such as Task Identity, Cycle Time and Mechanization, were rated as well. Workers also rated their jobs in terms of the same job design scales, which likewise were summed into an index of overall scope.

These data on job characteristics and their perception by workers were then compared with worker absenteeism rates and with a questionnaire measure of job satisfaction. Workers in jobs which were rated by observers as of larger scope were found to have better overall absenteeism records than those in narrower jobs, but not to differ in overall job satisfaction. In terms of the workers' perceptions, jobs experienced as having a larger scope were found to be associated with greater job satisfaction, but not with appreciably different absenteeism records than narrower jobs.

Investigating urbanization as a background factor, Turner & Lawrence found that, among workers in small towns, there was a pronounced positive relation between rated job scope and both job satisfaction and attendance; however, among the urban workers, job design factors had no appreciable relation to attendance, and two of the specific elements (Variety and Interaction) even were inversely associated with job satisfaction. There is some evidence in their data that the urban workers may experience given job attributes somewhat differently than do the small-towners, whose perceptions seem to have matched the observers' ratings more closely. The possibility that urban workers have different work motivations than non-urban workers was earlier suggested by Katzell, Barrett & Parker (1961), and receives support from Hulin & Blood (1968), who, like Turner & Lawrence, found a higher correlation between job level and satisfaction among non-urban than among urban workers. Other investigators have also made observations consistent with the foregoing (e.g., Kennedy & O'Neill, 1958). Turner & Lawrence also checked on the possible influence of other moderators, including pay level and worker age, but only urbanization played a significant role.

c. Patchen (1970) studied worker job perceptions in five geographically separated divisions of the Tennessee Valley

Authority. Two of them were engineering design units, and the other three were power plants. A sample of 337 employees were drawn from the former and 457 from the latter set of units.

Patchen's study is less comprehensive than that of Turner & Lawrence in that it lacks independent measures of task attributes, direct measures of job satisfaction, and measures of situational moderators. It is more complete in that it contains measures of mediating motivational levels.

The main aspects of job design studied by Patchen corresponded to Hackman & Lawler's four core dimensions of Difficulty, Identity, Feedback, and Control. Opportunities for personal development were also assessed. The last of those aspects turned out to have the strongest positive correlations with levels of work motivation (assessed by questionnaire measures of job interest and pride); it was also associated with better attendance records and with fewer reports of psychological stress. Of the more strictly job design features, Difficulty and Control were generally associated both with higher levels of motivation and better attendance, whereas other aspects of design failed to show clear-cut relations with either; relations with reported symptoms of psychological and physical stress were generally erratic.

In short, the study furnishes correlational evidence for the importance of personal growth opportunities, job difficulty, and control over one's job as conducive to both high motivation and better attendance. Other job design features were not found to be consistently related to either of those variables, which may account for why they were found not to be

highly correlated with each other, i.e., for a stronger correlation to emerge between motivation and attendance, it may
be necessary to compare jobs which are similar in job elements such as Feedback and Identity.  Higher motivation
levels were found to be significantly associated with lower
levels of stress, although specific job design features themselves did not generally have strong or consistent correlations with stress.

     d.  Hall & Lawler (1970) reported a correlational study
of engineers and scientists employed in 22 research and development organizations in Connecticut.  The sample contained
the 22 directors and 291 other professionals.  Various independent, take, mediating and satisfaction variables were
assessed by means of questionnaires and interviews, and were
compared to both objective and rated measures of performance.

     One major aspect of job design was "job challenge,"
which was discovered to be significantly associated with felt
pressure for high quality of work.  The latter in turn was
correlated positively and significantly with both job involvement and job performance.  Job challenge was inversely
associated with another feature of job design, the range of
projects on which the professional worked; challenging jobs
and jobs which concentrated on a relatively small range of
projects were found to be more satisfying in terms of needs
for esteem, autonomy, and self-fulfillment.

     Another major feature of job design studied was direct

responsibility for the customer. This was found to be associated with felt pressures regarding time and money. It was
also significantly correlated with overall performance and
with satisfaction, especially with respect to social and
esteem needs.

In broad strokes, then, the study showed that R&D professionals whose jobs incorporate the features of challenge,
limited range of projects, and direct responsibility for customers tend to be more satisfied and productive, in part
because those features are associated with certain motivating
forces like job involvement, and pressures for quality, financial responsibility, and getting things done on time. However, the correlational nature of the study prevents the
precise allocation of causality.

e. <u>Hackman & Lawler</u> (1971) described the most recent and
extensive of the prototype correlational studies. It is also
the most complete, in the sense of mustering data pertinent to
virtually all of the criteria for prototypes noted earlier in
the chapter. Based on their review of previous work, especially that of Turner & Lawrence, they identified as the "core
dimensions" of job design the elements of Diversity, Identity,
Feedback, Control, and Interaction (two aspects). All the
dimensions were studied in 13 jobs occupied by 208 workers in
an Eastern telephone company, including obtaining observers'
and supervisors' ratings of the content of jobs as well as
incumbents' perceptions. Workers also described their level of

motivation in terms of (1) interest in doing the job well and
(2) job involvement (Lodahl & Kejner, 1965). Dependent variables included measures of job satisfaction, supervisors'
ratings of the worker performance, and absenteeism.

Observers' ratings of job design elements were generally
reflected in workers' perceptions (less so in the case of
"Feedback"). The four core dimensions of jobs were found generally to be positively correlated with worker motivation, with
job satisfaction, with ratings of job performance, and with
attendance; the effects of these four dimensions were additive, i.e., the higher the composite rating on them, the
greater the levels of job satisfaction and performance. The
"Interaction" dimension was found to be positively correlated
with job satisfaction but not correlated with either motivation, job performance, or absenteeism.

The strength of the worker's "higher order" needs, i.e.,
those involving achievement and growth rather than comfort
and security, was found to be a factor which moderates the
foregoing relations of job scope to satisfaction and performance. The relations were stronger among workers with
greater needs for "higher-order" gratification.

f. <u>Miscellaneous Studies</u>. There have been many other
correlational studies over the years which, although not
qualifying as "prototypes" by our criteria, illuminate one or
another aspect of the picture. A number of them have investigated the correlations between job design elements and job

satisfaction. Thus, for example, studies have pointed to the dissatisfaction of workers with more repetitive, specialized, shorter-cycle jobs (e.g., Walker & Guest, 1952; Blauner, 1964; Kornhauser, 1965; Shepard, 1970). Shepard (1970) found that the inverse relation between job specialization and job satisfaction was not affected by size of the community in which his sample of blue-collar workers grew up or by their attitudes of work alienation; however, the latter measures were of dubious validity. In a related study, Shepard (1971) found that feelings of alienation were generally greater among mechanized than non-mechanized workers in both blue-collar and white-collar jobs.

More recently, Sheppard & Herrick (1972), in their widely publicized study of two samples of male, blue-collar workers, reported that those employed in jobs which were rated as being at higher task levels -- i.e., entailing greater autonomy, variety, and/or responsibility -- also more often described themselves as having higher overall job satisfaction (this finding is reported for one of their samples, but is not mentioned for the other); in both samples, workers at higher task levels reported greater attachment to (less readiness to quit) their present jobs than those at lower task levels. Form (1973) recently reported a study of the job attitudes of approximately 100 auto workers in each of four countries (U.S.A., Italy, Argentina, and India), in which he found, contrary to Sheppard & Herrick but like Blauner, that only a minority of workers were dissatisfied; however, dissatisfaction again proved to be greater among those at lower skill levels and those having less control over their work. Kennedy & O'Neill (1958) had earlier found that most workers in highly specialized jobs were not notably dissatisfied with them.

The most comprehensive study of the correlations between working conditions and worker satisfaction was performed by the Survey Research Center, University of Michigan (1970). Interviews were conducted with a national sample of 1,533 workers. Fifteen of the questions were deemed by the investigators to be relevant to job content, but a correlational analysis showed that only five might appropriately be combined into an internally consistent index of "Enriching Job Demands." Those five covered learning new things, variety, skill level, creativity, and planning. Two other items were also combined into a separate "Autonomy" index. Both of those indices were among the working conditions found to be most strongly correlated with overall job satisfaction, although even here the level of correlation was modest (about .30). The fact that satisfaction with pay was also associated with those aspects of job design illustrates the problem of inferring causality from correlational data. Fein (1973) also has pointed out that the importance of having interesting work varied for different occupational groups in the SRC sample, e.g., was greater for white-collar than for blue-collar workers.

The SRC study also obtained self-reports of various health-related symptoms. Overall job satisfaction was found to have a moderate or slight inverse correlation with reports of job-related tension (-.37), depression (-.24), and somatic complaints (-.15). More enriched and autonomous jobs tended to be associated with reports of slightly higher tension, and slightly lower levels of somatic complaints, depression and zestlessness. These trends, although they square to some extent with those of certain other studies (Gurin, Veroff, & Feld, 1960; Kahn et al., 1964), are not readily reconciled with those of Patchen mentioned above, except perhaps that mental and somatic complaints were in neither case strongly associated with job characteristics. However, it has been reported that job satisfaction is one of the most significant correlates of longevity (HEW, 1973).

Another set of correlational studies has been concerned with the relations between job satisfaction and avoidance or withdrawal behavior. The latter included mainly absenteeism and turnover, but it has been shown that a common thread runs through a number of such manifestations including, in addition to those two variables, visits to the dispensary, grievances, and work stoppages (Merrihue & Katzell, 1955). There have been excellent reviews of such studies by Brayfield & Crockett (1955), Herzberg et al. (1957), Vroom (1964), and Robinson, Athanasiou & Head (1969). By and large, that literature sub-stantiates modest inverse correlations between job satisfaction and avoidance behavior, e.g., workers with higher job satis-faction generally have better attendance and turnover records.

Those findings help confirm the view that the rate of withdrawal is lower in expanded jobs insofar as they generate
higher job satisfaction.  However, as we have already noted,
such reviews yield a more equivocal picture of the correlations between job satisfaction and productivity.

There have been several other correlational studies of
aspects of job design and aspects of job performance which,
because of limited scope, are not included among our prototypes
For example, Hill & Thickett (1966) found that most workers in
their small sample of millers were more productive on jobs
having longer cycle and setting times.   Waters & Roach (1973)
reported that dissatisfaction with work content was predictive
of absenteeism and turnover among clerical workers, and to a
greater degree than were a number of other job attitudes.
Dissatisfaction with the content of highly rationalized jobs
was also strongly implicated in both overall dissatisfaction
and voluntary turnover of female factory workers (Wild, 1970).
By and large, the picture based on the prototypes summarized
above tends to be confirmed by the non-prototype correlational
findings.

g.  Summary.  Our review of correlational studies suggests that certain job design characteristics are correlated
with higher job satisfaction of workers, especially intrinsic
aspects of job content associated with enlarged challenge or
difficulty, diversity, identity, control, and work-cycle time.
Opportunity for growth and advancement also appears to be

important, although strictly speaking, not an aspect of current job content.

The assertion by Herzberg, Mausner & Snyderman (1959) that those conditions are also associated with higher productivity but not with manifestations of avoidance (e.g., turnover or absenteeism), is not unequivocally supported by the findings. There is, for example, some correlational evidence that enlarged or enriched jobs are characterized not only by better productivity levels, but also by less absenteeism or disposition to quit. By now, enough facts have accumulated to indicate that conditions which improve job satisfaction are likely also to reduce avoidance behavior such as turnover and absenteeism. Contrary to the position originally expressed by Herzberg and associates, these would appear to include job-content "satisfiers" as well as contextual "dissatisfiers."

There are too few studies which correlate aspects of job design with productivity to serve as a basis for a firm conclusion, although there are some data suggestive of positive correlations with some features of job content. We will find in our next section, which deals with the redesign of jobs, additional findings bearing on this question.

## 2. Intervention Studies

The indications from the foregoing review of correlational studies were that jobs of expanded scope are likely to be occupied by workers with higher job satisfaction. There is also some reason to believe that incidents of avoidance, like absenteeism and turnover, are likely to be less frequent in such jobs, although it is not entirely clear whether that is due specifically to job content or to associated factors which happen to affect both job satisfaction and avoidance behavior (e.g., pay level). Further, although it has been claimed by some on the basis of correlational findings that productivity is greater in enlarged or enriched jobs, the supporting evidence is sparse, at best. Furthermore, the causal links are once again unclear, since variations in other important factors are often associated with differences in job scope, e.g., technology and pay.

If the proof of the pudding is in the eating, it is equally true that the confirmation of correlational findings lies in the results of their application. In brief, what happens when jobs are redesigned so that they have expanded scope?

In 1971, Rush reported on the experience of seven companies which undertook such experiments. The HEW report entitled Work in America (HEW, 1973) summarized 34 experiences, including those which had been reported by Rush. More recently, Glaser (1973) has reported 17 such studies, eight of which had been covered also in one or another of the earlier reports. Our search has located several other studies bearing on the same issue.

Regrettably, our review of all the foregoing reveals no

simple answer to the seemingly simple question of what happens
when jobs are redesigned to enlarge or enrich them. This is
mainly due to the fact that, in most of these instances, the
job change was undertaken to improve an ongoing work situation,
and not to answer a scientific question. As a consequence,
significant elements were changed in addition to job scope,
so that it is unclear to what to attribute the results. Moreover, since little attention was given to precise assessment
of the variables at issue, it is often the case that one
cannot even be sure what the results were.

In saying these things, our object is not to criticize
those who did the studies, for after all, their purpose in
doing them was primarily managerial, not scientific. In this
regard, it is to their credit that they were open to experi-
menting with new approaches. Nonetheless, we are obliged to
assess the validity of the resulting information for the sake
not only of the scientific community, but for that of practitioners and policy-makers who wish to know the significance of
those results for their own plans and actions.

When we applied the criteria noted earlier in this chapter, we found only nine intervention studies which satisfied
our minimum requirements. Those requirements, it may be recalled, included some to ensure sufficient internal validity to
enable us to say of a study that some definable aspect of job
redesign was responsible for any significant changes which may
have occurred in job performance as well as in job satisfaction

and/or work motivation.

Immediately below will be reviewed the nine "prototype" experiments which approximate those criteria, to be followed by a summary of those miscellaneous studies which provide interesting, but more limited, information.

a. Lawler, Hackman & Kaufman (1973) reported an experiment which, although one of the most recent, will be presented first since it comes closest to attaining our criteria for a "prototype." It therefore will serve as a reference point against which the results of other studies may be assessed. The major respects in which that study satisfied our criteria comprise (1) its inclusion of independent, take, mediating, dependent and moderating variables; (2) the quantitative nature of most of the data; (3) the analysis of statistical significance of differences; (4) a meaningful degree of external validity or generality; and (5) the use of control or at least comparison conditions. This is not to say that it is a perfect study, as the authors themselves recognize, but at least it tries to touch all the bases. Among its chief defects are the limited changes in job content, the absence of firm performance data, the absence of a good control group, and the fact that it is limited to certain special kinds of jobs occupied only by female workers in a public utility.

The study entailed redesigning the jobs of certain telephone operators in an eastern telephone company; also implicated were the jobs of service assistance personnel who, among

other things, had some supervisory responsibilities for the
operators. Operators' jobs actually consisted of two sub-jobs
between which they alternated: directory assistance (DA) and
toll operating functions. The former sub-job was redesigned,
whereas the latter remained unchanged, thus serving as a form
of control condition (albeit flawed by possible "spill-over"
effects between the two sub-jobs). The redesign entailed a
number of features which appeared to us to generate greater
diversity, identity, and autonomy when doing the DA sub-job.
"Before" data were obtained from the workers about two weeks
prior to the installation of the change (largely worked out and
imposed by high-level supervision with expert consultants), and
again six months afterward. "Before" data were collected from
24 operators and "after" from 17. The before-after comparison
of workers' perceptions of the content of the DA sub-job
revealed significant increases in Identity, Feedback, and
Interaction (the perceptions were confirmed in independent
ratings by supervisors); there were no significant changes in
any of these dimensions for the toll sub-job (control condition).
No significant changes were detected in measures of job involvement (or intrinsic work motivation) of the workers. Their
job satisfaction also did not change appreciably, except that
satisfaction with co-workers declined significantly.

In the case of the service assistants (whose reactions
to their own jobs had been studied separately, since they were
indirectly affected by changes in the DA job), no notable
changes occurred either in their perceptions of the content of

their jobs or in their job involvement. However, significant
decrements in satisfaction were detected with reference to job
worthwhileness, security, and here too, co-workers.

The possibility of moderating effects of various background characteristics of the operators was investigated, but
only tenure seemed to play even a small role: adverse effects
on attitudes were greater for longer service workers.

Regrettably, as regards job performance, only qualitative
impressions of management are cited by the authors (without
conviction as to significance) to the effect that productivity
and quality did not change over the period of the study,
although turnover and absenteeism declined, as did the general
economy at the time. Training time was said to be reduced
from five days to two, with a corresponding reduction in costs,
although the reasons are not entirely clear.

The results of the study, although essentially negative,
are nevertheless instructive. They alert us to the notion
that changes in job design may not necessarily have the intended impact or "take," or have corresponding effects on
motivation, and, under such conditions may not have any appreciable consequences for productivity or job satisfaction.
Further, there may be unanticipated side effects on relations
between workers in interdependent jobs, as witnessed by the
deterioration of attitudes toward co-workers, attributed by the
authors to the change in authority relationships between the
jobs of operators and service assistants, which may have been

aggravated by the absence of consultation. In short, the fact
that the study coped with the various panels of measures and
the controls deemed of importance by us helped even a negative
finding be instructive, since we have a fairly clear picture
of what happened and why.

We will continue now with additional intervention
studies which qualify as "prototype."

b. Ford (1969) wrote a widely-cited monograph reporting
a number of experiments done in various components of the
American Telephone and Telegraph Company. Although several of
them are suggestive of a linkage between job design, satisfaction and performance, two of them clearly lead the others in
terms of approximating our prototype standards. One involved
reorganizing the responsibilities of four groups of 38 line-
men so that both the Difficulty and Diversity of activities
were increased, as well as the Identity of completed work.
Some increase in Authority was also entailed, including that
for dealing with customers. A defect in the study is that no
readings were taken of whether the changes had the intended
impact on the workers. As was typical in the AT&T experiments,
the changes were largely designed and installed by higher levels
of supervision with the help of consultants.

Compared with four other groups whose jobs remained unchanged over the nine-month period of the study, the four experimental groups manifested several improvements in performance, most clearly in tardiness records, in amount of

overtime work needed, in production quality (errors), in the percentage of orders completed on schedule, and in the frequency of formal grievances. Several other aspects of performance either did not change or the extent of the changes is unclear (e.g., absenteeism and units completed per hour).

Since the jobs were rather extensively reorganized, it is possible that the improvements in productivity were due to improved efficiency of the new work methods rather than to increased worker motivation. Clear evidence of improvement in job attitudes would have provided a check on that possibility. Although a job attitude questionnaire was administered at the outset and toward the end of the period of study, relatively few members of the experimental groups completed it, thus somewhat diluting the import of the findings that there was an average improvement in job satisfaction among those groups as compared to some decline in the comparison groups. That decline may have been due to knowledge that the latter groups had of the experiment going on elsewhere in the company. The study is further weakened by the absence of analyses of statistical significance of differences, although some of the changes do appear to be substantial.

c. The second AT&T study reported by Ford (1969) which we shall include here was done in 1965 on 90 female clerical workers responsible for customer correspondence. Seven specific "vertical" changes were gradually made in jobs. The nature of the changes seems to us mainly to have increased the

autonomy and wholeness of the work, plus more personal responsibility for customers; however, in the absence of take
measures, this assessment remains conjectural. The changes
were made in two work groups, without the knowledge of the
workers or their first-line supervisors that a study was under
way. There were three comparison groups in which no commit-
ments for change were planned or, presumably, implemented.

Job attitudes of the workers were measured by a questionnaire administered shortly before the changes were initiated,
and again six months thereafter. Various objective measures of
performance were obtained over the six-month study period, as
noted below. The results were presented graphically, and without accompanying specification of whether they were statistically significant; hence the significance of any changes noted
below remains in doubt.

The "change" groups showed increases in average scores
on the attitude survey, including reports that changed jobs
were more satisfying and interesting. Some of the write-in
comments, plus impressions of the supervisors, suggest heightened levels of work motivation, but that mediator was not systematically measured in the study. On the average, the attitude scores of the comparison groups did not change appreciably
over the course of the study.

A factual index of quality of customer service, already
in use as a gauge of performance, showed improvement in the two
"change" groups, seemingly to a greater degree than was true of

the comparison groups. Without furnishing quantitative details, the report also claims that one or both of the "change" groups exceeded the comparison groups on a variety of criteria, such as turnover, productivity, lowered costs, lower absence rates, and source for managerial upgrading. Elsewhere it is noted that savings would result from elimination of an expensive verification step, from reduced turnover, and in training costs. The major incremental cost listed was a fraction of the salary of the project director, with the implication that the change was cost-effective.

     d. Rush (1971) prepared a Conference Board report entitled "Job Design for Motivation" in which he summarized current thinking on the subject. The publication contained case studies of job redesign in seven organizations. One of them more nearly approximated our criteria for a "prototype" than the others, namely that of the Internal Revenue Service. A highly repetitive clerical job of tax return examining was redesigned in ways that seemed pertinent to enhancing all of the key job dimensions, including autonomy. An experimental group was composed of 20 workers, and a control group of 24. Over the six-month period of study, no appreciable improvements were observed in production or in error rates either of the experimental or control groups (the overall production rate actually declined, which was attributed to the greater complexity of the work). Neither did job attitudes change appreciably over the period of the study. Commenting on the essentially negative findings, Rush reported informal evidence suggesting that the job changes had little or no impact on the workers, that worker involvement and satisfaction with the work were low to begin with, and that "bread-and-butter" or "hygiene" needs of workers were not being satisfied. The report therefore usefully addresses itself to the issues of take and mediating variables. However, the fact that motivation and satisfaction were rather low at the outset hardly limits the generality of the findings, since it is precisely to cope with such problems that job enrichment is usually undertaken. However, the fixation of these workers at the "hygiene" level does represent a significant limitation, since the effects might be different for workers who were more affluent and more ready for growth.

     e.  Bishop & Hill (1971) reported a study which, although technically sophisticated, suffers from superficiality of job changes, which seemed to be largely confined to the dimensions of Diversity and Identity. The absence of take measures, however, prevents a sure diagnosis on that score. The 48 workers in the study were performing a light short-cycle sorting job in a sheltered workshop, which creates a question of generalizability. The workers were divided into three small groups:  an experimental group whose jobs were enlarged, a control group whose jobs were changed but not enlarged, and a second control group whose jobs remained the same although they were aware

of the changes going on.*  The total period of study lasted
only five days.

At the end, both the quantity and quality of production
of the experimental group were below those of the two control
groups.  The latter groups wound up about the same in quantity
of production, but the no-change group was best of the three
in quality; this comparison is indicative of the potential
disruptive effect on production of introducing changes in job
methods.  The level of satisfaction of the workers with the
job content remained stable in the experimental group, increased in the change group, and declined in the unchanged
group.

The study, although limited in external validity because
of the special population and short duration, has some interesting implications, most notably that (1) enlarging jobs
may improve neither production nor job satisfaction; (2) the
mere change in job content may have more positive (or less
negative) effects on production and satisfaction than does
enlargement; and (3) workers whose jobs are not changed but are
aware that changes are being made elsewhere can suffer a decline in job satisfaction.  This last effect is illuminated by
data showing that those workers, on average, experienced

---

*This "extended control group" feature is highly com-
mended for adoption elsewhere, and could desirably be expanded
to include a third control group which was insulated from all
changes.

greater anxiety and lost some status in the eyes of their co-
workers. Also important are the findings that changes in
production levels among the groups did not parallel the
changes either in work satisfaction or in a measure of anxiety.

f. <u>Maher</u> (1971) edited a volume which contained reports
of experiences with job enrichment, including experiments
which he himself conducted. His study was a simulation conducted in a laboratory situation, which is amenable to
superior control and observation, thereby enhancing internal
validity, but inevitably open to questions of external
validity (Bracht & Glass, 1968; Frederiksen, Jensen, &
Beaton, 1972). Weick (1965) has pointed out that such limitations are not necessarily lethal. Maher's study utilized
college student volunteers who assembled electrical extension
cords in groups of five under a supervisor. One of the job
characteristics under study was segmentation (completing the
entire assembly vs. assemblyline-like operation), apparently
involving mainly key dimensions of Diversity and Identity. The
other main dimension studied was Autonomy (highly specified
work procedures vs. discretion in choosing procedures). Actually three experiments were performed entailing various combinations of the job characteristics of segmentation and
autonomy, in relation to their effects on production (usable
cords per man-hour) and job satisfaction over a total period of
four days.

The findings were essentially that productivity was

usually highest when jobs were largest (non-segmented and autonomous), usually lowest when jobs were most restricted (segmented and regulated), and usually intermediate for mixed combinations of those characteristics. However, the changes in production did not parallel changes in group job satisfaction, as the latter was typically approximately equal for the several conditions of work. This raises a question as to whether the productivity results were due to differences in motivation or differences in the efficiency of the work methods. The absence of "impact" or work motivation measures hampers the analysis here. The external validity of the study is dubious, especially as the "workers" had no permanent attachment to their "jobs," nor did their productivity have implications for pay, advancement, job security, or other rewards.

g. Kraft (1971) studied the redesigned jobs of teams of typists and 28 checkers in a bank, and reported the results in the volume edited by Maher. An article by Dettleback & Kraft (1971) seems to cover essentially the same study. The jobs of these workers (28 in each of the two jobs) were changed so as to enrich them by providing greater customer identification, group responsibility, personal accountability, and opportunities for performing harder operations. The extensive treatment appeared to entail changes in all of our job content dimensions, plus increasing autonomy and personal development as well. Various production data and responses to an attitude questionnaire were compared for findings prior to the change and again about six months later. Although statistical tests

of significance are not provided, there is evidence that the
workers did perceive the jobs as enlarged and also felt them
to be more satisfying, i.e., more interesting and worthwhile.
The production data cited in the two reports are not entirely
clear, nor is statistical significance reported, but there is
some evidence that there were improvements both in quantity
and quality of production in the experimental work groups.
Comparable data were unfortunately not furnished for control
groups whose jobs were not changed.  Although this would
appear to be a rather widely applicable study, its findings
are unfortunately somewhat equivocal because of the aforementioned weaknesses in internal validity.

     h.  Janson (1972) presented a report of a job enrichment
study in a large insurance company, which was subsequently
written up by Glaser (1973).  The study, which lasted a year,
included two groups of keypunch operators, one of which served
as the experimental and the other as the control.  The experimental group is mentioned as containing 83 employees, with no
corresponding figure given for the control.  Twenty-five job
changes were installed in the experimental group, drawn from
a brainstorming session of the group supervisor and the unit
leaders; the illustrative ones indicate rather extensive changes,
which include increases in discretion (autonomy), diversity,
difficulty, feedback, identity, and responsibility for dealing
with the client directly.  The experimental group showed improvements in rates of productivity, errors, and absenteeism,

all substantially greater than in the case of the control group
(although statistical significance was not reported). Turnover in the experimental group increased slightly over its low
reported level, whereas that of the control group declined
slightly from its initially higher level. Actual and potential
savings due to staff reductions (and associated reduction in
machine rental costs), were calculated as follows:

| Source | No. Staff Saved | No. Potential Additional | $ Saved | Potential Add'l. $ |
|--------|-----------------|--------------------------|---------|--------------------|
| 1. Improved Production | 2 | 1 | $11,354 | $ 6,245 |
| 2. Reduction of Controls | 7 | 14 | 40,465 | 81,588 |
| 3. Absenteeism Change | 2 | 1 | 12,486 | 4,104 |
| Totals | 11 | 16 | $64,305 | $91,937 |

Attitudes were measured by the same set of nine questions
employed in the Bankers Trust study reported above by Kraft
(1971) and Dettleback & Kraft (1971). Some of them assess take
("The job provides feedback"), whereas others more specifically
assess feelings ("The work itself is interesting"). When the
survey was conducted on a "before" basis, both groups showed
nearly identical scores, described as "average." Eleven months
later, the control group was said to have retained essentially
the same average score, whereas the experimental group's score
increased by what was termed a "significant" amount. Taped
interviews with members of the experimental group before and
after the change qualitatively reflected more positive attitudes
as well.

The study is noteworthy in the amount of quantitative information compiled on both an experimental and control group, thereby contributing to internal validity. Although it seems likely that some of the job changes produced more efficient work methods, the attitude data suggest motivational effects as well. The external validity of the study would appear to be reasonable, although lack of information about the company, location, etc., limit our ability to generalize.

i. <u>Davis & Valfer</u> (1966) changed the design of supervisory jobs in the civilian shops of a military establishment. The eleven shops were concerned with repair and overhauling of parts of aircraft systems, and contained from 18 to 30 workers each. The authors report that, prior to the experiment less attention was given to cost effectiveness than was officially prescribed.

In two of the shops, the supervisors' jobs were changed by allocating responsibility and authority for all functions required to complete the products being processed. This entailed not only a change in the supervisors' jobs, but associated changes in the organization of shops and training of workers, thereby obscuring the results of supervisory job redesign <u>per se</u>.

In another set of four shops, the supervisors' jobs were redesigned so as to give them greater responsibility and authority over quality of the work. This also involved giving rank-and-file workers and craftsmen greater self-control over

the quality of their work, again serving to  blur the effects
of supervisory job changes.

The above experimental groups, as well as the remaining
control groups, were compared with regard to a number of take,
mediating, and dependent variables obtained before, during,
and from 6 to 15 months after the experimental changes. Data
generated by observers and the supervisors themselves showed
that the changes indeed affected the way supervisors did their
jobs:  basically, they gave greater time and attention to technical and production matters, and functioned with greater independence of their own supervisors. As perceived by their
subordinates, the supervisors given increased quality responsibility exhibited more structuring and consideration behavior,
but the opposite was true in the product responsibility shops.

In the shops where supervisors were given more quality
responsibility, they reported increased job involvement and
job satisfaction, but the statistical significance of the
finding is questionable given the small number of cases. One
of the four shops demonstrated a significant improvement in
productivity, and two of them experienced significant reductions
in production costs.

In the shops where supervisors were given expanded
responsibility for production, supervisory job satisfaction
also reportedly increased, but there were no changes in
productivity that exceeded those of the control shops. Personnel problems, including absenteeism, lateness, grievances,

accidents, etc., did not change from their initial levels under either experimental treatment.

j. <u>Miscellaneous Studies</u>. The literature contains a number of studies of job design which we have not incorporated among our "prototypes" because they depart too far from the standards we have set for internal validity. These include a number of the examples reported by our three general references: Rush (1971), <u>Work in America</u> (HEW, 1973), and Glaser (1973). Building on the example of <u>Work in America</u>, we are summarizing these in Table VI-2 at the close of this section. For each study, we describe briefly not only the job change and its results, but the factors which, in our judgment, limit their internal validity, i.e., our ability to say that we are reasonably confident that a significant change in job performance and/or satisfaction was attributable to change in the specified job content.

To help the reader understand the relevance of our criteria, we will comment below on one of the studies listed in Table VI-2. It is selected not because it is either better or worse than the others, but because it provides clear illustrations of the points we wish to make.

Rush (1971) includes among his case reports that of the Weyerhaeuser Company. The program was installed in one of its paper manufacturing plants, which has many automated features. Its 300 employees are represented by five unions. The job enrichment program is called the "I am" plan. It was introduced in the context of the company's management having already attended a four-week development course featuring the motivational and problem-solving approaches basic to the plan. A full-time coordinator was appointed for installing the plan, and he and the plant manager programmed a number of steps to implement it, including:

1. Select a committee of 60 employees representing all levels of division.

2. Get feedback on the committee's perceptions of problems and needs.

3. Educate the committee about the nature of the plan.

4. Conduct a plant-wide job attitude survey, and feed back the results.

5. Select discussion leaders for work groups.

6. Train discussion leaders.

7. Hold group "improvement" conferences, including problem identification, brainstorming, and work simplification techniques.

8. Establish a Steering Committee on job and process improvement, based in part on data gleaned from Steps 4 and 7.

9. Set up and train project teams to work on particular internal problems; training includes work simplification, problem-solving, and decision-making.

10. Establish problem-solving by project teams as an on-going process.

11. Hold refresher courses relevant to foregoing.

It is presumably as a direct outgrowth of steps 9 and 10 that job enrichment occurs in a specific work group. Typically this entails adding planning and controlling elements to the work of members of the group; each group monitors its productivity, machine utilization, quality control, the productivity and contribution of individual members, and behaviors such as absence, tardiness, and interpersonal interaction.

The plan was inaugurated in 1968, and at the time of the report (period of about two years?) it was said to have "shown a rate of productivity exceeding that of comparable plants." It was also said that employees' grievances had dropped appreciably. A company executive commented that the better productivity record could not be attributed to a greater market for its products or increased automation, and concluded that the "I am" plan is responsible. It was admitted that the "Hawthorne effect" might be responsible, but that regular continuation of these activities is planned (which would presumably help maintain the stimulation resulting from attention and change).

The following problems may be noted as placing limits on our ability to illuminate the hypothesis that job enrichment was responsible for increased work job motivation, or satisfaction, or performance.

1. The "I am" plan involved many features in addition to

the enrichment of jobs, including management and worker training, an attitude survey and feedback, work simplification, and financial incentives (via a contract which provides for additional compensation for high-producing groups).

2. The absence of impact or "take" measures makes it impossible to tell which of the above features were salient.

3. The absence of motivational or attitudinal measures prevents one from knowing whether, how much, or in what ways motivation was changed.

4. Since the attitude survey was not repeated (nor other such data furnished), we cannot tell whether the "quality of working life," as experienced by the workers, in fact changed.

5. The productivity and grievance information is vague and impressionistic.

6. Hardly any information is given about the other plants with which productivity was compared.

7. There is no assessment of the statistical significance of changes.

We are not denying that important and worthwhile things may have happened at the Weyerhaeuser plant. All we can say is that we cannot be confident, in light of the above limitations, that job satisfaction and/or performance in fact improved and, if they had, that it would be attributable to the motivational impact of specified changes in job design.

We reach similarly ambiguous conclusions in connection with the other reports listed in the Table VI-2.

## 3. Influence of Worker Characteristics

We noted earlier several instances where worker characteristics were studied as factors moderating relationships between
job design and outcome variables. In this section, we will
review various studies bearing on this issue, since it is
important to know whether job redesign is a more useful
strategy with certain kinds of workers than it is with others.
For example, we reported earlier that Turner & Lawrence (1965)
found that scope-of-job ratings correlated positively with
both job satisfaction and attendance among blue-collar workers
in small towns, but not in urban samples, and that Hulin &
Blood (1968) reported similar results, which they ascribed to
greater alienation of the latter from middle-class work norms.
The relevance of alienation is thrown into question by
Shepard's (1970) study, in which alienation as measured by
questionnaire did not appreciably affect the relationship between job specialization and satisfaction. The contradictory
results serve to point up the elusive quality of the concept
of "alienation."

We also noted earlier the finding of Hackman & Lawler
(1971) to the effect that the relationships of job-scope factors to satisfaction and performance were greater among workers
with stronger "higher order" needs (achievement and growth)
than among those oriented more toward comfort and security. In
a similar vein, Fein (1973) has asserted that, in the national
sample included in the Survey of Working Conditions, the

importance of interesting work was stronger among workers in higher-level and white-collar jobs than among rank-and-file blue-collar workers. Lawler, Hackman & Kaufman (1973), in their study of the effects of redesign of jobs of telephone operators, failed to detect differences based on growth needs, work orientation, educational level, or age of workers; however, that negative finding may have been due to the relative homogeneity of the sample with respect to those background considerations. Turner & Lawrence (1965) also failed to detect a moderating influence of age in their correlational study of blue-collar workers.

A related set of studies has been concerned with differences among various groups of workers in what they want in their jobs. For example, it has been found that, on average, greater emphasis is placed on such "extrinsic" factors as pay, security and working conditions by workers from lower socio-economic groups, those who have less education, and those raised in urban communities than is the case with their middle-class, better-educated, rural or small-town counterparts; the latter groups in turn are likely to place greater stress on social service, self-realization, and opportunities for achievement (Morse & Weiss, 1955; Stefflre, 1959; Gay et al., 1971).

The previously noted tendency for blue-collar samples to be less responsive to intrinsic or work-content considerations than white-collar workers has also been detected in studies by

Friedlander (1964, 1965). It has also been found that those
at higher occupational levels tend to have greater interest
in intrinsic job factors, such as work content, self-
expression, and prestige, and less in such extrinsic factors
as earnings and security, than do those at lower levels
(Centers & Bugental, 1966; Wollack, Goodale, Wijting, & Smith,
1971).

Age trends are less clear. The Minnesota surveys of the
mid-1960's (Gay et al., 1971) found that younger workers, on
average, placed less emphasis on such intrinsic factors as
achievement and ability utilization than did those at the older
end of the sample; however, the latter also put more emphasis
on such extrinsic considerations as compensation, company
policies, and supervision. Middle-aged workers in that study
were the ones not concerned with the intrinsic factors of advancement, authority, and responsibility. However, the more
recent study of blue-collar workers by Sheppard & Herrick (1972)
reported that job-content factors such as variety, responsibility, and autonomy were more salient to those under 30 than to
older workers. They also cited findings from the SRC Survey of
Working Conditions to the effect that younger workers place
greater emphasis on job content, less on comfort, and no difference compared to older ones in regard to pay and security.

The change in the pattern of age differences in the
studies done about 1970 compared to those done about 5 years
earlier may be associated with the changing attitudes of young
people toward work recently noted by Yankelovich (1972, 1974).
These include less disposition to accept tradition, authority,

and the idea that hard work will pay off, and a higher level of expectation about what is due them. Of late, these trends may be accelerating more sharply among young people having less education and in blue-collar jobs.

## General Conclusions on Job Design

1. The terms "job redesign," "job enrichment," "job enlargement," and the like have been employed rather loosely to embrace a wide variety of working conditions and practices. These have included not only a congeries of activities and responsibilities at which the worker spends a bulk of his time and which are normally considered his "job," but a number of peripherally-related considerations such as methods of compensation, voice in decisions, and identification with the company product. We believe that those interested in the effects of redesigning job content _per se_ would do well to focus on the core activity dimensions of Diversity, Difficulty, Identity, Feedback, Interaction, Cycle Time, and Self-Regulation. In combination, these comprise what may be regarded as "job level" or "scope."

2. There have been some 40 instances where jobs having different scope have been compared for effects on worker attitudes and performance. Most of them are case studies in on-going situations which, although usually reporting improvements in job attitudes and/or performance, are individually unconvincing because of inadequacies in research design. In

aggregate, they do suggest that something along those lines
may really be happening, but that impression must be tempered
by the realization that (a) the changes often entail more
than the redesign of jobs, e.g., changes in pay or work technology are also often involved, and (b) the case literature
is testimonial in nature, so that negative experiences may not
be volunteered. In essence, we find that the results of the
majority of case studies of job redesign, although suggestive,
are inconclusive because of low internal validity.

    3. There have been 14 studies that are methodologically
more adequate than those case studies; 5 were correlational,
and 9 entailed the redesign of jobs. Their results are summarized in Table VI-1.

        a. Most of them found that workers in expanded
           (enlarged or enriched) jobs have higher job
           satisfaction or job attitudes that were other-
           wise more favorable than is the case in more
           restricted jobs.

        b. In about half of the studies, aspects of produc-
           tivity were found to be better in addition to
           better attitudes. In 6 of the studies where job
           satisfaction was higher, manifestations of with-
           drawal (turnover or absenteeism) were typically
           better, i.e., less frequent.

        c. In only one study (Davis & Valfer) did job atti-
           tudes improve while job performance, on balance,

| Finding | Supporting Studies | Studies Failing to Support |
|---|---|---|
| Better attitudes (motivation and/or job satisfaction) | Herzberg, Mausner & Snyderman[1] (professionals) | Internal Revenue Service (clerks) |
| | Turner & Lawrence[1] (blue collar) | Maher (students) |
| | Patchen (various) | Bishop & Hill (blue collar) |
| | Ford[2] (frame men) | Lawler, Hackman & Kaufman[1] (telephone operators) |
| | Ford[2] (clerks) | |
| | Hall & Lawler (engineers) | |
| | Hackman & Lawler (various) | |
| | Kraft[2] (clerks) | |
| | Janson (clerks) | |
| | Davis & Valfer[2] (blue-collar supervisors and workers) | |
| Better productivity | Herzberg, Mausner & Snyderman | Internal Revenue Service |
| | Ford[1,2] (framemen) | Bishop & Hill |
| | Ford[2] (clerks) | Lawler, Hackman & Kaufman[1,2] |
| | Hall & Lawler | Davis & Valfer[1,2] |
| | Hackman & Lawler | |
| | Kraft[2] | |
| | Janson | |
| | Maher | |

Table VI-1 - Continued

| Finding | Supporting Studies | Studies Failing to Support |
|---------|--------------------|-----------------------------|
| Less withdrawal | Herzberg, Mausner & Snyderman | |
| | Turner & Lawrence[1] | |
| | Patchen | |
| | Hackman & Lawler | |
| | Janson | |
| | Lawler, Hackman & Kaufman[2] | |

[1]Results mixed, i.e., not the same in all measures or samples, but generally favor the inference.

[2]Statistical significance not reported or doubtful.

did not, but those results were not unequivocal.
Conversely, in one study (Maher) performance was
found to improve when jobs were enlarged but attitudes did not; however, this was a laboratory
study in which job satisfaction has limited
significance.

d.  In three instances, job redesign failed, on bal-
    ance, to significantly improve either job atti-
    tudes or performance.

e.  When this last result is coupled with the incon-
    sistent or questionably significant relationships
    noted in several of the studies classified as
    showing positive results and the fact that the
    clearest support for the value of job enrichment
    came from correlational studies rather than ex-
    periments in redesign, we must conclude that job
    expansion is not regularly associated with signi-
    ficantly better job attitudes and performance.

f.  The studies of Hall & Lawler, of Ford, of Hackman &
    Lawler, and of Janson furnish what is probably the
    clearest support for the thesis that job expansion
    is associated with both better attitudes and better
    performance; those of the Internal Revenue Service,
    of Lawler, Hackman & Kaufman, and of Bishop & Hill
    most clearly show lack of impact.   Contrasting
    these two sets of studies is instructive since it

highlights some of the factors which may
account for the differences between them.  It is
apparent that, compared with the other studies, the
first set involved extensive and pervasive changes
in jobs; also, in three of the four instances,
greater authority was given to workers not only
over their own jobs but also over responsibility
for customer service.  By constrast, in the three
instances where attitudes and performance both
were unaffected or declined, the job changes were
so trivial as to be hardly perceptible to the
workers.

4.  Some of the prototypes, together with the other literature, suggest additional conditions which may be favorable to
beneficial results of job redesign; these include:

a.  Not all workers are equally responsive to design
features; enlarged jobs seem to have more favorable effects on workers whose "bread-and-butter"
needs for security have been met, those who have
stronger needs for self-expression and growth,
those who are younger, those coming from non-
urban and work-oriented culture patterns, and
those in higher-level jobs.  Among workers representing opposite poles of those characteristics,
who are more likely to be occupying blue-collar,
lower-level jobs, enlargement of jobs may have
negligible or even adverse effects.

b.  Other factors which may moderate the effects of
    job enrichment or enlargement derive not from the
    workers but from the work situation. These appear
    to include the extent to which organizational
    policies and practices have already accommodated
    "hygiene" needs for job security, income, and the
    like. Fein (1973),for example, questions whether
    the favorable results reported in some companies
    would be duplicated at organizations having less
    progressive labor histories; in a similar vein,
    those responsible for the IRS study hypothesized
    that its negative results might have been due in
    part to the low "hygiene" level of the organiza-
    tion. The nature of the technology would also
    seem to place boundary conditions on enrichment,
    as Fein has also noted; it is of interest that the
    prototype cases of improvement in both attitudes
    and performance typically entailed jobs which are
    not closely tied to a complex, interdependent
    machine technology (including telephone framemen,
    clerks, key-punch operators, and professionals).

c.  There are instances where redesign of jobs may at
    times have inadvertent negative side effects on
    other workers, or on relations between those whose
    jobs are changed and other workers (including
    their supervisors).

5. The overall message to be learned from the above studies is as follows:

The most consistent evidence that the scope of job content relates to worker motivation, job satisfaction, and job performance comes from correlational studies of workers whose jobs already differ in scope, thus possibly implicating other contaminating causes such as pay level, worker values, and technology. Efforts to redesign jobs have not produced results that are generally persuasive in validity or consistent in direction, although there are tantalizing bits of evidence, including the results of 4 prototype experiments, which suggest the potential value of the approach to both the quality of working life and economic performance. Those who wish to experiment should be prepared to make major job changes, for it is apparent that to do less is likely to be ineffectual. Moreover, evidence also suggests that such experiments are likely to succeed only if (a) workers are psychologically "ready" for it, which is more likely to be true of young, affluent, and better educated workers, and (b) the production technology lends itself to such change. The key ingredients of a generally motivating job, as suggested by the above data, include:

    a. sufficient difficulty to be challenging;

    b. sufficient diversity to be interesting;

    c. constructive interaction with others;

    d. a work cycle sufficiently long that the work is not repetitive or monotonous;

  e. sufficient identity or wholeness of the task to
     to represent a meaningful share of the product
     or service;

  f. regular and frequent feedback concerning the
     consequences of one's work;

  g. considerable self-control over one's own work;

  h. direct responsibility for the welfare of others
     outside one's immediate work group, especially
     customers or clients -- a concept sometimes
     termed "stewardship."

Various students of the subject have set forth their
recommendations for how jobs should be redesigned, including
Davis (1966), Herzberg (1968), Foulkes (1969), Myers (1970),
Glaser (1973), and Walters (1973). In addition to the eight
job dimensions noted above, elements mentioned in one or more
of such papers include:

  i. financial compensation of the workers commensurate
     with their contributions to the value of the
     service or product;

  j. democratization of the control and decision-making
     structure of the organization;

  k. continual or periodic expansion of job boundaries,
     lest adaptation sap the motivating effect.

Not all of the experts in the field are in agreement on
the proper practices. Herzberg, for example, warns against
contaminating the motivational value of enrichment of jobs by
incorporating diversification (horizontal enlargement), or

"hygienic" improvements, including human relations and, presumably, compensation. Fein (1971), however, has argued that most of the favorable effects attributed to job enrichment have probably been due more to the associated increases in efficiency of work methods and/or in compensation, and that these should therefore be the critical targets for improvement. Rush (1971) also included work simplification among his list of features of job redesign.

We are inclined to the view stated by Herzberg to the effect that the concept of job enrichment had best be confined to the motivating aspects of intrinsic job content. This is not to say that factors like compensation, democratization of control, and methods efficiency are unimportant. But work rationalization is not basically a strategy for improving job attitudes, which is central to concerns of this review. The re-distribution of control and changes in compensation, although motivational in intent, are conceptually and procedurally different from changes in job content per se, and therefore are to be treated separately in this report.

Table **VI-2**. Summary of Miscellaneous Case Reports

There follows a presentation of miscellaneous case studies. For each study, the following information is furnished where available:

1. Source or reference
2. Organization name and type
3. Workers studied (numbers, jobs, etc.)
4. Technique or nature of change in job design
5. Key job dimensions affected, i.e., Difficulty Diversity, Feedback, Identity, Autonomy, etc.
6. Results of impact or take measurements
7. Results of motivational measurement
8. Job satisfaction results
9. Performance results
10. Limitations of external validity (generalizability)
11. Limitations of internal validity, i.e., doubts as to whether the claimed results are acurate and/or are attributable to the moticational impact of job re-design. The nature of these doubts are entered in the case presentations according to the following key:

A  dubious measurement or operationalization of independent variables
B  dubious measurement or operationalization of impact variables
C  dubious measurement or operationalization of intervening variables
D  dubious measurement or operationalization of performance variables
E  dubious measurement or operationalization of job satisfaction
F  inadequate statistical tests of significance of differences
G  inadequate control group(s)
H  small samples
I  short time for assessing results
J  problems in inferring whether results are due to motivational effects of job re-design or to other factors, i.e.

$J_1$  efficiency of work methods
$J_2$  equipment changes
$J_3$  different pay system
$J_4$  participation
$J_5$  training
$J_6$  recruitment or selection practices
$J_7$  other

These limitations on validity are <u>in addition to</u> those stemming from absence of measurements listed in categories 5, 6, 7, 8, and 9, above.

Note: Information <u>estimated</u> in the cited source or by the present writers is shown in parentheses.

## Case 1

1. Source:  Rush (1971)

2. Organization:  Monsanto Co., Textile Division - nylon manufacturing plant

3. Workers:  45 hourly and five salaried chemical operators

4. Technique:  Job re-design by task force with representative operator participation

5. Job Dimensions:  (Difficulty, Diversity, Feedback, Identity, Autonomy)

6. Impact:  None reported.

7. Motivation:  None reported.

8. Job Satisfaction:  (Employees reported as being enthusiastic.)

9. Performance:  Quality of output improved; productivity improved; turnover and absenteeism unchanged; suggestions increased

10. External Validity:  Non-union

11. Internal Validity: D, F, G, H, I, $J_1$, $J_4$, $J_7$

## Case 2

1. Source:  Glaser (1973)

2. Organization:  Donnelly Mirrors, Inc. - auto mirror manufacturing

3. Workers:  600 employees

4. Technique:  Massive organization-wide intervention, including job re-design, Scanlon Plan, and other changes

5. Job Dimensions:  (Job Design, Interaction, Control, Group Autonomy, Group Responsibility, Group Influence, Opportunity for Growth, Pay)

6. Impact:  None reported

7. Motivation:  None reported

8. Job Satisfaction:  None reported

9. Performance:  Productivity increased; quality improved; tardiness and absenteeism reduced.

10. External Validity:  Non-union; family-owned company; has been on Scanlon Plan for 20 years

11. Internal Validity:  D, F, G, J

## Case 3

1.  Source:  Rush (1971)

2.  Organization:  PPG Industries - fiberglass yarn manufacturing

3.  Workers:  92 frame operators and 28 frame cleaners

4.  Technique:  Jobs re-designed with employees input.

5.  Job Dimensions:  (Diversity, Interaction, Feedback)

6.  Impact:  None reported

7.  Motivation:  None reported

8.  Job Satisfaction:  (Personnel and production managers report morale is high.)

9.  Performance:  Increased productivity; absenteeism and turnover unchanged.

10.  External Validity:  Non-union

11.  Internal Validity:  E, F, G, $J_1$, $J_4$

## Case 4

1.  Source:  Rush (1971)

2.  Organization:  Weyerhauser Co. - paper manufacturing plant

3.  Workers:  300 employees

4.  Technique:  Massive organization-wide intervention under full-time coordinator

5.  Job Dimensions:  (Job Re-design, Worker Control, Opportunity for Individual Growth, Pay)

6.  Impact:  None reported

7.  Motivation:  None reported.

8.  Job satisfaction:  None reported

9.  Performance:  Higher productivity compared to other plants; fewer grievances.

10. External Validity:  Strong union-management cooperation

11. Internal Validity:  D, $J_1$, $J_3$, $J_4$, $J_7$

## Case 5

1. Source:  Rush (1971)

2. Organization:  Monsanto Co. - agricultural chemicals plant

3. Workers:  12 bagging technicans

4. Technique:  Job re-design by task force which included technicans

5. Job Dimensions:  (Diversity, Identity, Feedback, Individual Control, Group Control)

6. Impact:  (Investigator reports little change in technology but increase in work planning and control.)

7. Motivation:  None reported

8. Job Satisfaction:  None reported

9. Performance:  Increased productivity after initial drop.

10. External Validity:  Non-union

11. Internal Validity:  B, G, H, I, $J_4$

## Case 6

1.  Source:  Glaser (1973)

2.  Organization:  Kaiser Steel Co. - pipe mill

3.  Workers:  Pipe mill workers

4.  Technique:  Technique not described

5.  Job Dimensions:  (Job Re-design - no description given, Worker Control, Pay)

6.  Impact:  None reported

7.  Motivation:  (Author reports impressions of increased Self-determination, Need for Achievement, Effort, and Concern for Job Security.)

8.  Job Satisfaction:  None reported

9.  Performance:  Increase in productivity

10. External Validity:  Threat of shut-down; strong union-management cooperation

11. Internal Validity:  C, D, $J_1$, $J_2$, $J_3$

Case 7

1.  Source:  Powers (1972)

2.  Organization:  W.R. Grace & Co., Cryovac Division - technical manufacturing

3.  Workers:  33 salaried workers; 9 machine operators; 18 inspector packers; 6 service personnel

4.  Technique:  Job re-design by committee comprised of department superintendent and first-line supervisors

5.  Job Dimension:  (Identity, Feedback, Control, Job Skills)

6.  Impact:  None reported

7.  Motivation:  None reported

8.  Job Satisfaction:  None reported

9.  Performance:  Increase in "units produced per dollar"; (Improved quality)

10.  External Validity:  Possibility of a typical employee group resulting from low selection ratio and unique recruitment procedures.

11.  Internal Validity:  D, F, G, H, $J_1$, $J_3$, $J_5$

Case 8

1. Source:  Rush (1971)

2. Organization:  Syntex Corp., Arapahoe Chemicals - small-
   jobs shop

3. Workers:  Chemists

4. Technique:  Not described

5. Job Dimensions:  (Diversity, Difficulty, Feedback,
   Individual Autonomy, Individual Responsibility)

6. Impact:  None reported

7. Motivation:  None reported

8. Job Satisfaction:  (Management reports higher morale
   among chemists and also among salesmen, the primary
   customer contacts.)

9. Performance:  (Management reports higher productivity,
   less turnover, prompter deadlines.)

10. External Validity:  Higher specialized employee group;
    small job shop organization.

11. Internal Validity:  D, E, F, G

Case 9

1. Source: Rush (1971)

2. Organization: Texas Instruments

3. Workers: Approximately 50 male and 25 female cleaning and janitorial personnel

4. Technique: Previously contracted-out jobs were taken over by T.I. and re-designed

5. Job Dimensions: (Diversity, Feedback, Interaction, Group Influence, Group Responsibility, Training, Pay)

6. Impact: None reported.

7. Motivation: None reported

8. Job Satisfaction: None reported

9. Performance: Cleanliness improvement over contractor's level; turnover lower than contractor's level; cost decreased; number of personnel needed fewer than contractor needed.

10. External Validity: Organizational climate conducive to change; start of new department rather than change in existing one

11. Internal Validity: D, F, G, $J_1$, $J_2$, $J_3$, $J_5$, $J_6$, $J_7$

CHAPTER VII

PATTERNS OF CONTROL

The very essence of social organization is coordinated control over the behavior of organization members. The absence of such control would quite literally produce disorganization.

The significance of control was therefore not lost on administrative management theorists, who were much concerned with the issues of the allocation of authority, the scalar principle of hierarchy, unity of command and span of control. Political theorists were also cognizant of the centrality of issues of power and control to the nature and operation of the state.

Unlike the situation in Europe, where political theorists were long concerned with issues of control in organizations, American students of organizational behavior remained aloof from concerns with control until the time of World War II, when ideological issues were thrust to the fore. And even then, the subject of control surfaced initially in the benign contexts of the motivational force of self-determined and group goals and of the effects of different leadership patterns.

Even today, many analysts and critics of American organizational practices have skirted the problem of control. For example, Sheppard & Herrick (1972) largely ignore it, while

Work in America (HEW, 1973) treats autonomy and participation merely as one of several aspects of job enrichment.

This is not to suggest that the subject has been completely disregarded in the U.S.A. A recent popular work written by Jenkins (1973), entitled Job Power, is concerned with the following theme: "The central idea of industrial democracy is the re-distribution of power...the key is power over decisions" (page 3). A more radical position is featured in another recent work, Workers Control (Hunnius, Garson & Case, 1973), where it is stated that "Workers' control means democratizing the work place....It means that a firm's management should be accountable to its employees" (page ix).

Those two books illustrate the traditional dual sources of interest in the topic. Hunnius et al. are oriented mainly toward ideological concerns, seeing workers' control of industry as nothing less than social justice. Jenkins, on the other hand, emphasizes the pragmatic theme that "democratic methods are more productive, and therefore more profitable, than autocratic methods" (p. 302).

Our concern here will be descriptive and will be addressed first to conceptualizations of control in organizations, to be followed by a summary of studies which bear on the effects of various control patterns on the job attitudes and behavior of workers.

## Theory of Organizational Control

The distribution of control among the members and groups which compose an organization is one aspect of its structure. In terms of our theoretical framework, control, like other structural festures of organizations, is likely to affect either the ability or motivation of workers, or both, and thereby affect their productivity and satisfaction. Organization theorists have suggested that the effects of different control structures may operate through one or more of the following specific dynamics:

- Goals or courses of action which individuals and groups have set for themselves generate stronger motivation for accomplishment than those imposed by others.

- Self-determined goals are likely to be clearer than those imposed by others.

- Organization members want to exercise control, and therefore experience satisfaction to the extent that the control system affords such opportunities and dissatisfaction when it does not.

- Participation in shaping organizational decisions helps insure that the decisions take into account the interests and needs of those participating, thereby serving to elevate their level of commitment to those courses of action.

- Participation in shaping organizational decisions helps ensure that they take into account all of the available knowledge and ideas of those participating.

- Some patterns of control require more time to reach decisions than others.

- Some patterns of control require more time to implement decisions than others.

- Patterns of control differ in the extent to which they fit the functional requirements of different situations, and hence have different outcomes depending on characteristics of the situation.

Although terminology varies somewhat from author to author, the following definitions and conceptualizations may be distilled from literature on the subject. All pertain to aspects of control structure, and may therefore be employed later in our discussion of studies relating control patterns to worker attitudes and behavior.

1. "Control" is the act or process whereby a person, group, or organization intentionally determines or affects what another person, group or organization does. (It is equivalent to what some authors regard as successful influence, the term "influence" being used for any change in behavior induced by another whether intended or not). Thus control may be regarded as the inverse or reciprocal of "freedom."

2. "Power" refers to potential control, that is, control is based on power and occurs when power is used. Power is defined by the presence of certain conditions which constitute the means by which control may be effected, sometimes called "types" or "bases" of power. These include:

a. <u>Legitimate</u> power, or the acknowledged "right" to control by virtue of one's office or position;

b. <u>Expert</u> or persuasive power, stemming from the perception by others that one has supervisor knowledge or ability;

c. <u>Referent</u> or personal power, dependent on special charisma which attracts followers or believers;

d. <u>Reward</u> or utilitarian power, which depends on one's ability to dispense or withhold rewards;

e. <u>Coercive</u> power, which depends on ability to dispense or withhold punishments or aversive conditions;

f. <u>Situational Power</u>, which is a property neither of persons nor their offices but rather of the situation or circumstances which evoke previously programmed behavior.

3. <u>"Authority"</u> is the power that one holds by virtue of the role, position, or office he holds, and entails a combination of legitimate, reward, and coercive power. Some authors refers to it as "position" or "official" power. Thus, the use of authority represents one from among several ways in which control may be exercised in organizations.

4. <u>"Leadership"</u> refers to power stemming from personal rather than positional attributes, drawing mainly on expert and referent bases. It is equivalent to what Etzioni (1965) terms "informal power." Katz and Kahn (1966) consider it as "incremental influence," i.e., the effects that a person has

on others for reasons beyond those attributable to his role or office, and thus capable of manifestation by anyone irrespective of his job in an organization.

Although leadership is a factor in the control of organizational behavior, it is an _interpersonal_ process separate and different from the structure of work and the programmed relationship among organization members irrespective of who they are and what kinds of personalities they may have. Leadership is thus a phenomenon of organizational life which operates irrespective of authority relations, and may in fact operate counter to them. From the standpoint of organizational management, it is strategic to have leadership and authority relations coincide, so that the former supplement and reinforce rather than disrupt the latter. Techniques for accomplishing that lie in the realm of selecting and developing managers in such a way that they may also be effective leaders. But this is a quite different matter than programming a system of relationships of people at work based on authority, i.e., on the agreed-upon _right_ to make decisions and determine what others do and to invoke rewards and sanctions in accordance with conformity to those decisions. For these reasons, the amount and distribution of control in organizations might not coincide at all closely with the leadership styles of its supervisors. Evidence of this was reported in the study by Tannenbaum _et al_. (1974); they found only a modest relationship between participativeness as an interpersonal style of supervisors and the perceived level of worker influence.

For several reasons, we will not undertake to analyze here the hundreds of studies done in recent decades on the nature and effects of leadership styles:

- As noted earlier, the focus of our study is on the programmed structure of work and work relationships; leadership and other informal human relationships on the job fall outside that purview, since they entail a different strategy of intervention;

- As noted above, organizational control structure only partly reflects leadership patterns whereas the structure of formal authority for decisions is even more central; hence our focus will be on authority and control, which are amenable to re-structuring by those responsible for the design of work;

- The literature on leadership styles as related to worker attitudes and performance has already been recently summarized and evaluated by others (especially Dubin et al., 1965; Fleishman & Hunt, 1973; Stogdill, 1974).

5. Distribution of Control refers to who has how much control. There are two aspects of distribution:

    a. Level or Amount of Control, i.e., in absolute terms to what extent does any given person or group determine a certain outcome;

    b. Gradient or Balance of Control, i.e., with respect to any given outcome, what is the relative degree to which it is determined by each of the several persons or groups of interest.

These two features of control structure have been the focus of the "control graph" approach developed by A.S. Tannenbaum and his associates (e.g., Tannenbaum, 1962; Smith & Tannenbaum, 1963). Basically, the control graph summarizes the responses which organization members give to a question like, "How much say do _____ have over what goes on here?", the blank being filled in by reference to a given hierarchical segment of the organization such as top management, or supervisors, or workers. The respondent answers the question on a scale ranging from 0 (no say) to 10 (complete say). The average answers of all respondents then can be portrayed on a graph as follows:

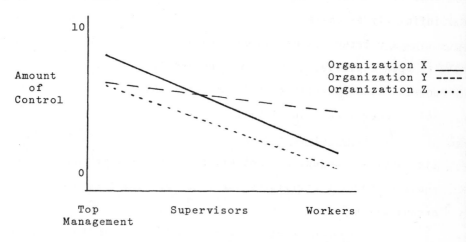

Our example simultaneously shows the curves for three hypothetical organizations. In each case, the amount of control is revealed by the average level of the line in terms of the ordinate or vertical axis; thus organizations X and Y show approximately equal amounts of control, whereas Z has less than the others. The slope of each line portrays the balance or gradient of control, the more horizontal or flatter it is (e.g., Y) the more egalitarian the control, while the more vertical or steeper (e.g., X) the more hierarchical or centralized the control. Note that total control is not necessarily fixed, i.e., there is not necessarily a finite pie available in any given organization, so amount and balance can vary independently of one another. In game-theoretical terms, control over decisions may be envisioned as a non-zero-sum game, i.e., when one person or groups "wins" another need not necessarily "lose" the same amount. On the other hand, the control "pie" is probably not infinitely expansible.

A related set of concepts regarding allocation of control has been expressed by Paré, who refers to four structures of power: Boss Power; System Power; Peer Power; and Goal (or Self) Power (see Rush, 1969).

6. Scope of Control pertains to which topics or activities are the subject of control, since control may not extend equally over all activities performed by a person, group, or organization.

7. Domain of Control refers to the notion that control is exercised over some person, group, or organization, so that in analyzing control patterns it is necessary to stipulate who is being controlled by whom. There are three domains of interest in the present connection:

a. Control over what goes on in the specific position or job filled by an individual;

b. Control over what is done by and in a work group
   or department;

c. Control over what is done by and in an organization, such as a plant or company.

The specific <u>methods</u> of shaping control patterns, as well
as of studying them, depend somewhat on the domain, i.e.,
whether control is at the level of the individual job, the
work group, or the organization:

a. Individual Job:  In Chapter VI on Job Design, we
   saw that "autonomy" is widely regarded as one of
   the core dimensions of the enriched job.  Jenkins
   (1973) does not regard such increased autonomy as
   equivalent to increased influence or democracy,
   preferring to define the latter in terms of "the
   extent to which employees are allowed to deal
   directly with their...environments," and not just
   "...within the strict limits of the management-
   created fixed 'job'..." (p. 242).  Perhaps the
   essential difference is whether or not control is
   exercised over others, i.e., is an <u>interactive</u>
   process (Lowin, 1968).  Job autonomy entails less
   control of workers by management, but does not in
   itself increase their direct influence on managers.
   This may be largely a definitional matter, but we
   will in this report follow the practice of con-

sidering changes in job autonomy under the heading of job design rather than in the present chapter.

One aspect of control in the domain of the individual job which does involve a shift in inter-positional influence is when superior and subordinate jointly enter into the redefinition of the latter's job, and to some degree often the former's as well. That process, often formalized under the label of "Management by Objectives" (MBO), therefore falls within the scope of the present chapter.

b. The Work Group: When members of work groups obtain greater control over their own operations, we have a situation analogous to MBO. This is an aspect of what has been traditionally termed "decentralization," and has more recently been given the label of "autonomous work groups." Like job autonomy, it is typically accomplished via redefinition of the scope of authority.

c. The Organization: Control processes, of course, ramify the organization as a whole and may be designed and investigated at that level. There are two major strategies for accomplishing this. One is structural, including such properties as organizational size, number of hierarchical or statu levels, span of control, etc. The other is normative and, as in the case of job and work-grou

autonomy, consists of legitimizing (agreeing on)
the making or participation in the making of certain classes of decisions by various organizational members or groups of members. Where distribution of authority is widespread through the
organization, terms like "consultative management,"
"industrial democracy," and "participation in
decision-making" have been applied. Policies
governing such procedures may either be informal
or formal (e.g., collective bargaining).

To illustrate the semantic confusions on this subject, we
may note that Work in America (HEW, 1973) reserves the term
"participative management" to workers' participation in decisions
on "aspects of work intimately affecting their lives," i.e.,
processes relating to job and work-group autonomy; however, that
definition leaves in limbo sharing of control over larger,
organization-wide issues of central concern to writers like
Jenkins (1973) and Hunnius et al. (1973).

We will review experiences with various control patterns
below by grouping the studies under rubrics corresponding to
the foregoing three domains:  individual jobs (MBO), work
groups, and total organizations.

## Management by Objectives

The term "Management by Objectives" (MBO) is employed to
describe various programs that have in common the following

elements (Wikstrom, 1968; Beach & Mahler, 1972; Carroll & Tosi, 1973):

1. definition and communication of organizational goals and objectives;

2. setting objectives and goals for individual workers in relation to the above;

3. participation both by the individual and his superior(s) in setting the objectives for his job;

4. periodic review and feedback of the individual's performance in comparison to those objectives.

There appear to be at least two ways in which MBO may affect the pattern of control: (1) by giving workers a greater voice in defining and revising the objectives of their jobs; and (2) by affording them greater freedom in devising ways of attaining those objectives. As Beach & Mahler (1972) state: "Management by objectives...demands descentralization to some degree. It means surrendering authority...the key to making it work is participation" (p. 235).

In addition to changing the allocation of control, MBO also can in theory affect other dynamics of performance, including: clarification of goals, better planning, and more frequent and complete feedback on performance.

Three sets of studies on MBO stand out as prototypes, namely those conducted at the General Electric Company, Purex Corporation, and Black & Decker Manufacturing Company. We will discuss these next, to be followed by briefer consideration of some additional studies of MBO.

## Prototype Studies of MBO

a. <u>General Electric</u> studies are summarized by Meyer, Kay & French (1965) and Meyer (1972), and are reported in greater detail by Kay, Meyer & French (1965) and French, Kay & Meyer (1966).

One of the earlier experiments involved 92 exempt employees occupying a variety of jobs in a large GE plant. The conventional procedure of conducting in a single annual appraisal session a consideration both of salary and future performance was changed so that the two topics were covered in separate reviews held two weeks apart. Employees received one of two forms of the performance review: one in which the employee's superior (the appraiser) was instructed to afford the employee a high degree of influence in formulating a list of performance objectives for the future, whereas for the second group of employees, as customary, appraisers had the greater influence in determining the final list of objectives. Information about what went on in the performance review was gathered by observers and by questioning the employees via interviews and questionnaires. The difference in treatments had their intended effects on relative influence, as reported both by observers and by the employees; thus, this form of MBO may be said to "take" as a method of changing control over job goals.

Both groups of employees reported heightened acceptance of goals for the future, but the authors state that the increase was greater on the part of those afforded greater influence than those afforded less influence. The acceptance of goals may be considered as an expression of motivation to attain them. In keeping with that interpretation, the more participative group about 12 weeks later reported achieving a greater proportion of their improvement goals than did the other group. The former also expressed more favorable attitudes toward their managers and certain aspects of their jobs, including the appraisal system. The advantages of the participative method in terms of goals attainment appeared to be particularly stronger for employees who had customarily experienced participative management and for those who were subject to less criticism during the appraisal process. There was also evidence that improvement was more likely to occur when improvement goals were defined specifically rather than vaguely.

A later study at GE tested the Work Planning and Review (WPR) procedure which grew out of the preceding experience. As Meyer (1972) describes it: "This new approach differed from the usual program in that (1) there are more frequent discussions of performance, (2) there are no summary judgments or ratings, (3) salary discussions are held separately, and (4) the emphasis is on mutual goal planning and problem solving."

In one department of the company, about half the managers chose to adopt the new program, whereas the others decided to continue with the conventional annual performance appraisal. A questionnaire survey was made of the affected employees before any changes were introduced, and was repeated a year later during which time the two contrasted appraisal programs were in operation. The attitudes of the unchanged group remained essentially the same, but those in the WPR program changed in several respects, including increased acceptance of the goals set for the future (a mediating variable, as noted earlier), and more favorable attitudes toward their superiors and toward the performance reviews. The authors also report "strong evidence" that employees in the WPR program were more likely to have done things to improve their performance, but this assertion is not documented in detail.

A third GE study was aimed at learning how the ways in which WPR interviews are conducted are related to improvement in job performance. Fifty-six WPR sessions were observed. Each employee in the study completed a questionnaire and was interviewed, as were the superiors involved. In addition to illuminating what goes on in such interviews, the study discovered certain features which were associated with improvement in job performance as reported 14 weeks later; for example, in the case of below-average performers, subsequent improvement was likely to be greater where subordinates more actively participated and where they received proportionately more positive than critical statements about their past performance.

Meyer (1972) concludes from the GE experience that the following two features of MBO serve to motivate improvement of those appraised: (1) the specification of goals and expected results, and (2) the participation by each employee in appraising results of his past performance and in planning future improvements.

We would concur that the foregoing program of research supports the favorable effects of such actions on employees' perceptions and attitudes, especially as compared to conventional appraisals; however, the benefits of such programs on job performance and effectiveness were not clearly documented by that research since it relied largely on subjective reports. It should also be noted that MBO was studied only in samples of exempt employees, primarily lower level supervisors and professionals.

b.  Purex Corporation studies have been reported by Raia (1965, 1966). They were conducted at a number of plants of the company, starting approximately in late 1961 or 1962. Two surveys were conducted of the perceptions and opinions of participating managers, one about a year after the program had been initiated (N = 112), and the second about another year later (N = 74); all of the findings are limited by this retrospective feature. The second survey furnished "take" data, indicating that nearly two out of three managers reported either setting their own goals or playing the dominant role in doing so in the planning and review sessions with their superiors; as to frequency, plant managers reported receiving such reviews on the average of every three months, but lower-level managers received them on the average of nearly every six months. Although "before" data were not furnished, these findings suggest that the frequency and nature of review sessions moved in the direction intended under the MBO program.

A content analysis of questionnaire responses of participants indicated to Raia the importance of two mediating
mechanisms activated by the program: "It improves management
planning and control on the job, and provides motivation to
improve individual performance" (1966, p. 56). This suggests
that MBO may in part serve to improve the ability of managers
to do their jobs, and in part to increase their motivation to
do so, the latter ostensibly resulting largely from improved
goal-setting and feedback. However, these inferences are
essentially based on impressions rather than detailed factual
data.

The work at Purex is of particular interest because it
furnished objective data on performance of the plants studied.
In fiscal 1963, average performance in meeting budgets ran
about 5% below the goals set, whereas in 1964 it averaged 15%
above that level (and 10% above the revised goals that had been
set upward). Productivity during the period from April 1962 to
April 1964 showed an average increase of 9% over the preceding
13-month base-line period, and the trend line was continuing to
move upward. Unfortunately, comparison data are not reported
for plants in which the MBO program was not installed, so that
it is not possible definitely to attribute the economic improvements to the MBO program.

  c. <u>Black and Decker Co</u>. study has been reported by
Carroll & Tosi (1969, 1970, 1973). It involved 129 managers at
all levels in the company. The study was commenced a year after
an MBO program had been introduced, so that no true before and

after comparisons were feasible; the study therefore mainly
serves to illuminate the internal dynamics of MBO, rather
than assessing its overall impact.

Two sets of take variables were measured by brief questionnaires, one concerning participant perceptions of the
goal-setting process, including their own influence in the
process; the second set concerned their perceptions of the
review and feedback process. Mediating variables were also
assessed by brief questionnaires, one concerning self-assessed
increase in effort and the other with subordinates' reports
of their bosses' reactions to poor work on their parts.

Dependent variables, like those in the GE study,
were limited to the perceptions of the participants, thus
raising a question of internal validity because of the possible circularity of relationships. In the present study, they
were measured by questionnaires whose brevity occasions questions of reliability and content validity. The topics covered
comprised self-assessed success in achieving goals, relations
with superiors, and evaluation of the MBO program.

Correlational analysis of the data reveal the following
main results:

(1) Features of the MBO process (take variables) which
had the clearest association with the dependent variables were
those pertaining to the review process, i.e., frequency of
feedback and amount of positive feedback; these tended to have
moderate positive correlations (often statistically significant) with self-reported success in achieving goals, with

improved relations with supervisor, and with attitude toward the MBO program. The take variables describing MBO generally failed to show appreciable or meaningful relationships with the mediating variables, so that the mechanisms connecting MBO to the above outcomes remain obscure.

(2) Differences in participants' perceptions of influence over goal-setting were not significantly correlated either with motivational mediators or with the dependent variables. This is particularly noteworthy, since presumably MBO operates via its enhancement of self-control. However, it should be recalled that the study provides no comparison of control before and after the inauguration of the MBO program, so that the foregoing finding pertains to differences in perceived influence among participants who all are participants in MBO; conceivably, they all may have experienced more influence than they had previously.

(3) Certain characteristics of the subordinates and of their reported participation in decisions appear to moderate the above relations between influence and other variables. Giving workers greater control over goal-setting appears to have favorable effects if they are relatively self-assured and if they are normally afforded opportunities to participate in decisions on the job. Otherwise, the effects are negligible or even negative.

## Miscellaneous Studies of MBO

MBO programs have been adopted in a number of additional

companies.  A report by Wikstrom (1968) described in considerable detail the nature of five of them.  In several of those
instances, favorable results were claimed.  The following is
an example:  "Certain definite values seem to stand out, in
the department's evaluation of management by objectives.
First, better work is done.  Quality has improved, costs are
lower, delivery schedules are met....Management by Objectives
[also] has tended to eliminate the 'political' atmosphere....
has allowed for individual creativeness on how to get the job
done...has improved [communication] tremendously...and most
important..., has provided for greater employee commitment"
(p. 60).  However, since the report does not describe specifically the investigations or the data on which such conclusions were based, its case studies do not serve our evaluative purpose.

A study of the effects of MBO on need satisfactions in
the jobs of managers was conducted in two companies by
Ivancevich, Donnelly & Lyon (1970).  Using a questionnaire
which got at perceptions of satisfaction of needs for security,
social relations, esteem, autonomy and self-actualization,
they found statistically significant improvements in satisfaction after the installation of MBO as compared to the level
which had existed before.

Carroll & Tosi (1973) summarized a dissertation study
by Mendelson on the relationship between participation in goal-
setting and the subordinate's job understanding and rated

effectiveness. The degree to which goal-setting was manifested was studied by a questionnaire administered to 25 pairs
of superiors and subordinates in 8 companies. The degree of
goal-setting was found not to be correlated with the subordinates'
understanding of their supervisors' expectations, suggesting
that this is not a critical factor in the results of MBO-type
programs. The relation of goal-setting participation to
ratings of subordinates was not consistent, since it was
insignificant with ratings of performance but positive with
ratings of promotability.

A study by Ivancevich (1972) suggests that two factors
which may help enhance and maintain the favorable effects of
MBO on job attitudes are (a) implementation of the MBO program
via top management rather than via a personnel department, and
(b) periodic "booster" training of those involved. The
empirical findings of the study provide some not unequivocal
support for those seemingly sensible propositions.

## Conclusions Regarding Management by Objectives

The following conclusions regarding MBO are extremely
tentative, given the small number of empirical studies:

a. MBO programs represent a way of increasing employees'
understanding of and perceived control over the goals and
objectives of their own jobs.

b. Those perceptions are likely to induce higher motivation to achieve the goals. This conclusion, drawn from field
studies, is consistent with the results of a number of labora-

tory studies on goal-setting, especially those conducted by Locke and his associates (Locke, 1968).

c. Another effect of MBO is to increase the frequency and clarity of feedback employees receive from their superiors.

d. The foregoing effects lead recipients of MBO to have more favorable attitudes toward their superiors and toward the method by which they are evaluated.

e. The few studies of effects of MBO on broader aspects of job satisfaction indicate that they also are positive.

f. Effects of MBO on work effectiveness have not been conclusively demonstrated. There are subjective reports of better goal attainment and of actions taken to improve performance, but those do not provide concrete results. There are also impressionistic accounts of better productivity and performance, but they lack sufficient documentation. The single study which furnished objective performance data indicated positive results following installation of MBO, but it is not conclusive because it lacked adequate controls.

g. MBO is not without its critics. Among the concerns which have been voiced is that: (1) it may serve as a device for imposing the hidden agenda of supervisors on their subordinates, thus, on balance, increasing relative control over the latter; (2) subordinates often do not push their views as actively as supervisors, thereby resulting in "participation" which is more fictitious than real; (3) its application is mainly to managerial and exempt employees.

## Work Group Control

We move now to studies concerned with control over the goals and activities of primary work groups, starting with those studies which meet our criteria for prototypes.

### Prototype Studies

a. The initial, and by now classic, study of changing control patterns in the work-group domain was reported by Coch & French (1948). Performed at the Harwood Manufacturing Company, a sleep-wear manufacturing plant, the study stemmed partly from the theories and laboratory experiments of Kurt Lewin, especially a famous one on the effects of democratic, autocratic, and laissez-faire styles of leadership (French, 1950; Marrow, 1972). The Coch & French study employed the Lewinian approach in analyzing and trying to reduce resistance to changes in work methods as manifested by sharp declines and slow rates of recovery in productivity and by high rates of turnover. The major variable was degree of worker participation (control) in changing the work methods and associated piece-rates. In one experiment, three levels of participation were employed in comparable groups of factory workers: (1) the usual minimal participation; (2) consulting with worker representatives on the changes; (3) involving all workers in the change process. Compared to the participative groups, the no-participation group manifested slower recovery in productivity, attainment of a lower ultimate level of productivity, and higher turnover during the 40 days of the study. Of the former, participation by all workers appeared to result in more rapid recovery of output (we say "appear" because results throughout were reported in words and graphs and without tests of statistical significance). A supplementary experiment reported by Coch and French showed that the above results were not due to the recalcitrance of the no-participation group, since when they were later able to participate in another job change, the results were similar to those of the earlier participation groups.

Although Coch & French interpreted the Harwood results in motivational terms, no direct assessment of motivational states was furnished. The study also did not include measures of the workers' perceptions of change in conditions ("take" measures) or of job satisfaction. In these respects, the study fails to qualify as a "prototype" by our standards, but is cited nevertheless both because of its historical interest and its illustration of participation as a method of affecting workgroup control.

b. Morse & Reimer (1956) reported the second classic study which will be described here, not only for its historic interest but because it meets our prototype standards. The study was an outgrowth of the continuing interest in leadership by Lewin's successors, by then centered at the University of Michigan. A set of correlational studies summarized by Katz & Kahn (1951) had indicated that supervisors who are participative in style have work groups characterized by

higher morale and performance than those who keep control to
themselves. This led to an experiment in which the structure
of control changed in four divisions of a large insurance
company headquarters. This was done by focussing not on personal leadership style, but on changing the allocation of
authority. In two divisions, decision-making authority was
delegated down the line so that decisions affecting such matters as replacements and vacation schedules were made by rank-
and-file workers (called the "Autonomy program"). In two
other divisions ("Hierarchical program"), the aim was to
increase control by supervisors even more than had existed in
the past.

That these treatments had the intended significant impact
on perceptions of control and influence was shown both by
questionnaire responses of the workers and by observations of
the changes in participation activities.

Questionnaires administered at the beginning and end of
the study (nearly two years later) showed that motivation to
meet organization goals was greater in the Autonomy than
Hierarchical program. Workers in the Autonomy program showed
significant improvements in the following attitudes, whereas
those in the Hierarchical program declined: general satisfaction with working for the company, attitudes toward management,
and feelings of self-actualization. There was also a slight
decline in intrinsic job satisfaction in the Hierarchical program, but, interestingly enough, no significant change under the

Autonomy one.  Cost effectiveness improved in both programs,
but significantly more in the Hierarchical then the Autonomy
one.  Turnover showed evidence of being higher in the former
than the latter program, but the difference was not statistically significant.  Although the authors (and Likert, 1967)
suggest that the Autonomy program may have proven superior in
performance given a longer period of time, this possibility
remains moot.

The authors' interpretation of their findings is that the
more participative system "increased the motivation of employees
to produce" (p. 128), and thus led to decisions producing
greater cost effectiveness.  Although the necessary facts are
not furnished, it may be supposed that the lower motivation of
workers in the Hierarchical program was offset by better decisions of the supervisors, either whose motivation to have an
effective group presumably increased or whose ability to implement cost-effective decisions was facilitated.  The possible role of increased experience or other factors improving
the capability of both sets of workers was not considered.
Another factor possibly detracting from internal validity is
that workers under each program were apparently not unaware of
the other program; that circumstance may have induced a special motivation to "look good" on the part of the Autonomy
workers lest their system be changed to that of the more disliked Hierarchical one.

    c.  <u>Seashore & Bowers</u> (1963) and <u>Smith & Jones</u> (1968)

reported an experiment which was generally similar to that of Morse & Reimer, except that it was conducted in a large manufacturing plant. Using supervisory training and counseling together with supervisor-subordinate meetings, an attempt was made to move three departments toward Likert's (1961) "participative group" organization pattern. Two unchanged departments served as controls. Questionnaires were administered to employees prior to the change in 1958, during the change program in 1959, and again two years later. Eleven "take" variables were measured, having to do with perceptions of interaction and of influence among work-group members, degree of participation in decision-making, control activities, and several aspects of supervision. Seven of the eleven were found to have changed in the expected direction. Controlgraph measures showed some increase in total control, but not in balance of control. In terms of effects on dependent variables, increases were noted in job satisfaction, machine efficiency, and attendance in the experimental group but not the control groups.

We turn now to several more recent studies of workgroup participation which also qualify as prototypes.

d. Powell & Schlacter (1971) did a study which, like that of Coch & French, permitted comparison among different modes of participation. The experiment involved six field crews installing electrical utilities in a highway system. Prior to the experiment, work was scheduled by assignment

from a central operations office. Without announcing that
an experiment was being performed, management instituted
changes in the method of work shceduling:  in the case of two
of the crews, it now was done by having the supervisors confer with the operations office; in the case of two other
crews, members as a group conferred with a representative of
that office; the remaining two crews were given complete
responsibility for their own work schedules.

Neither "take" nor mediating variables were measured,
so we are in the dark as to the dynamics set in motion by
these changes. However, the two crews given complete responsibility reported significantly higher levels of satisfaction of
both their hygienic and motivation needs (in Herzberg's terminology), but their productivity declined. The crews afforded
the more modest increase in control did not change significantly either in their job satisfaction or productivity.  The
program adversely affected absenteeism in five of the six crews.

c.  Oster (1970) reported a classically designed study
involving experimental and control groups with before and
after measures of "take," attitudinal, and performance variables.  It was performed in a "medium" sized manufacturing
plant of plastic parts.  The workers comprised 105 press
operators, both male and female and all of them black; there
were 11 supervisors of the work groups, all of them white.
The experimental treatment involved 16 weekly group meetings
at which work problems were discussed and production goals

occasionally set. The supervisors had been instructed separately in how to increase worker participation by means of the meetings.

Before and after "take" questionnaires revealed that, as hypothesized, workers in the experimental program perceived significantly greater increased participation whereas those remaining under the control conditions did not. Job satisfaction, measured before and after treatments by means of the Job Description Index (Smith, Kendall & Hulin, 1969), improved significantly more in the participation as compared to the control condition. The specific facets of job satisfaction which improved were Supervision and Co-workers, but not Work Itself, Pay, or Promotions.

Absenteeism in the participation group during the 16 weeks following the experimental period declined significantly by 22%, whereas the control group declined an insignificant 2%. Although the difference between the groups in turnover rates appeared substantial (11.8% under participation and 19.5% under control conditions), the difference was not quite statistically significant in view of the sample size.

Need for Independence (Vroom, 1960) was measured for each of the workers, and was found to be a significant factor in both their perceptions of participation and changes in job satisfaction. Those expressing a stronger need for independence were more likely to feel that they were indeed participating under the experimental conditions, and also to

manifest greater increase in total job satisfaction and satisfaction with supervisors and co-workers. Sex did not seem to
be an important factor affecting either perceptions of participation or the aforementioned aspects of satisfaction. The
moderating role of personality factors supports other findings
that such factors enter into determining how workers respond
to control and freedom in their work groups (Tannenbaum &
Allport, 1956; Vroom, 1960).

The studies reviewed above all involved a planned change
in the patterns of control over what goes on in the work group.
Although they usually showed significant improvements in job
behavior and/or satisfaction as a result of those treatments,
the mediating mechanism of improved motivation was only inferred or at most only sketchily treated. The next study to
be reported focussed more directly on how differences in
control affect the motivational variable of job involvement;
unlike the previous studies, the design was correlational
rather than experimental.

f. Siegel & Ruh (1973) surveyed 2,628 employees (about
equally divided between male and female) of six midwestern
manufacturing companies. A questionnaire assessed their perceptions of the amount of influence they had over decisions
affecting their jobs. All also completed a questionnaire on
job involvement, 7 of the 8 items coming from the Lodahl &
Kejner (1965) scale. An appreciable and significant positive
correlation was found between perceived influence and job
involvement (r = .51), although this may be spuriously high

since both variables were measured by self-reports of the
same sample of workers.  The degree of correlation was
slightly higher for employees having city as compared to
small community backgrounds, and for those having some college education; the magnitude of the correlation may be an
indication of the salience of participation as a factor in
job involvement.

Job performance data were available in a blue-collar
sample from one of the participating companies.  Here, job
involvement was found to have a low but statistically significant correlation with voluntary turnover during the 22-
month period following questionnaire administration ($r = -.17$).
Correlations between job involvement and both absenteeism and
productivity (per cent of standard production) were negligible;
however, since many of the jobs in the sub-sample were on
assembly lines, the extent to which productivity was under
the control of individual employees is questionable.

## Miscellaneous Studies

In this section we will briefly treat several studies of
work-group control patterns which fail to satisfy our criteria
as prototypes because of limitations in the scope of variables
measured, but are nonetheless instructive because of the
nature and extent of some of the relationships found.

French et al. (1958) published a later report of experiences with worker participation in methods changes at

Harwood. There were some favorable effects on productivity and turnover but they are not conclusive because they were not entirely consistent nor were control groups employed.

Lawrence & Smith (1955) undertook to analyze further the dynamics of participation as reported by Coch & French by performing a similar study in another factory. One group of workers participated in discussions of work-related issues, whereas another also participated in setting production goals. Both improved in productivity, but the latter gained more than the former.

Sorcher (1969) has more recently reported the productivity benefits to be gained by increasing factory worker participation in setting production goals -- in this instance, quality goals. Although not attributable solely to participation (some redesign of jobs and training were also involved), average weekly cost savings were estimated at $1,000, outweighing by a factor of about 50:1 the estimated annual incremental cost of $1,000.

Fleishman (1965) reported a study which in several respects resembled that of Coch & French, including its setting in the garment industry -- in this instance a dress factory. The subjects of the study were female sewing-machine operators who were unionized. In an attempt to reduce the losses in productivity (and in piece-rate earnings) typically found in a style changeover, increased participation of a group of 20 experienced operators was enlisted in designing the production processes for a changed style; a matched group of 20 continued under the customary less participative method of planning the work.  As hypothesized, the loss in productivity of the experimental group was less than that ordinarily manifested; the effect also carried over to a later change even though it was done by the old method.  The meaning of the results is obscured by the fact that the findings were duplicated in the control group of operators.  This result was ascribed to the control group's knowledge of the participation experiment and therefore the perception that they were participating through representation by their co-workers.  However, it is also possible that the "Hawthorne effect" was partly or completely responsible for the results, rather than the motivating effect of increased participation directly and/or by representation.

Two situations have been reported where the key topic of participation was the nature of a financial incentive plan. One of them was at the Harwood plant (Marrow, 1972).  About five years after the experiments reported by Coch & French, the plant supervisors were invited to work out the details of a cost savings incentive plan in which they would share with top management reduction in current production costs, which had risen considerably above the standard.  The procedure eventually devised involved a Cost Control Council which was responsible for reviewing costs and searching for ways to reduce them. A variety of plans were implemented for improving work methods, layouts, absenteeism, mechanical breakdowns, etc.  Marked improvements were reported in employee turnover (53%) and absenteeism (12%), in make-up pay (58%), and in average hourly production (9%). These, of course, were not due solely or mainly to increased motivation of the workers, since changes in methods and procedures, i.e., in capability, were the central mechanisms of improvement. However, it does seem that the motivation of the supervisors to cut costs was increased, although it is unclear to what extent that was due to participation, to the opportunity to increase earnings, to the pressure or challenge of the escalating production costs, or to other possible factors mediating variables and control groups.

In the second set of studies on participation in planning incentives, Lawler & Hackman (1969) described a program in which part-time janitorial personnel participated in designing an incentive plan to motivate better attendance. The employees included about equal numbers of men and women, were mostly members of minority groups, and had little formal education. Three groups of workers (N = 27) designed their own plan; two groups (N = 39) had the identical plan imposed on them; four control groups (N = 51) had no incentive plan, i.e., were paid on a straight time basis. Attendance in the participative groups improved significantly during the 16 weeks following adoption of the plan, whereas that in the groups where it had been imposed and in the control groups remained unchanged. The authors suggest that a possible reason for the failure of the plan to work when imposed is that it was not well understood by those groups. However, without "take" or mediating measures, the dynamics of the results remain obscure.

A follow-up to the foregoing, reported by Scheflen, Lawler & Hackman (1971), revealed the following:

1.  In the single participative group where the incentive plan remained in effect, attendance was still at its high level, even though most of the present members had not worked there when the plan was adopted.

2.  In the two groups where the plan had been imposed, attendance eventually improved, although it still had not attained the level of the participative group.

3.  The plan had been discontinued by management in two of the groups which had adopted it participatively; in those groups attendance after discontinuation deteriorated to levels even lower than at the start of the experiment.

Conclusions Regarding Work Group Control

The findings of the studies reviewed above are summarized in Table VII-1. The findings indicate that:

a.  Work groups whose members have more of a say over the group's production goals, work, and working conditions usually have higher average job satisfaction than those having less control.

b.  There is some evidence that members of participative groups also have stronger work motivation.

c.  There are instances where increased work control was associated with reduced turnover or absenteeism, but in at

Table VII-1

Correlates and Consequences of Greater Work Group Control

| Finding | Supporting Studies | Studies Failing to Support |
|---|---|---|
| Better job attitudes (satisfaction and/or motivation) | Morse & Reimer (clerks) | |
| | Seashore & Bowers (factory workers) | |
| | Powell & Schlacter[1] (blue-collar) | |
| | Oster[1] (factory workers) | |
| | Siegel & Ruh (factory workers) | |
| Better productivity | Coch & French[2] (factory workers) | Powell & Schlacter[1] |
| | Morse & Reimer[1] | |
| | Seashore & Bowers | |
| | French et al.[1] (factory workers) | |
| | Lawrence & Smith (factory workers) | |
| | Sorcher (factory workers) | |
| | Fleishman[1,2] (factory workers) | |
| Less withdrawal (turnover, absenteeism) | Coch & French[2] | Powell & Schlacter |
| | Morse & Reimer[2] | |
| | Seashore & Bowers | |
| | Oster[1] | |
| | French et al.[1,2] | |
| | Lawler & Hackman (janitors) | |

---

[1]Results mixed, i.e., not the same in all measures or samples, but generally favor the inference.

[2]Statistical significance not reported or doubtful.

least one case, absenteeism increased.

    d.   Productivity is usually, but not always, higher in groups having more control. Even where it is higher, the dynamics are not always clear. It is possible that participation in methods changes makes a group more amenable to improved work rationalization (Gomberg, 1966), reduces members' fears of failure, or increases their motivation to succeed. In some studies, there was also the possibility that the Hawthorne effect or the desire to look good during an experimental period might account for temporary performance gains. In any event the results of one study suggest that improvements in worker productivity may not be greater than those achieved by vesting greater control in the supervisory staff.

    e.   Two conditions that seem effective in improving productivity via changed control patterns are when work groups are given a greater say in goal-setting and in determining modes of pay for performance.

    f.   Work group participation appears to function better with people whose personalities "fit" that control pattern, e.g., those who have need for autonomy and are non-authoritarian.

    g.   There has been a large number of studies on control patterns in temporary groups studied in the laboratory, as summarized by Lowin (1968). Although many show positive results of participation, others are more equivocal. We have not reviewed them here not only because the aforementioned excellent summary already exists, but because we share Lowin's assessment

of their dubious external validity for policy-making purposes
in organizations. We also wish to remind the reader that some
experiments in job redesign and in systems redesign include
increased work-group autonomy; when they are suitable for our
purposes, such studies are reviewed in the chapters dealing
with those topics.

## Organizational Control Structure

In our review of organization-wide control patterns, we
shall survey first an important set of correlational studies
which employed as a "take" variable the technique known as the
control graph. That will be followed by a review of several
additional prototype correlational studies employing other
ways of assessing perceived control. The second section will
cover studies which compare different organizational features
affecting control, i.e., "independent" variables: although we
may state now that relatively few of the studies which correlated differing perceptions of control with various outcomes
delved into the variables which accounted for the differences
in perceived control. A third section will be addressed to the
rather sparse evidence that the effects of control structures
are moderated by characteristics of the situation. The fourth
section will be devoted to a single experiment which involved
the planned re-allocation of control in a work organization as
the primary element of change, and which in other respects
qualifies as a prototype. Finally, we will turn to studies of

the effects of formal participation plans, including unionization.

## Correlational Studies of Control Patterns

Starting in the mid-1950's investigators at the Institute for Social Research, University of Michigan, undertook an important series of studies of organizational control patterns employing a technique called the control graph. As explained in the theoretical introduction to this chapter, that technique, which is based on a questionnaire, permits the depiction and calculation of the total amount of control perceived as being exerted by organization members on each other, and its distribution across hierarchical levels. Several of those studies qualify as prototypes, and are summarized in the following section. It will be followed by a review of several additional correlational prototypes in which control patterns were assessed by other means.

a. <u>Smith & Tannenbaum</u> (1963) drew together the results of three correlational studies employing the control graph in work organizations: a package delivery firm, a labor union, and an auto sales company. Each had a number of geographically separate branches, which constituted the units under analysis. Each study also included some measures of organizational performance (dependent variable) and a measure of motivational or attitudinal level of the members which may be regarded as a mediating variable. The perceived amount of distribution of control in the graph are, of course, essentially "take" variables indicating the impact of the control system used in the organization being investigated. Below we will summarize the main correlations obtained when the measures were compared for the various branches of each of the four organizations.

(1) Total amount of control was found to be associated with more positive job attitudes of members in two of the three organizations, and with effectiveness of performance in those same two organizations; the sales company was the exception.

(2) Slope of control (sharpness of the gradient from higher to lower hierarchical levels) was correlated with attitudes.

(3) Agreement between higher and lower echelons on amount of perceived control also tended to be associated both with attitudes and performance in most organizations, but agreement on slope showed few substantial correlations.

(4) The degree of disparity between preferred and perceived control patterns showed some inverse correlations with attitude and performance; this suggests that dissatisfaction with control allocation is implicated in low work motivation and performance.

Based on those and other studies conducted in the late '50's to early '60's by the Michigan group, Tannenbaum (1962) concluded that more productive units typically showed higher total control or mutual influence than do less productive ones, but that no consistent differences appear in the distribution of control among hierarchical levels. He hypothesized that higher control operates by increasing self-respect and ego involvement on the job. He suggested that there may be two dilemmas posed by that state of affairs: (i) more total control means not only greater influence on the part of organization members but also a greater amenability to being influenced; and (ii) whereas greater job involvement may enhance the joys of success, it may also exacerbate the frustrations of failure.

A number of more recent studies along the same general lines have been reported by the Michigan group since the overviews summarized above. We will now review those which serve to add to the original findings.

b. Bowers (1964) reported a study performed in 40 sales agencies, regional offices and the home office of an insurance company, involving 920 individual respondents at four hierarchical levels. The study is of particular interest because of the extensive data available on economic performance, including two indices of agency development, plus one each of growth of business, costs, and business volume. Several other dependent variables were also included, as noted below.

Total control correlated positively, appreciably, and significantly with executive ratings of agency effectiveness, and, among the specific economic criteria, with cost effectiveness and with agency development, but not with staff turnover. Total control also correlated positively, appreciably, and significantly with five aspects of agent job satisfaction which were measured: company, job itself, income, regional manager, and fellow agents.

Neither slope of control nor discrepancies between ideal

and perceived control correlated strongly or consistently
with dependent variables.

    c.  <u>Bachman, Smith & Slesinger</u> (1966) reported a study
involving 36 sales offices of a firm selling intangibles.  Only
two hierarchical levels were involved:  managers and salesmen.
The salesmen were paid in part on a commission basis.  Again,
perceived total control was found to be highly correlated both
with average performance and job satisfaction of the salesmen
among the branch offices.

    In addition to the standard questions concerning control
over the organization (office), a parallel set of questions
asked managers and salesmen about their control over people
at the other hierarchical level, i.e., a measure of inter-
hierarchical or inter-personal rather than total control.
This measure, when averaged for each office, was also found
to correlate positively with both office sales performance
and average satisfaction, if anything even more strongly than
the measure of total control.

    An interesting supplementary set of data concerned the
salesmen's reports of the basis for the managers' control.
The reported use of expert and referent power (as described
in the theoretical introduction to this chapter) was prevalent
in offices having higher average production and satisfaction,
whereas in lower-scoring offices the prevalent bases of power
were primarily reward, coercion, and/or legitimacy.

    A non-prototype study which reinforces some of the

findings of the preceding one was published by Ivancevich (1970).
It was done on insurance agents, and also utilized perceptions
of total and inter-hierarchical control. The dependent variables were self-reports of the degree to which needs for
status, autonomy, and growth were being satisfied. Both
aspects of control were found to be positively correlated with
all three categories of need satisfaction.

    d. In the most recent of the control-graph prototypes,
Tannenbaum et al. (1974), published a monograph reporting
their comparative analysis of control patterns in samples of
large and small plants in five different countries (U.S.A.,
Italy, Austria, Israel, and Yugoslavia). Although we are not
generally covering the foreign literature in this report, we
will summarize those findings which characterize their U.S.A.
sample and/or which obtain for the most part irrespective of
national location.

    On a within-country basis, the amount of total control
as calculated for each of 52 plants was found to correlate
significantly negatively ($r = -.25$) with a composite index of
the disparity in motivation among hierarchical levels, i.e.,
the higher the total control, the greater the similarity among
workers and managers in such attitudinal reactions as responsibility for performance, alienation, and job satisfaction.
Thus on a plant-wide basis, total control appears to be associated with conditions favorable to performance, whereas distribution of control was not. However, no measure of
economic performance was actually included in the report.

The data permitted a breakdown of what aspects of hierarchy are associated with job satisfaction, which here as well as in numerous other studies was found to be higher, on average, the higher one goes up the hierarchical ladder. A multiple regression analysis of data from American plants showed that the amount of authority and influence which respondents report for themselves is a net predictor of job satisfaction irrespective of their hierarchical level, seniority, salary, job opportunities, and similar factors. Conversely, the respondent's hierarchical level in and of itself had nothing to do with his job satisfaction apart from its association with influence, job opportunities, working conditions and the like.

The study also generated some data which help to underscore our previous point concerning the differences between control structure and participativeness as an aspect of supervisory style. Their questionnaire contained questions pertaining to the latter as well as the former. Across plants, the reported average interpersonal participativeness of supervisors correlated only .44 with total organizational control and only -.30 with the slope of gradient of control. Hence, supervisory style and organizational control patterns are more independent of than related to one another.

We turn now to several prototype investigations employing correlational designs but where aspects of control structure were measured by methods other than the control-graph.

e.  <u>Smith</u> (1970) did a study which extends the analysis

of control patterns to an engineering research organization.
The organization contained 15 divisions, each composed of
between 20 and 150 scientists. The scientists reported on
the degree of decentralized influence delegated to divisions
regarding technical and administrative decisions, and also
on the extent to which influence was shared <u>within</u> their
division.

Both of these kinds of measures of influence were found
to have significant relations with one or more of various
mediating and dependent variables:  the more decentralization
of divisional decision-making a scientist reported and the
more sharing of influence with the division, the greater was
the level of self-rated job involvement and also the higher
was at least one of five variables relating to scientific
productivity. Not all aspects of control were related equally
strongly to all productivity variables, suggesting that the
optimum control system depends on the weights given to different
outcomes.

f. <u>Farris</u> (1969) studied 151 engineers working for a
large electronics firm. They reported their perceptions of
six organizational factors, one of which had to do with perceived influence on work goals (take variable) and another with
job involvement (mediating variable). The former had a negligible correlation with the latter. Dependent variables consisted of two supervisory evaluations, number of patents, and
number of technical reports. All variables were compiled twice:
in 1959 and 1965. The perception of job involvement correlated
positively,significantly, but not strongly, with rated useful-

ness and patents both in 1959 and in 1965, and the 1959 perception of involvement predicted those two dependent variables
about as well in 1965. The study also indicated that participation was positively associated with some aspects of concurrent performance, but that its effects did not carry over to
performance five years later; apparently, the level of
participation needs to be sustained.

Frost, Wakely & Ruh (1974) have described a set of studies
pertaining to the Scanlon Plan which will be discussed further
in our chapter on system-wide studies. In the present connection, we wish to note that they found that the level of perceived participation on the part of 2,488 employees in 15 plants
correlated positively, appreciably, and significantly with three
attitudinal measures of work motivation. One of the latter
variables, Job Involvement, was found to have no appreciable
correlation with objective measures of job performance or
absenteeism, and a low but significant correlation (-.17) with
turnover; however, the authors note that problems in measuring
those performance variables suggest caution in drawing conclusions from those findings. Personal values of the employees
were not found appreciably to moderate the relations between
perceived participation and work motivation.

## Correlational Studies with Independent Variables

The foregoing correlational studies all entailed comparing
existing differences in workers' perceptions of control with

some mediating and/or dependent variable(s), without describing
the practices or conditions which may have accounted for perceptions of control. We now report a handful of studies which
attempted to illuminate this question of the "independent
variables" associated with control; leaving for a later section the variables of formal representation plans.

a.  The previously noted international study by Tannenbaum
et al. (1974) addressed itself to how cultural and political
differences among nations (which may be regarded as independent
"variables") are associated in various aspects of hierarchy,
including control.  They reported that in "participative"
cultures (Yugoslavia, Israeli Kibbutzim) plants generally
showed higher levels of participation by rank-and-file workers,
as well as flatter or more egalitarian control graphs, than
was the case in the three "private economy" countries (U.S.A.,
Italy, Austria).  Those culture differences do not explain why
the non-supervisory workers in the U.S.A. reported having
about as much influence as those in the "participative"
countries; among the suggested reasons are the influence
afforded American workers by their unions and, informally, by
democratically-oriented supervisors.

b.  Indik (1965) analyzed how organizational size (independent variable) affected the distribution of control ("take"
variable), and, in turn, dependent variables reflecting withdrawal activity (attendance, turnover, presence at meetings).
The data were apparently drawn from three of the organizations

previously reviewed by Smith & Tannenbaum (1963) and summarized
above: 32 branches of a package delivery firm, 36 automotive
sales offices, and 28 chapters of a membership organization.
The hypothesis that the larger units would be characterized by
relatively greater control at higher organizational levels was
not clearly supported, although the correlations tended in
that direction. Organizational size was found to be inversely
correlated with the aforementioned dependent variables reflecting withdrawal activity, i.e., members of larger organizations were more likely to be absent, to quit, or not to show up
at meetings; but this was apparently only to a minor degree
because of the effects of control structure. Porter & Lawler
(1965) have reviewed the literature on the effects of organizational size on job satisfaction and withdrawal behavior;
they concluded that job satisfaction tends to be somewhat lower
and absenteeism and turnover to be greater in larger than in
smaller organizations, but that the trends were neither sharp
nor consistent.

c. A re-analysis by Smith (1966) of control-graph data
from six organizations previously studied also shed some light
on the independent variables which may shape the control graph.
The ratio of the number of supervisory employees to the total
number of employees in each branch was computed. That ratio
was then compared to the degree of hierarchical control (slope)
perceived by members of branches. The results failed to show
a general trend. Another independent variable which was

analyzed by Smith was the degree to which the unit's goals reflected the interests of its employees or members, as rated by external observers. The correlations between those ratings and degree of hierarchical control were significantly negative (between -.28 and -.37) in four of the six organizations, i.e., branches rated as having goals less reflective of members' interests tended to be seen as involving greater control from higher levels. The two instances where the correlations were positive were of insignificant magnitude (union locals and insurance agencies). The basic problem of correlational designs, namely determination of what is cause and what is effect, is particularly at issue in this relationship.

d. A study by <u>Carpenter</u> (1971) examined the effects of the independent variable of the degree of hierarchy ("tallness") of the organizational structure of school systems. A questionnaire administered to teachers in six systems obtained their ratings of discrepancies between optimum and existing conditions, some of which related to the perceptions of influence and control ("take") and others to assessments of outcomes (job satisfaction). "Tall" structures were perceived as permitting significantly less than optimum exercise of professional authority, participation in setting school goals, and determining teaching methods than were medium or flat structures. Satisfaction in tall structures was also less with respect to several of the issues raised, including feeling of self-esteem and of professional prestige and opportunity to help people. The index of "tallness" employed was based largely on the extent to which the organization chart entailed relations among peers reporting to the same supervisor, and thus may be closer in conception to "span of control" than to height of the structure. In this connection, it may be noted that a classic correlational study by Worthy (1950) found morale and performance to be higher in those branches of a retail chain having flat than in those having tall organizational structures. A later study of managers indicated that the relationships may be more complicated: flat organizations appeared to be more satisfying for personal and growth needs and tall ones for security and social needs (Porter & Lawler, 1964). In a laboratory study, simulated organizations having a taller structure were found to be more "profitable" than those with a flatter structure, apparently because the former facilitated certain aspects of task performance; motivational and attitudinal aspects were not studied (Carzo & Yanouzas, 1969).

## Correlational Studies Involving Situational Moderators

Katzell (1962) on theoretical and empirical grounds questioned the generality of control pattern effects, hypothesizing that various situational parameters would moderate the consequences of directive or participative patterns of organization and supervision. Katz & Kahn (1966) similarly agreed that hierarchical control patterns, featuring steep gradients from top to bottom, would be more effective than equalized control where interdependence among units and members is high,

where creative or problem-solving requirements are minimal,
and where identification with organizational goals is weak.
Walsh (1973) has noted numerous examples in the literature
where satisfaction and/or performance are dependent on the
fit or interaction between the person and the environment in
which he operates. Lichtman & Hunt (1971) have examined the
subsequent literature and concluded that it supports Katzell's
thesis both with respect to the personal disposition of organization members and systemic properties of the organization (including task and technological attributes). Lowin
(1968) has reviewed both the laboratory and field literature
on participative decision-making, and concluded that its
effects are moderated by a number of characteristics of the
situation. Dalton (1971) makes the related point that control
systems must be designed to fit the following three aspects of
the situation: (a) the organization's task; (b) the kinds of
people involved; and (c) the existing social system.

In previous sections of the present chapter, we have
noted that certain personal and/or environmental factors
moderate (whereas others fail to moderate) the effects of MBO
and of work-group participation. Several recent prototype
studies examined similar situational variables as possible
moderators of the effects of organization-wide control patterns, and these will be summarized in the following section.

a. Ritchie & Miles (1970) surveyed 330 managers, comprising sets of superiors and subordinates, in six divisions

of a firm. The "take" measures consisted of perceived participation in several kinds of decisions. Respondents also indicated satisfaction with the immediate supervisor, which was
the sole dependent variable reported. An additional variable
was the evaluation by each superior of the capabilities of
their subordinates in relation to their own, which may be interpreted as a measure of trust in subordinates. The results
showed that:  (1) managers who see themselves as actively
participating in decisions are more satisfied with their immediate supervisor than those whose participation is less;
(2) managers whose immediate supervisors trust their subordinates' capabilities (i.e., rate them highly) are likewise more
satisfied with those supervisors than where trust is lower.
These two effects on satisfaction with supervisor are linearly
additive, there being no significant moderating effect of trust
on the effect of participation.  The authors regard the effect
of trust on satisfaction as indicating that the quality of
participation as well as the amount of participation is important, although other explanations are also conceivable.

    b. <u>Weiss</u> (1969) published a study of 213 elementary
school principals in a single school system who reported their
perceptions of their participation in decisions.  Principals
who had higher scores on a measure of authoritarian personality had significantly lower perceptions of participation,
whereas those scoring higher on a personality measure of independence tended to have slightly higher perceptions of partici-

pation (not statistically significant). The greater the perceived participation, the higher their job satisfaction turned
out to be. However, contrary to the moderator conception, the
relation between perceived participation and job satisfaction
was not significantly affected by level of authoritarianism
or independence. Of course, there always remains the question
of the accuracy with which such elusive personality traits
are measured in a mass survey such as this one. There are
also statistical and methodological problems which may distort
moderator effects, as noted by Zedeck (1971).

c. <u>Pritchard & Karasick</u> (1973) investigated the moderating effect of a personality variable similar to independnece,
namely, need for autonomy. In this instance, the measure was
a standard personality inventory, the Edwards Personal Prefer-
ence Schedule. The investigation was conducted among 46 managers
in five regional offices of a national franchising chain, and
30 managers in a manufacturing company. Perceptions of degree
of centralization of decision-making (steepness of gradient
of control) were obtained, and generally corresponded to the
reports of two consultants; the latter data may be regarded as
an independent variable and the former as a "take" variable.
For each manager, job satisfaction was assessed by the
Minnesota Satisfaction Questionnaire, and ratings of performance were made by a consultant using performance data and
interviews with superiors. In the franchising company, an objective index of economic performance for each of the five

regional offices was also available.

The latter index of performance was found to be generally lower in the branch offices that were seen as more centralized (rho = -.70; p < .10). Average job satisfaction was generally higher in the more centralized offices, but with only five cases the appreciable coefficient of -.60 did not reach statistical significance. When the data from the two companies were pooled, managers reporting greater centralization of decision-making did not differ in performance ratings from those reporting decentralization, but did tend to have significantly lower job satisfaction (r = -.39). Guion (1973) has suggested that this last correlation may be due to the fact that both sets of data came from the same survey and may simply reflect two ways of expressing job dissatisfaction -- a criticism which is plausible but which should be tempered in this instance by the reported correspondence between respondents' perceptions and consultants' descriptions of centralization.

Finally, taking account of the managers' Autonomy need did not significantly alter the foregoing picture. This finding and the ones reported by Weiss and by Frost, Wakeley & Ruh, above, do not parallel those reported by Tannenbaum & Allport (1965) and by Vroom (1960), where workers having stronger tendencies toward independnece, non-authoritarianism, and related personality characteristics were found to be more responsive to participation at the work group level. It may be that personality factors are more potent in governing responses to

control patterns at the level of the work group than that of
the organization, perhaps because the latter are more
structural than interpersonal in nature.

## Experimental Change in Organizational Control

The prototype studies of organizational control structures reviewed above have all been correlational in design.
Several experiments which induced planned change either were
done at the work group level (e.g., Coch & French; Morse &
Reimer; Sorcher; Lawrence & Smith; Hackman & Lawler), or did
not include our required range of variables (e.g., Marrow, 1972).
There do exist several more studies where changes were made in
organizational control patterns, but as part of extensive
changes in several other sets of variables; several of these
are considered in our chapter on system-wide studies. We have
located only a single field experiment which focussed essentially on changing the control structure of an organization and
which qualifies as a prototype. It was performed in the R & D
center of a division of a large technology-based corporation,
and was reported in a monograph by Dalton, Barnes & Zaleznik
(1968). It is summarized in this section.

A new director of the center believed that it suffered
from problems of low productivity, low morale, and inefficient
utilization of staff, to which a cumbersome, top-heavy organization structure was a major contributor. He formulated a
reorganization plan, discussed it with the senior managers of
the center, and, after some modifications, implemented it with

their help.

The basic hypothesis of the study concerned the benefits of redistribution of control, i.e., "where the gap between degrees of authority from the top to the bottom of the organization decreases, the motivation to work hard increases and will be reflected in measures of productivity and satisfaction" (p. 3). The design of the study involved the implementation of the reorganization plan in part of the organization, with some work groups left unchanged although not isolated from the others. Certain measures were obtained on a retrospective basis only at a later time, whereas others were obtained before and again after the change; the measures are listed below:

(1)  Independent Variables. These were shaped by the reorganization, which had the following features:

(a)  elimination of one level of management, namely the middle one of three levels below the director;

(b)  project groups made the central unit of organization, each headed by a Junior Manager;

(c)  redefinition of the authority of Junior Managers (JM) and Senior Managers (SM), so that former were to have greater authority for operations and budgeting, whereas latter were to have less authority for administration but more for long-range technical planning;

(d)  committees were established at the JM level to coordinate several functional areas.

In brief, it would seem that the above changes would
serve to increase personal autonomy and work-group control at
the level of JM and non-supervisory scientists, while decreasing the control of SM's; effects on authority of top
management of the center seem mixed: increasing in some
respects and decreasing in others. The net effect would be
flattening the control gradient or slope, with no deliberate
effort to change total control.

(2) Take Variables. Evidence that the above changes
had their intended effects is that more workers (including
JM's) in the experimental than the comparison groups reported
increased autonomy and local control (although this was less
true at lowest levels). The effects on the SM's were unclear,
due in part to the small number of cases.

(3) Mediating Variable. Workers in the experimental
groups were more likely to report increased job involvement
than those in the comparison group.

(4) Dependent Variables. A variety of perceptual
(subjective) measures were obtained from the participants,
the key results of which may be summarized as follows:

(a) ratings of organizational effectiveness: no
significant difference between experimental and
comparison groups;

(b) satisfaction with superior: no significant
difference between experimental and comparison
groups;

(c) gains in job satisfaction: more frequently re-
    ported by members of experimental than com-
    parison groups;

(d) gains in personal productivity: more frequently
    reported by members of experimental than com-
    parison groups;

(e) gains in group productivity: ditto;

(f) decline in reported unwillingness to consider
    other job offers: ditto.

Differences in the above dependent variables were generally greater and more consistent in the case of JM's and SM's
than non-supervisory Junior Scientists; the former were also
the sub-samples which reported more pronounced increments in
authority and in job involvement. These data again underscore
the point that the effects of changes in work structures can be
understood only when measures are obtained also of their impact
on the perceptions ("take" variables) and motivations (mediating variables) of the workers.

In general, the outcomes of the study appear to have supported the hypothesized benefits of authority redistribution,
provided one accepts the validity of the subjective assessments
of personal and group effectiveness and does not interpret them
as merely another expression of the improvement in job
attitudes.

## Conclusions on Organization Control Structure

The results of the prototype studies of organizational

control described above are summarized in Table VII-2. Since most studies did not adequately distinguish total control from equalization of control, the findings are stated in terms of perceived greater control on the part of the workers studied, irrespective of whether workers at other organizational levels experienced changes in control as well.

a. Organizations whose members see themselves as having a relatively high level control over their work lives are usually more productive than those characterized by lower control. However, with only one exception, the studies on which that conclusion is based are correlational, so that the causal direction is uncertain.

b. Organizations whose members see themselves as having higher control also usually have employees who express greater job and need satisfaction. Again the direction of causality is uncertain.

c. There is evidence which indicates that the foregoing relationships between amount of control and the dependent variables are due to the former's positive association with the work motivation of the organization members.

d. There is no clear evidence in the literature regarding which organizational policies and practices account for differences in control structures. One clue is that workers have better attitudes toward control when control by supervisors is based mainly on expert and referent sources of power, rather than on legitimacy or coercion; the power of superiors

Table VII-2

Correlates and Consequences of Greater Organizational Control by Workers

| Finding | Studies in Support | Studies Failing to Support |
|---|---|---|
| More favorable attitudes and/or job satisfaction | Smith & Tannenbaum (blue-collar) | Smith & Tannenbaum (sale... |
| | Smith & Tannenbaum (white collar) | Farris (engineers) |
| | Bowers (sales) | |
| | Bachman, Smith & Schlesinger (sales) | |
| | Tannenbaum et al. (factory) | |
| | Smith (professional) | |
| | Frost, Wakeley & Ruh (factory) | |
| | Ritchie & Miles (managers) | |
| | Weiss (school principals) | |
| | Pritchard & Karasick[1] (managers) | |
| | Dalton, Barnes & Zaleznik (professionals) | |
| Better productivity | Smith & Tannenbaum (blue collar) | Smith & Tannenbaum (sa... |
| | Smith & Tannenbaum (white collar) | Pritchard & Karasick[1] |
| | Bowers | |
| | Bachman, Smith & Schlesinger | |
| | Smith[1] | |
| | Farris[1] | |
| | Dalton, Barnes & Zaleznik[1] | |
| Less withdrawal | Dalton, Barnes & Zaleznik[2] | Bowers (sales) |

[1]Results mixed, i.e., not the same all measures or samples, but generally favor the inference.

[2]Statistical significance not reported or doubtful.

[3]Attitudes toward changing jobs, rather than actual behavior.

and their immediate subordinates to influence one another also
seems to play a part, as does the feeling on the part of individual workers that they personally wield appropriate influence.
A structural feature that appears to produce the perception of
greater control on the part of lower-ranking members is reduction in the number of hierarchical levels (i.e., creating a
"flatter" organization).

e.  Most studies do not distinguish between two major
aspects of control structure:  total level of control, and
equalization of control.  In those which have, total control is
generally found to be positively correlated both with attitudes
and performance, but this is less consistently true of equalization of control.

f.  The positive effects of high levels of total control
in organizations appear to be rather general, and no moderating
qualifier has yet been demonstrated.  However, it should be
noted that few of the studies have utilized factory workers, so
that special caution is needed in generalizing the results to
this type of population.  The inconsistent consequences of
equalization of control have led to hypotheses that it works
best when the personalities and culture of participants are
egalitarian, when task requirements are neither especially
inter-dependent nor innovative, and where a high level of commitment to organizational goals exists; however, firm empirical
verification of such hypotheses is not yet at hand.

g.  In the absence of sufficient study, no conclusions

can be stated about the relations between control structure
and withdrawal.

h.   In addition to the field studies on which the above
conclusions are based, there have been several laboratory
studies of control patterns in simulated organizations, most
of which have been covered in Lowin's (1968) review. A more
recent one has been addressed specifically to the control-
graph dimensions of amount and slope of control (Levine &
Katzell, 1972; Levine, 1973); it confirmed the beneficial
effects of high total control on satisfaction and productivity,
and the somewhat less potent effects of equalization. However,
limitations of external validity and generalizability lead us
again not to cover the latoratory literature here.

## Formal Participation in Organizations

In our introductory section, we observed that a major
strategy for allocating control is by agreement among members,
i.e., the prescription of authority to various organizational
roles. This "normative" approach, in turn, may either be implemented informally or by some legitimized and publicly
stated formal system. In that connection, Strauss & Rosenstein
(1970) noted that "For the most part, American advocates of
participative management have ignored formal power relations
and structure. The participation they envisioned occurs
[mainly] in face-to-face relationships within the normal hier-
archical-bureaucratic channels..." (p. 202). They noted that
this is essentially the method that characterizes McGregor's

Theory Y or Likert's System 4,* although they have some structural features as well.

Outside the U.S.A., however, organization-wide participation more often takes the form of representative mechanisms
through which workers influence or control organizational
decisions. As described by Roach (1973), such formal plans
may be grouped under three rubrics:

1. Worker representation on boards of directors or
   management boards at higher levels.

2. Joint or cooperative labor-management committees
   or councils.

3. Collective bargaining and related forms of union-
   management activities.

Although fairly widespread in Europe and Israel, the direct
presence of workers on boards of managers or owners ("co-
determination") is almost unknown in the U.S.A. A well-known
exception is the "multiple management" system which has been in
operation for almost 40 years at McCormick & Co., food product
manufacturers (McCormick, 1949). However, even this is not a
classical case of worker participation since representation on
the various boards which the system entails is limited essentially to upper echelons of employees. Given our focus on experience in the U.S.A., we will therefore move on to a consideration of the other two types of formal representation

*Excellent non-technical summaries of these and related
systems of thought are presented by Rush (1969).

plans.*

a. <u>Labor-Management Committees and Councils</u>. Although
joint committees have been often mentioned in the American
literature (e.g., Sturmthal, 1964), the factual assessment of
their effects in the U.S.A. is limited to two studies: a 25-
year old survey of experience in many companies, and a study of
the system employed at TVA. They will be reviewed in this
section.

(1) <u>AMA Survey</u>. In 1949, an American Management
Association published the report of a survey conducted under its
auspices by Dale (1949) and entitled "Greater Productivity
through Labor-Management Cooperation." The study focussed on
formal programs of cooperation between management and labor on
matters of joint interest, essentially aiming at raising productivity and thus presumably increasing the financial "kitty"
available for distribution to labor and management. While
the survey and its findings were not limited to unionized companies, nearly 90% of the 201 companies providing data turned
out to be unionized. Although it is not reflected in this
survey, note should be made of the view expressed by Harbison
& Coleman (1951, p. 90) to the effect that union-management
cooperation of this kind is not common, and is likely to be

---

*Readers interested in further information on foreign
experiences with councils, co-determination and similar plans
are referred to Jenkins (1973), Hunnius <u>et al</u>. (1973), and
Sturmthal (1964).

limited to small plants and those which are in financial trouble.

Cooperation in the sense used in the survey is different from collective bargaining, mainly in that the former is based solely on "good faith" rather than on contractual agreements. Although most of the plans were initiated by management, and quite a few by a union, it should be noted that labor-management collaboration in increasing productivity had been a policy urged by the War Production Board in the years immediately preceding the survey. As also noted by Dale, expenditures for running the committees and carrying out their decisions during that period mattered little when the government was paying for it.

The form of cooperation typically entailed formation of one or more committees or task forces to deal with particular problems or objectives which had been identified. The degree of influence ranged from information-gathering, through consultation and recommendations, to equally shared decision-making by labor and management representatives.

Interviews with company and union officials and with a small sample of employees regarding their views of the cooperative programs showed about two-thirds of respondents were pleased with results. Company officials cited as major benefits improved productivity and better mutual understanding. Union officials mentioned economic benefits as well as better understanding. There were also citations by union officials and rank-and-file workers of participation, pride, sense of contribution, and recognition.

Dale's report is noteworthy in that a strong effort was made retrospectively to obtain before-and-after data on the concrete results of the programs. He points out, appropriately, not only the difficulties of obtaining suitable information but also problems of evaluating it even when obtained. The latter include isolating the effects of cooperation, stability of other factors over the period of measurement, lack of comparability among groups, possible moderating effects of background factors, and the need for longer periods of observation. Within those limitations, he gathered and summarized evidence of the effects of cooperative programs in various problem areas.

The principal findings are summarized in Table VII-3.

Table VII-3

AMA Survey of Labor-Management Committees

| Area of Cooperation | Company(ies) | Tangible Results Cited |
|---|---|---|
| Job Evaluation | U.S. Steel | Reduction in wage-related work stoppages. |
| Absenteeism | 9 companies | Absenteeism approximately halved. |
| " | 2 comparable companies* | Absenteeism about twice as great in company using a union-management committee as in one using foremen and peer control. |
| Suggestion System | Illinois Central Railroad | Number of suggestions increased, as did % adopted and size of award. |
| Safety | Jos. E. Seagram & Sons | Accident frequency reduced. |
| " | Pulp & paper industry in State of Washington | " " " |
| " | 26 companies in various industries | 17 of them improved their industry-wide positions on accident frequency. |
| " | 3 woolen companies | Accident frequency rate declined to rate markedly lower than industry-wide. |
| " | 2 steel companies | Accident frequency rate declined to rate markedly lower than industry-wide. |
| " | Colonial Beacon Oil Co. | Improvement in various safety statistics. |
| " | Libby-Owens-Ford Glass Co. | " " " " " |
| Waste Reduction | Westinghouse Electric (Springfield, Mass. plant) | Ratio of defective productive labor costs halved over 2-year period. |

*Reported by Fox, J.B., & Scott, J.F. Absenteeism: Management's Problem. Boston, Harvard Graduate School of Business Administration, 1943.

In addition to those reported in the table, benefits were reported in several other respects which are not summarized here because specific data were not furnished; these included productivity, promoting understanding, discipline, and training. Of particular interest is the report that three-fourths of the companies asserted that they had received from moderate to a large amount of aid from the unions in increasing productivity. This result was said to be due mainly to improving workers' "attitude on the job," leading to "better personal efforts" (p. 66), i.e., increased work motivation.

From the standpoint of our evaluation needs, the AMA survey suffers from lack of sufficient information on the "take" and mediating variables, and from the interpretative problems which Dale himself noted. There is also the sampling problem: how many of the hundreds of other companies believed to have tried cooperative programs found them to be useless or worse? The age of the survey is also a problem, especially since the use of such formal committees seems no longer to be widespread in the U.S.A.

(2) Brown (1969) reported a study involving the cooperative conference system employed at the Tennessee Valley Authority. Each of the branches of TVA has a set-up wherein employees' representatives confer regularly with management representatives to discuss work problems outside the scope of the union contract (see also Tannenbaum, 1965). Brown studied as a "take" variable the degree to which employees at each of

26 branches perceived themselves as having the opportunity to participate in organizational matters. Also measured were the employees' identification with the organization and its goals (mediating variable), their satisfaction with various aspects of their jobs, and absenteeism records. Analysis of average scores on the above measures among 26 branches showed that perceived influence correlated .46 (significantly) with organizational identification; however, the latter did not correlate significantly either with average job satisfaction or with absenteeism. The above association between perceived influence and organizational identification (implying motivation) within a participation system indicates that it does not necesarily work equally well in all organizations, for reasons not apparent from the study.

b. <u>Collective Bargaining with Unions</u>. Sturmthal (1969) has noted that the principal formal method of allocating greater participation to workers in the U.S.A. is collective bargaining with labor unions. He cites the weighty opinion of Sumner Slichter and his associates to substantiate the proposition that this is indeed a method of sharing control:

"An important result of the American system of collective bargaining is the sense of participation that it imparts to workers....It is true that few workers participate" (Slichter, Healy & Livernash, 1960, p. 960).

Tannenbaum (1965) points out that union-management cooperation "implies increased influence or control by the union....However, it does not mean less control by management" (pp. 739-740). In short, he envisions that collective bargaining could contribute to elevating the total amount of organizational control via the increased reciprocal influence of managers and workers. Elsewhere (p. 722), however, Tannenbaum recognizes that increased total control may not characterize all union-management situations. For example, he cites Kerr's (1954, p. 231) assertion that cooperation is more likely to occur in periods of prosperity when conflict over the size of the financial pie is minimal.

In addition to the amount of influence, another relevant parameter as noted in our introduction is the scope of issues over which control is exercised. Salpukas (in Rosow, 1974) has noted a recent tendency for collective bargaining to move gradually into newer "non-economic" areas, including job design, decisions regarding overtime work, and appeals from preemptive decisions by management. In this regard, UAW Vice-President, Irving Bluestone has observed: "Emphasis in qualitative improvement of life on the job is, I believe, the next step on the road toward industrial democracy. Two distinct, somewhat overlapping, directions are indicated. One relates to 'managing the enterprise'; the other relates to 'managing the job'" (1973, pp. 15-16).

After noting that American advocates of participative management have tended to ignore formal power relations,

Strauss & Rosenstein (1970) express the opinion that they have also tended to ignore unions. Some explicitly exclude unionism from their purview of industrial democracy because, for example, "unions do not exercise decision-making power" (Jenkins, 1973, p. 3). We therefore are unable to locate more than a handful of studies which included unions as a factor in the control structure of organizations. Hence, we can report only sparse factual data concerning the question of the role of unions in affecting the perceptions of control on the part of employees, or their work motivation, attitudes, or performance. We will summarize below the few relevant studies we have located.

(1) <u>Effects of Presence or Absence of Union</u>. A fundamental question is whether the presence or absence of a union in an organization affects the perceptions, attitudes, or performance of employees. Data bearing on parts of this question exist in some early studies. For example, in 1947, the <u>National Industrial Conference Board</u> asked employees in six manufacturing companies to check which of 71 factors were among the top five in importance in determining their attitudes toward their jobs. "Labor unions" was ranked first by only about 1% of the respondents, and among the top five by about 6%. The most frequent top choices, by comparison, were "job security" (31% first choice), "Compensation" (9%), and "type of work" (7%).

<u>Stagner</u> (1952) surveyed the job attitudes of 715 railroad workers with the cooperation of both management and the union.

In a special analysis of a subsample of 100 drawn at random, he identified the 50 who had the higher levels of aggregate job satisfaction based on 15 questionnaire items, and the 50 who had lower levels of satisfaction. The two items which most clearly differentiated between the two groups were those pertaining to satisfaction with union-management relations and with grievance handling. Stagner noted that this finding needs to be interpreted in the context of a highly unionized industry. We may also note that the survey was conducted in a period when the issue of collective bargaining was prominent, as witnessed by the controversy surrounding the Taft-Hartley Act.

Walker & Guest (1952) reported findings relevant to the questions of the effects of unionization in their classic study entitled The Man on the Assembly Line. The automobile plant which they studied had been unionized in 1949 shortly after it started operations. They intensively interviewed a representative sample of 180 assembly-line workers, during which attitudes toward the union as well as the job were investigated. Attitudes toward the union were rated as generally favorable on the part of 2/3 of the workers. However, coinciding with the results of the NICB survey summarized above, only 2 of the 180 interviewees cited the union as the most important reason for liking their jobs, with the factors of pay and steady work again leading the list. Nevertheless, Walker & Guest concluded that the presence of the union was important in helping to compensate for the lack of intrinsic job satisfaction, and that it served as "a kind of psychological bulwark against impersonality of management" (p. 133). The last, of course, points to the union's role in the power picture of the plant as a factor in positive attitudes toward work.

The national Survey of Working Conditions (Survey Research Center, 1970), performed under U.S. Department of Labor auspices by the University of Michigan, found that about half of the 655 blue-collar workers in the sample worked under collective bargaining contracts. The presence or absence of collective bargaining was not significantly associated with "zest" for work or with overall job satisfaction. However, those working in non-unionized situations were appreciably and significantly less satisfied with their pay (eta = .27, p $<$ .001). Similar comparisons were not reported for white-collar workers, although about 1/4 reported working under union contracts.

Katzell and associates (Katzell, Barrett & Parker, 1961; Cureton & Katzell, 1962) investigated an unusual situation in which a company had 72 decentralized warehouses doing essentially the same work under similar policies, except that 40 of them were unionized and 32 were not. The mean number of production workers per warehouse was 35. The unionized warehouses tended to be somewhat less productive and profitable, but were not significantly different from the non-unionized warehouses in errors of work or in personnel turnover. The employees of unionized plants also had lower average job satisfaction. However, unionization tended to be confounded with several other situational variables: compared to non-unionized warehouses, unionized ones tended to be larger, to be located in larger communities, pay higher wages, and have more male employees. Hence, the authors felt that the situations were best characterized in terms of a complex of all five characteristics, namely urbanized vs. small-town patterns, with unionization as part of the former. An oblique factor analysis of the situational and performance variables showed that they could be considered as constituting two related sets: one was characterized primarily by smaller plant size and included also higher productivity and profitability; the second (which correlated .44 with the first) was dominated by the situational variables of lower wage rates and (to a lesser degree) more female workers and not being unionized. The latter had little relationship to performance variables except for turnover, which tended to be higher. Thus the relations between unionization and performance in this company were not pronounced; what association existed was apparently due largely to certain other contextual variables which also were present.

The case of the Weldon Company (Marrow, Bowers & Seashore, 1967) involved extensive changes in management methods, production methods, and personnel practices, and will therefore be reviewed in detail in Chapter VIII. It is worth noting here that one of those changes included unionization of the plant. Because of the many variables involved, it was not feasible to isolate the consequences of that particular change, and the

authors made no effort to do so. However, one "take" variable
which might be expected to have been particularly sensitive to
that change is the control graph; comparison of graphs of the
plant measured before with those measured almost five years
after unionization showed no appreciable gain either in total
control or in control by rank-and-file workers relative to
management. As will be seen in that chapter, other factors
were also aimed at increasing the influence of workers, mainly
in relation to the confines of their own jobs and work. All
this suggests is either that the control graph is an instrument
of low sensitivity, that the efforts to raise employee power
(including unionization) were ineffectual, or that perceptions
of control are strongly resistant to change.

The inference from the foregoing set of studies is that
the presence or absence of a union in and of itself appears not
to play a major part in the overall job satisfaction of workers,
although unionized workers are somewhat more satisfied with
their pay than non-unionized workers. It is generally believed
that unions serve to enhance worker influence, but the limited
before-and-after results in a single plant showed no gain in
perceived say over what goes on. A study in which the productivity of unionized workers was compared to that of non-
unionized ones in similar organizations found that the latter
were slightly more productive than the former, but other contextual factors were implicated along with unionization.

It is conceivable that the impact of unions on productivity

is not direct, but indirect. For example, Chamberlain (1948) suggested that the presence of a union pushing for higher wages and other economic benefits may compel management to operate more efficiently. It is also possible that the presence of the union may affect production not by increasing it, but by relieving some of the forces which might otherwise decrease it. These and related kinds of effects on productivity would not be revealed by the "micro" level kinds of studies reviewed here, if indeed they could be proven at all.

In assessing workers' reactions to the presence or absence of union, note may be taken of the fact that in 1972 union representation petitions to NLRB exceeded petitions to decertify existing unions by a ratio of about 10:1, and that only about 10,000 workers terminated their union representation through NLRB out of some 19 million union members (Henle in Rosow, 1974). That last figure is about one-fourth of the eligible work force.

(2) <u>Union-Company Relationships</u>. The foregoing literature pertained to the question of the ways in which the presence or absence of a union is associated with job attitudes and performance of employees. As we noted, there is little in the way of scientific information bearing on this issue. Somewhat more data are available on the subject of the ways in which features of an existing union or of its relations with management affect the job attitudes and performance of employees.

<u>Gottlieb & Kerr</u> (1950) reported the results of an attitude

survey of employees of the Buchsbaum Company which nearly 10 years earlier had initiated a turnabout in union-management relations from conflict to cooperation (Buchsbaum et al., 1946). Although evidence was cited for improvements in performance in the interim, including markedly increased sales volume and reduced disciplinary problems, the median job satisfaction of 467 employees in three Bauchsbaum plants was only about average compared to results of surveys elsewhere. However, the workers' job satisfaction was strongly associated with their evaluation of the union (r = .74). Likewise worker attitudes toward their supervisor and their shop steward were significantly correlated (r = .31). These findings led to the conclusion that "mutual emotional acceptance and cooperation between management and union had tended to structure employees' satisfaction attitudes along integrated rather than divisive lines" (Kerr, 1954). Such integration or positive relationship between attitude toward company and union has come to be known as "dual allegiance" (Purcell, 1953; Stagner et al., 1954).

Purcell (1953) conducted interviews with 202 packinghouse workers at Swift & Company (Chicago), which had recently entered a period of labor harmony after one of conflict. He found that 73% of the sample had positive attitudes toward both the company and the union, whereas the remaining 26% were nearly equally divided between those who had favorable attitudes toward one and unfavorable attitudes toward the other. Practically no one felt negatively about both the company and the union. Similar results were later reported for the workers at Swift plants in Kansas City and East St. Louis (Purcell, 1960). It should be noted that the foregoing kind of relationship between attitudes toward company and union is extremely non-linear, so that it cannot properly be inferred that attitudes toward the company paralleled attitudes toward the union, as was found by Gottlieb & Kerr, above. As a matter of fact, when the Chicago sample was subdivided into 12 groups based on various characteristics, the average degree of favorability toward management and toward the union among the groups correlated -.48, i.e., groups having more positive attitudes toward the union tended, on the average, to have less favorable attitudes toward the company.

Purcell (1960) also reviewed the results of 12 studies by other investigators who had compared worker attitudes toward their company and union, and reported that in 8 of them the investigator found that dual allegiance existed. In four other instances, however, there was evidence of polarization one way or the other in those allegiances. As noted before, however, evidence that most employees feel one way toward their company and the same (or the opposite) way toward their union, is not in itself, evidence that the latter is a factor in the former; such evidence would at least require concomitant variation, i.e., that employees who feel more favorably than others toward their union also feel more favorably toward the company. The data produced by Purcell do not satisfy that requirement,

although it does refute the common notion that the two allegiances are necessarily opposed. Also, as Rosen (1954) has
pointed out, studies reporting dual allegiance have typically
studied situations where the workers' roles as employees and
union members have not been incompatible, and may not predict
what would happen if a choice had to be made.

In addition to the evidence on dual allegiance,
Purcell's (1960) report furnishes some comparative data among
the three Swift plants. In relative terms, these are summarized in Table VII-4.

Table VII-4

Comparisons Among Three Swift Plants

| | Plant Averages | | |
|---|---|---|---|
| | Chicago | East St. Louis | Kansas City |
| Attitudes toward Company* | 1.6 | 1.5 | 2.0 |
| Attitudes toward the job* | 1.8 | 1.6 | 1.9 |
| Attitudes toward the union* | 2.0 | 1.2 | 1.3 |
| % Absenteeism (White Male)** | 19 | 14 | 5 |
| "   "   ( " Female)** | 28 | 1 | 7 |
| "   "   (Negro Male)** | 26 | 11 | 27 |
| "   "   ( " Female)** | 63 | -- | 29 |

*Scale:  1.0 = Very favorable
        2.0 = Favorable
        3.0 = Neutral
        4.0 = Unfavorable
        5.0 = Very Unfavorable

**Absenteeism estimated in terms of percentage of employees who worked less than 52 weeks during the year.

It is apparent from Table VII-4 that average attitude differences among the plants were not large; furthermore, the differences were not tested for statistical significance. Nonetheless, it would appear that the Chicago plant, where workers had the least favorable attitude toward the union, was not the one which had the lowest attitudes toward the company and job (Kansas City); however, Chicago did have the poorest absenteeism record. Chicago had the best turnover record of the three, but so many relevant factors differed among the plant locations that Purcell was loath to draw conclusions about turnover.

In 1954, Derber and his associates published their classic study of labor-management relations in eight companies in a mid-western community which they called "Illini City." Among the subjects of inquiry were the influence of the union representing the workers in each company, and the determinants, correlates, and consequences of that influence. Union influence was measured by means of a rating procedure completed by the investigators on the basis of their case studies and double-checked by company and union officals.

Among the chief findings were:

1. Favorability of attitudes held by employees at all levels toward their companies (a dependent variable) were positively and significantly correlated with those toward their unions, especially on parts of foremen and of union officials, as shown by the following:

Correlations between attitudes toward company and union

For top management:                                    +.48

For foremen:                                           +.82

For union officers                                     +.77

For rank-and-file workers                              +.33

That pattern of positive correlations between attitudes toward company and union is supportive of the notion of dual allegiance (and dual disaffection).

2.  When the average data for the eight plants were compared, rank-and-file workers' attitudes toward the company were highly and significantly correlated with union influence (measured as noted above), and also with two aspects of average worker income:

Correlations with attitudes toward company

Influence of union                    +.74

Average hourly earnings               +.65

Average annual earnings               +.54

The authors inferred that "these (four) key aspects of labor-management relations not only supplement each other but also may serve as determinants of one another" (Vol. 2, p. 216). These and other data also suggest that union influence may have determined more favorable job attitudes in part because of its role in better satisfying worker needs and expectations.

3.  Factors associated with greater union influence included:

a.  Management and union norms favoring union
    influence;

b.  Skill in bargaining and leadership on the part
    of the union officers, provided the collective
    bargaining situation lends itself to such skills;

c.  The absence of a well-integrated management or-
    ganization for dealing with the union (unless
    management favored close cooperation with the
    union);

d.  A work force that is unified and outspoken;

e.  Local union autonomy;

f.  Favorable management attitudes toward the union.

These factors may to some extent be determiners (independent
variables) of union influence, but the authors noted the possibility that their relationship to union influence may also
be circular.

Wass (1962) studied the attitudes of 1,817 employees of
a large mid-western Company described as experiencing labor-
management conflict. Attitudes toward the union correlated
negatively with attitudes toward management in the case of
hourly and supervisory personnel, but positively in the case of
salaried non-supervisory employees. The author suggested that
the direction of the relationship probably depends on how the
personnel in question perceive the climate of labor-management
relationships, i.e., on the "take" variable which here was
estimated rather than measured.

Wass's study is one of the few that compared the attitude
toward the union with other dependent variables. The directions
of those correlations are summarized below, with the correlations of the same variables with attitudes toward management
listed alongside for comparison:

Correlations with attitudes toward:

|  | Union | Management |
|---|---|---|
| Accident frequency | Positive | Positive |
| No. health & accident claims | " | Negative |
| Absenteeism rate | " | " |
| Life satisfaction attitude | Negative | Positive |

Thus, in this conflictful situation, employees expressing relatively favorable attitudes toward the union were generally
rather sour on life in general, tended to hold less favorable
attitudes toward management, and to be more often absent, have
more accidents, and lodge more health and accident claims -- a
generally negative syndrome. Apparently, however, not all
classes of personnel experienced the climate of labor-
management relations similarly, and this may make a difference
in the above picture. These findings suggest that the existence of dual allegiance may depend on a climate of harmonious union-management relations.

    c.  Conclusions on Formal Participation.

       (1)  In the U.S.A., formal methods of providing for

participation by non-managerial workers may be grouped into two main types: collective bargaining contracts and labor-management councils.

(2) The former is quite widespread, with about one-fourth of American workers being covered by such contracts. Those workers generally express favorable attitudes toward the presence of the union in their work situation, and the absence of strong dissatisfaction is indicated by the rarity of de-certification actions. However, workers rarely cite the union as one of the chief features contributing to job satisfaction.

(3) There are only scattered data which speak to the question of whether job attitudes and/or performance of union-ized workers differ from those of comparable non-unionized workers. What little there is suggests that the union is not a major factor in those respects, except for making a contribu-tion to somewhat greater satisfaction with pay. Where unions cooperated in labor-management councils, there was a general impression among company officials that the union contributed to improved productivity by raising the level of work motiva-tion, but this information is by now 25 years old and largely anecdotal.

(4) Workers' attitudes toward company and union are typically positively correlated, especially if there is a climate of labor-management harmony. This depends partly on the perceived influence of the union and its instrumentality in meeting workers' needs and expectations.

(5) There is evidence that the scope of union influence
is gradually increasing to include such issues as job design
and working practices in addition to the traditional concerns
with economic and safety issues.

(6) Labor-management committees cooperating to solve
problems which fall outside of collective bargaining contracts
were fairly widespread in the U.S.A. in the 1940's, sparked by
policies of the War Production Board. We found no statistical
data on their prevalence currently, and it may be that their
former functions have been largely absorbed either into informal consultative managerial practices, into the collective
bargaining format, or have disappeared.

(7) Studies of labor-management committees and councils
have in general not provided the quality of data needed to make
definitive statements. However, such as it is, it suggests
that the practice of labor-management committees was perceived
by workers and their union officials as furnishing a desirable
mode of participation, and by company officials as helping to
improve the work motivation of workers as well as serving as a
source of ideas for solving problems. Generally uncontrolled
experiments of unknown representativeness suggest that such
arrangements may have contributed to improving safety, wastage,
and suggestions.

(8) Although formal representation is generally believed
to be a vehicle for the exercise of greater influence by rank-
and-file workers, limited factual data do not clearly show that

workers under such conditions see themselves as having greater influence. This circumstance raises a note of caution as to whether formal representation plans, whatever their other benefits, are dependable ways of increasing the perception of influence of the rank-and-file in organizational affairs. It is also possible, however, that the potential value of such plans as mechanisms for increased influence by workers has not yet been fully exploited.

### Discussion and Conclusions Regarding Control Patterns

In this chapter, we have seen that the pattern of control -- who has a say over what and whom -- is a central concern of organizational life. We have endeavored to discern what consequences follow from different patterns of control in terms of the issues to which this review is addressed, i.e., the job attitudes and performance of organization members.

We earlier noted that it is useful to divide questions of control into the three domains or levels at which it operates: the individual job, the work group, and the organization. Our review of the literature was accordingly organized under those major rubrics and, at the end of each, we summarized the conclusions that we could infer from the findings. It will therefore not be useful to repeat those conclusions here. Rather, we will endeavor below to bring into focus those trends which ramify issues of control at all levels. In trying to draw broad conclusions embracing many specific findings, it must be understood that the generalizations are only approximately true, i.e., on average and not in every case.

1.  Workers who perceive themselves as having greater control over what goes on in their jobs, their groups, and their organizations, generally feel greater involvement in and commitment to those features of their working lives than do workers who believe they have less control.

2.  The former also tend to be better satisfied with their jobs than the latter.

3.  The former are less likely to quit their jobs.

4.  Statements about the effects on productivity must be less global.  Those aspects of control patterns which appear to be conducive to productivity include relatively high levels of: (a) self-control (autonomy) with respect to doing one's job; (b) collective influence on the part of work group members over the work goals and methods of compensation of their group; and (c) mutual influence among all levels of an organization. Equalization of control among hierarchical levels is not generally correlated with productivity.

5.  A variety of means have been employed to increase the climate of mutual influence or participation, some informal and some formal.  No scientific basis exists for evaluating their effectiveness relative to one another.  However, it does appear that any given approach has at times worked better in some situations than in others.  That may be because the method better fit the context of certain situations than others (e.g.,

technology or work force), or because its logic was implemented more competently in some instances than in others.

      6.  The present state of knowledge is such that the restructuring of control along various of the lines discussed above may be undertaken with greater confidence that it will improve employee job satisfaction and turnover than that it will increase productivity.

CHAPTER VIII

PATTERNS OF COMPENSATION

People work for many reasons, but they can be grouped
under two main headings: (1) because they like it (involving
notions like "commitment" and "intrinsic satisfaction," which
depend on job features discussed in Chapter VI) and/or
(2) because of its instrumentality in getting something else
that they want. The latter category contains a number of goals,
including security, prestige, approval, etc., but notably the
one that would be most frequently mentioned in our society is
"money," i.e., financial compensation for work. The topic of
"money" is therefore fundamental to a consideration of work
motivation, and its consequences of job satisfaction and performance. And, since money in the form of wages is a major
cost factor in industry, the question of the return on the
payroll dollar is central to the issues of productivity and
profitability.

The question of why people want money -- a question of
key importance to maximizing return on the payroll dollar --
is not at all as simple as it would seem at first glance, and
a number of theories have been invoked to answer it. Opsahl
& Dunnette (1966) and Lawler (1971) concluded their reviews of
that literature with the belief that the most useful approach
is to regard money as a symbol of and instrument for attaining
other desired outcomes. This view is probably close to the

common-sense explanation that most people would have. In turn, it leads to several questions whose answers should help in the design of compensation plans which could lead to improved satisfaction and performance:

1.  <u>What does money mean</u> or symbolize to various kinds of people, including its importance to them?

2.  On what <u>basis</u> should money be paid? There are two fundamental bases for payment in use in capitalistic countries: <u>time</u> and <u>production</u>, each with a variety of systems or plans of administration. (A third basis, having to do with <u>need</u>, has been proposed by Marxists but not systematically implemented by them; it is often informally a factor in determining the compensation of certain workers under capitalism.)

3.  <u>How much</u> money should be paid? In turn, this question can be divided into one pertaining to <u>absolute</u> levels of compensation and another about <u>relative</u> levels.

4.  How do <u>increments</u> or raises in pay affect workers?

5.  The last two questions generate the issue of <u>equity</u>. In recent years, there has been increasing attention to the proposition that the role of compensation in determining job satisfaction and performance is not just a matter of its instrumentality for other outcomes, but also of its internal equity. That is to say, the effects of money are a function of the extent to which a person receives what he thinks he is entitled to, and not just how much of other things it will buy for him.

In the present chapter, we will review the literature

bearing on the foregoing issues. Since questions of financial compensation are old ones, much of the fundamental research on it was done more than ten and even twenty years ago. It will not serve any useful purpose for us to repeat the several excellent reviews of that literature already done (e.g., Whyte, 1955; Haire, Ghiselli & Porter, 1963; Opsahl & Dunnette, 1966; Lawler, 1971). Instead, we will here cite those fundamental conclusions of those authors with which we agree, and examine in detail only particular studies which, because of their criticality and/or recency, raise further issues of present additional findings.

It should also be mentioned that we have located virtually no studies of compensation which qualify as "prototypes" by our definition. Although there are some technically sound researches, they have typically covered only two of the relevant panels of variables. Studies which have touched on a wider number of variables have been in the form of case reports which leave much to be desired in precision and specificity of data -- especially pertaining to take and mediating variables -- and in experimental controls.

Before proceeding with our review, the reader may be interested in the relation between our topic and the literature on job evaluation. That literature concerns methods for determining the monetary worth of particular jobs, taking into consideration its requirements in terms of incumbents' skill and effort, and is useful for that purpose. However, there have been no precise empirical studies that we have encountered which assess the impact of job evaluation or its components on the mediating or dependent variables of concern to us. Readers interested in looking further into that field may wish to refer to such publications as Belcher (1962), Otis & Leukart (1954), and Sibson (1967).

When we review the literature on compensation, we will consider first the issue of the effects of absolute pay level, second the effects of relative pay level, and finally the effects of the various pay plans. However before proceeding with a review of those topics, it is instructive to consider the more fundamental question of what money means to people -- or put differently -- "Why do people want money?"

### The Psychological Meaning of Money

Opsahl & Dunnette (1966) discussed the following theoretical interpretations of the role of money.

1. Money acts as a conditioned reinforcer or incentive due to the pairing of money with other reinforcers and incentives throughout an individual's life.

2. Money acts as an anxiety reducer -- due to the fact that cues indicating the absence of money lead to anxiety and the actual presence of money produces cues for the cessation of anxiety.

3. Money acts as a "hygiene factor"; Herzberg et al. (1959) proposed that money serves to forestall both economic deprivation and the feeling of unfair

treatment. Thus, money performs the hygienic role
of helping to avoid pain and dissatisfaction, but
it does not promote heightened motivation or
satisfaction.

4. Money acts as an instrument for gaining desired outcomes; the extent to which money motivates behavior
is a function of:

   a. the extent to which behaving in a certain manner
      leads to money;

   b. the extent to which that behavior leads to other
      outcomes; and

   c. the extent to which these outcomes are desired or
      not desired.

Opsahl & Dunnette concluded that the evidence in favor or
against any one of these views remains ambiguous, with the possible exception of the "hygiene" view, which they regarded as
deficient. They stated that it is probably best to view money
symbolically and as an instrument for gaining other desired
outcomes.

One of the consequences of viewing money as an instrument
or as a personal symbol is that it assumes the importance of the
individual -- his personal life, background, motives and goals
-- in determining the motivating quality of money. Gellerman
(1963), for example, stated, "Money acts as a symbol in different ways for different persons and for the same person at different times" (p. 166). In fact, Gellerman argued that money

can be interpreted as a projective device in that a person's reaction to money is a function of his life to date -- including his early economic environment, his competence training, the various non-financial motives he has acquired, and his current financial status. In a later paper Gellerman (1968) stated, "Whatever symbolism money has for the individual and whatever presumptions and illusions he has about how added income would affect the way he lives, are as much a part of the increment for him as is the money itself" (p. 144). Opsahl & Dunnette (1966) also stressed the importance of measuring the personal, situational and job parameters that may define more fully of what money is the symbol and to what its attainment is instrumental.

Wernimont & Fitzpatrick (1972) performed a key empirical study which is pertinent to the discussion of individual differences in the meaning of money. A "semantic-differential" scale consisting of a list of 40 pairs of adjectives regarding money was administered anonymously to 533 individuals. An analysis of responses yielded 7 statistical factors underlying the connotations of money:

1. Money is a source of embarrassment and degradation.
2. Money is a socially acceptable, an "OK" thing.
3. Money is something that is not very important.
4. Money has negative moral implications.
5. Money means comfortable economic security and practical usefulness.

6. Money is associated with social undesirability.

7. Money connotes conservative business values.

As expected, people differed in these factor scores, depending on their backgrounds of employment, education, occupation, socioeconomic level, and sex. In general, employed groups viewed money more positively, as a good, desirable, important and useful thing. Unemployed groups and college students took a more tense, worried, unhappy view of money. They also tended to downgrade the importance of money and to look down on those who value money highly.

As the authors of the study stated, it is difficult to relate these findings to any theoretical statement about money, such as those reviewed by Opsahl & Dunnette (1966) which were discussed earlier. However, it may be concluded that money does apparently mean different things to different people, in terms of the 7 connotative dimensions discerned in the study, and that its use as a motivator of work should take such differences into account. For example, it probably should not be relied upon as much for those groups which tend to perceive it as unimportant or undesirable. However, the study is limited to the cognitive connotations of money, and does not speak to the point of whether different groups of people actually _respond_ differently to money in relation to work.

This leads us to our next question: How does the level of monetary compensation affect workers? First, we will consider absolute pay level and then relative level.

Absolute Pay Levels

## Absolute Pay Level and Job Satisfaction

Recent data reported in the Survey of Working Conditions by the Survey Research Center (1970) bears on the issue of the relationship between pay level and job satisfaction. As previously mentioned, the survey involved personal interviews with a national sample of 1,533 currently-employed workers. The study included 2 measures of overall job satisfaction, plus 5 pertaining to particular aspects of the job including pay.

The survey data indicated that annual income from workers' primary job was positively and significantly associated with the two measures of overall job satisfaction ($r = .15$ and $.20$). Moreover, the relations are linear: the more income people get, the proportionately more they like their jobs. Other studies which have reported positive correlations between job satisfaction and wages include Smith & Kendall (1963) and Centers & Cantril (1946), the latter also on a national sample of workers.

As might be expected, the survey found income level to be even more strongly correlated with satisfaction with pay than with the overall job ($r = .33$). Lawler (1971) likewise concluded that: "So many studies have shown a strong relationship between pay and pay satisfaction that it is not necessary to review all of them to establish the validity of this effect..." (p. 228).

It may be noted, however, that the degree of correlation between level and overall satisfaction is not as high as might

commonly be supposed, with pay usually accounting for only
about 4 or 5% of the variance in level of job satisfaction.
In the Survey of Working Conditions, factors like the quality
of supervision and of resources, and the level of autonomy in
decisions affecting one's work were found to be more strongly
correlated with job satisfaction than was income. Nevertheless,
among "labor standards" types of issues, the Survey found that
problems of income ranked in importance only behind those of
health and safety in the views of workers.

In line with that result, it may be noted that pay is
usually the aspect of work with which employees most often
express dissatisfaction (Lawler, 1971, p. 218). Figures on
the percentage of workers who are dissatisfied with their pay
vary somewhat from study to study, but figures around 80%
are not infrequent (Porter, 1961; Lawler, 1965).

The Survey of Working Conditions correlated income levels
with other elements reflecting the quality of working life, and
found that it was modestly and positively associated also with
indicators of mental health and of overall life satisfaction.
However, people at higher income levels tended a bit more to
experience job-related tension.

It should be noted that numerous other job and personal
factors are associated with earning higher income, including
security, prestige, future prospects, challenge, social
status, life style, etc., and that the above correlations may
be due to some degree to those associated variables rather than

to pay itself. On the other hand, to the degree to which income symbolizes or makes possible those other conditions, it is inextricably bound to them.

We have seen from the foregoing that income level is clearly associated with the level of satisfaction with pay. The latter, in turn, has been found to correlate with other dependent variables of interest, as will be summarized in the immediately succeeding sections.

a. Pay Satisfaction and Job Satisfaction. Lawler (1971) reports that employees usually report that pay satisfaction influences their job satisfaction (e.g., Walker & Guest, 1952; Evans & Laseau, 1950). In reviewing the literature testing Herzberg's et al. (1959) 2-factor theory of job satisfaction, House & Wigdor (1967) conclude that satisfaction with pay can contribute to positive job feelings, and dissatisfaction with pay to negative feelings toward the job. Moderate positive correlations between pay satisfaction and job satisfaction have been reported by several investigators, including Armstrong (1968), Wernimont (1966), and Hulin & Smith (1967).

b. Pay Satisfaction and Turnover. Lawler (1971), having reviewed the literature on this subject, states: "In general the studies have found that pay dissatisfaction is a good predictor of turnover, but that it is not as good a predictor as total job satisfaction" (p. 234). As we have seen, the latter is also related to level of pay. Penner (1966), for example, reported that employees dissatisfied with their pay are twice as likely to consider changing jobs as those who are satisfied.

Hulin (1966), on the other hand, found an inverse relationship between overall job satisfaction and turnover among
female clerks, but little relationship between pay dissatisfaction and turnover; however, in a follow-up of the original
sample of clerks, Hulin (1968) found that when pay satisfaction increased among the employees, turnover dropped substantially. Lawler (1971) found some evidence to suggest that
the relationship between pay satisfaction and turnover may be
affected by general employment conditions, and that pay dissatisfaction will be more strongly related to turnover in
times of full employment than in times of unemployment.

     c. <u>Pay Satisfaction and Absenteeism</u>. Lawler (1971)
also reports some support for the contention that absenteeism
can result from pay dissatisfaction. For instance, Metzner &
Mann (1953) reported that only 43% of white-collar workers
who were absent 4 or more times in 6 months were satisfied
with their pay, whereas 69% of those who were absent once or
not at all were satisfied with their pay. Van Zelst & Kerr
(1953) found that pay satisfaction correlated -.17 with number
of days absent. Lawler (1971) also cites some evidence for an
inverse relationship between absenteeism and overall job satisfaction, which in turn related to level of pay.

     d. <u>Pay Satisfaction and Performance</u>. Schneider and
Olson (1970) found a correlation of .25 between adequacy of
job performance and pay satisfaction in a hospital where pay
level was tied to merit, but no correlation in a hospital
where pay was based on seniority and not merit. Porter &

Lawler (1968a) report similar results for managers.

    e.    Pay Satisfaction and Strikes.  Lawler (1971) states
that dissatisfaction with wages, hours, and fringe benefits
is given by unions as the principal cause of between 70% to
80% of all strikes.  In support of this, he cites a study by
James (1951), who found a direct relationship between pay dissatisfaction and strike behavior in a study in which he compared a group of striking workers with a comparable control
group of non-striking workers; the strikers showed much higher
levels of pay dissatisfaction than did controls.

## Pay Level and Worker Motivation or Performance

    Perhaps our first impulse is to assume the obvious --
that the strength of a worker's motivation to perform his job
well is directly related to the amount of his pay.  This
assumption would be consistent with some laboratory data.
However, reviews of the work literature by both Vroom (1964)
and by Lawler (1971) indicate that there is no reliable
evidence that either worker motivation or worker performance
are directly related to pay level alone, all other things
being equal.

### Relative Pay Levels

    Several investigators have proposed that workers are
strongly motivated to obtain a just or equitable return for
their contributions to the job, quite apart from the absolute
level of their compensation (Adams, 1963a, 1965; Homans, 1961;

Jaques, 1961; Patchen, 1961; Sayles, 1958; Zaleznik et al.,
(1958). All make some form of the point that compensation
either above or below the level which the employee perceives
as being fair or equitable will result in tension due to the
existence of a state of imbalance. This tension will, in
turn, motivate the worker to seek to create balance by the
use of a number of behavioral or cognitive methods. This
general view has been given the label of "equity theory."

Another feature of equity theory is the element of
social comparison. The concept of social comparison is that
a worker's perception of equity or inequity is not based
solely on the balance between his own perceived contributions
(inputs)* to the job, and his own perceived return (outcomes)**
from the job, but rather he also evaluates the balance between
other relevant employees' inputs and outcomes compared to his
own. A person will perceive that he is being equitably com-
pensated if his input/outcome ratio equals that of relevant
others. Inequality between these two ratios will be perceived
as inequity -- which will lead to feelings of tension caused
by the cognition of discrepancy. The employee in turn will be
motivated to reduce inequity by:

---

*"Inputs include anything the individual perceives as
an investment in the job and as worthy of some return. They
might include effort, education, or time" (Campbell et al., 1970,
p. 349).

**"Outcomes are anything that is perceived as a return
from the situation. Money, recognition, and working
conditions might be examples" (Ibid., p. 349).

1.  increasing or decreasing his inputs -- by, for
    example, increasing or decreasing the quality
    or quantity of his work, and/or

2.  increasing or decreasing his outcomes -- by, for
    example, attempting to get more money from his
    employer, and/or

3.  cognitively distorting his inputs or outcomes/
    or others' inputs or outcomes, and/or

4.  changing the comparison person, and/or

5.  leaving the situation [Adams, 1963a, 1965].

To these we should add the sixth alternative that, in
real-life situations, workers may attempt to counter the
source of the inequity, i.e., by changing the pay system.
Adams postulates that the method for reducing inequity that is
most likely to be employed depends on the least perceived cost
to the people involved -- in terms of effort, self-esteem,
security, etc.

## Laboratory Research on Relative Pay

Most of the research on equity theory consists of
laboratory investigations having seriously limited external
validity to work organizations, and often having conceptual
and/or methodological weaknesses which attenuate their internal validity as well. Typical weaknesses include the
following:

Most studies used student subjects and not actual workers;
the tasks which the subjects were required to perform (e.g.,

proofreading, checking data, and interviewing) were limited in
variety and complexity, and not very much like real-world work;
the studies were short in time-span compared to the time-spans
involved in real-world work; most studies failed to control for
contamination by other variables (e.g., maintaining self-esteem
rather than equity); and there was often no "take" measure of
equity effects.

Pritchard (1969) has comprehensively and critically reviewed that body of research; the reader interested in further
discussion of its validity will find it in that paper.

It may serve to illustrate as well as update that body of
research if we were to summarize a recent study which endeavored to extend and correct some of the earlier work. The
study by Pritchard, Dunnette & Jorgenson (1972), because it
simulated a real work situation in the laboratory, also was
more applicable than most to organizational problems. Nevertheless, caution must be exercised in generalizing even from
this study since students, not actual workers, were the subjects
and since the study was not done in an actual, on-going work
situation. Furthermore, the nature of the experimental task --
which was data-finding and recording -- illustrates the limited, unrealistic kinds mentioned above. Underpayment, overpayment and equitable payment conditions were manipulated by
either (a) affecting perceptions of equity outcomes,
or (b) changing actual amounts of outcomes during the course of
the study. Performance was found to be affected by the

inequity manipulations, but only for the second type of manipulation, i.e., changing actual amounts. In an hourly pay treatment, overpaid "workers" decreased performance less than equitably paid ones, who in turn decreased less than underpaid ones. Under a pay-for-performance treatment, overpaid "workers" increased their inputs by working more for a given level of reward than did those in the other two equity conditions. Underpayment inequity, when compared to equity, resulted in greater dissatisfaction with pay and greater overall dissatisfaction with the "job." However, overpaid individuals did not differ in the satisfaction they expressed with pay when compared to equitably paid $\underline{S}$s, but did display lower overall job dissatisfaction than did equitably paid $\underline{S}$s. Dissatisfaction with overpayment as well as underpayment had been predicted by Katzell's (1964) theory of job satisfaction. Adams (1965) has noted that over-rewarded individuals generally show less tension or discomfort than do under-rewarded ones.

Table VIII-A summarizes the results of the key laboratory studies done on the subject of inequitable pay levels.

Table VIII-1

LABORATORY STUDIES OF RELATIVE PAY LEVELS

| Finding | Studies Which Support This Finding | Studies Which Do Not Support This Finding |
|---|---|---|
| Compared to equitable payment: | | |
| 1. Overpaying in an hourly pay system leads to a greater quantity of performance and/or quality of performance. | Adams & Rosenbaum (1962) Arrowood (1961) Pritchard, Dunnette, & Jorgenson (1972) | Friedman & Goodman (1967) |
| 2. Overpaying in a piece-rate pay system leads to a lower quantity and/or higher quality of performance, but only for a short time period. | Adams & Rosenbaum (1962) Adams (1963) Adams & Jacobsen (1964) Lawler, Koplin, Young & R. Fadem (1968) Pritchard, Dunnette, & Jorgenson (1972) | Andrews (1967) |
| 3. Underpaying in a piece-rate pay system leads to a greater quantity of performance and/or a lower quality of performance. | Andrews (1967) Lawler & O'Gara (1967) | |
| 4. Underpaying in an hourly pay system leads to a lower quantity and/or lower quality of performance. | Pritchard, Dunnette, & Jorgenson (1972) | |
| 5. Underpaying leads to pay dissatisfaction and/or job dissatisfaction. | Pritchard, Dunnette, & Jorgenson (1972) | |
| 6. Overpaying leads to pay dissatisfaction and/or job dissatisfaction | Pritchard, Dunnette, & Jorgenson (1972) (only overall dissatisfaction) | |

Field Studies of Relative Pay

In addition to numerous laboratory studies, there have been several correlational studies in work organizations which bear on the problems of relative levels of pay. These are reviewed in the present section.

a. Homans (1953) performed the initial study on this subject, using clerical workers in the billing departments of a large company. The cash posters performed the routine job of entering paid bills on customers' accounts, whereas the ledger clerks did more varied, interesting work. An employee had to be a cash poster for several years before she became a ledger clerk. Despite the fact that ledger clerks had higher status, they were paid the same as cash posters. Approximately 75% of the ledger clerks indicated that they felt that the situation was unjust in that they should receive more money because of their higher seniority and greater skill. Curiously, there was no reported general dissatisfaction with pay. In fact, 11 of 19 ledger clerks voluntarily reported that they liked their pay. Thus, the same pay for jobs differing in skill and seniority levels (independent variable), led to perceived inequity (take variable), but possibly not to differences in job satisfaction (dependent variable). The last finding runs counter to the laboratory study of Pritchard, Dunnette & Jorgenson (1972), mentioned above. However, Homans did not measure satisfaction systematically, nor was job performance studied. In addition, the study suffers from having a small sample.

b. <u>Clark</u> (1958) interviewed two groups of employees of a supermarket. Female cashiers worked full-time and had higher status and better pay than older, part-time male package packers -- many of whom were college students. Clark found that when interviewed, the packers were explicit about experiencing inequity and furthermore reported that they attempted to achieve equity by decreasing their inputs in the form of lowered effort and productivity. Clark also studied cashier-packer pairs in several different stores, and for each store he determined the average discrepancy between input-outcome ratios for all the pairs. He found that the lower the average difference between ratios for the pairs, the greater was the productivity of the store. This study supports those in the laboratory which found that underpayment under a time-rate system leads to lower satisfaction and productivity. However, again the validity of the study is limited by the small size of the sample.

c. In a study by <u>Patchen</u> (1961), skilled and unskilled workers (N = 489) in a Canadian oil refinery were asked to name and describe two persons, either inside or outside the company, whose yearly earnings were different from their own earnings. The workers were also asked whether the "comparison person" earned more or less than himself, about the comparison person's occupational level, and the worker's satisfaction with his own earnings. Actual pay rates were also determined. Results indicated that workers who chose higher-earning comparison persons showed a consistent trend to be less satisfied with their pay the closer the comparison person's occupational level was to their own. In other words, the more similar in occupational level a comparison person is, the more dissatisfied the comparer is with earning less. Those employees who were satisfied with their comparisons based their feelings of satisfaction on perceived consistency between the wage difference and other related differences between the workers (education, seniority, etc.). The above findings support the notion that perceived equitable payment relative to one's contribution is a source of satisfaction.

Another finding of Patchen's study was that workers who were actually relatively low in pay were less satisfied than others with the comparisons they made. Also, as a worker's promotion chances improved, they would more frequently choose potentially dissonant comparisons and be more dissatisfied with the idea of remaining below their comparison person in wages; however, this was less true of workers who had good promotion chances <u>within</u> the company than of workers who saw their chances as better <u>outside</u> the company. Patchen believed that the difference between the two groups largely depended on whether advancement had to be fought for or was assured. If it was assured (i.e., the within-company promotable group), dissonant comparisons were not needed as justification for advancement or as a protest against one's present status, but when advancement must be fought for, these reasons become more salient. Therefore, we see here the

interaction between perceived advancement and satisfaction
with relative pay.

    d. <u>Andrews & Henry</u> (1963) studied 228 managers in five
companies. They found that, at a given level of management
in a company, satisfaction with pay was more highly related to
the similarity between their pay and the average pay of managers in the other four companies, than to the similarity
between their pay and the average pay of other managers in
their own company. In short, comparisons appeared to be based
on the pay of managers at a given level regardless of company.

    The last two field studies reviewed above indicate the
importance and difficulty of defining the bases of equity
comparison in terms of (a) which people are chosen for comparison, (b) along which dimension these people are compared,
and (c) what personal and environmental factors influence the
wage comparison.

    The field studies as a whole appear to give limited sup-
port to the theoretical conceptions and laboratory research
related to equity theory, as well as to extend some of the
notions. In addition, everyday experience with wage administration supports most of the tenets: the importance of balance between contributions and rewards and of social comparisons; the restriction of output when incentive rates become
"loose"; dissatisfaction with underpayment and discomfort with
overpayment; low quantity and/or quality of production when
pay rates are inequitably low. Other ways of coping with

inequity, predictable from theory but undocumented in laboratory research, are experienced in real-life settings, including withdrawal (turnover) when pay is inequitable and/or
attempts to change the system such as through bargaining,
grievances, and work stoppages. However, it must be noted
that, with the few exceptions noted, there has been virtually
no "prototype" research on pay inequity in organizational
settings, so that the aforementioned "verification" of equity
theory is not supported by a sufficient number of high-quality
studies to be regarded as firm.

## Pay Increases

Our introductory section pointed out that the effects of
pay are theoretically not limited just to the stable level
being received but also to pay increases which are ordinarily
expected in a job. In the Patchen (1961) study summarized
above, we further saw that the co-worker comparisons on which
workers based their assessments of satisfaction with pay depended in part on their expectations regarding promotion (which
normally carries a pay increase); those with better chances
were more likely to make potentially dissatisfying comparisons
with others. We also saw earlier that satisfaction with pay
correlates with job performance when pay (including increases)
is based on merit, but not when it is not based on merit; this
suggests that the method for determining pay increases may be
an important factor in employee satisfaction and/or performance.

Important as this topic is, however, it has been given little research attention, beyond various studies which show that satisfaction with promotional prospects (having associated pay implications) is a factor both in overall job satisfaction and in turnover.

There has been a study by Giles & Barrett (1971) which examined the relationship between the size of merit pay increases and satisfaction with the increases. The study was designed to examine the concept of "diminishing utility" for each added dollar of merit increase received by 64 professional-level personnel employed at a medium-sized Eastern electronics company. Thirty-one of the employees were classified as engineers, and 33 as non-engineers in various functional specialties. The employees were asked to indicate their expected satisfaction with each of 13 hypothetical amounts of merit increase as compared to their self-reported most equitable hypothetical merit increase. Results did not support the concept of diminishing utility for each added dollar. On the contrary, each dollar of merit increase had increased utility for satisfaction ($r = .79$). It was also found that the engineer/non-engineer distinction had a significant moderating effect on the above relationship (for engineers $r = .77$, and non-engineers $r = .82$). Neither age nor length of service acted as a moderator. It is of relevance to equity theory to note that in about 10% of their sample a point was reached where larger hypothetical increases did not generate greater expected satisfaction; comments by those people indicated that excessive increments in pay would be unearned and that there might be corresponding performance expectations which they could not satisfy.

One limitation of the above study is that only hypothetical increments were investigated. One reported by Hinrichs (1969) examined employees' evaluations of actual pay increases, and found that the judged magnitude of an increment was inversely proportional to one's salary, although this relationship was not as clear when increments were large.

Recently, Greene (1973) published the only prototype which we have located on the subject of merit increases. He studied 62 first-line managers employed in various line and staff functions of a large manufacturer of business and communications equipment. Correlations were computed among the following:

(1) Independent Variable: amount of annual salary increase (less cost-of-living adjustment), expressed as a percentage of the previous year's salary; this was considered a measure of "merit" pay.

(2) Job Satisfaction: measured by the 10-item scale published by Bullock.

(3) Job Performance: ratings of quality and quantity of work by two of each manager's peers, on a specially devised research scale.

Each of the above measures was obtained twice, approximately one year apart.

The statistical procedure was designed not only to ascertain the degrees of relationship among those variables, but also the probable direction of causation. The last was based on the assumption that the correlation between a causal variable at time 1 and a dependent variable taken at time 2, should be significantly higher than measures of the same variables taken either in the reverse sequence or concurrently.*

The results disclosed that the amount of merit pay increment was substantially and significantly associated with job satisfaction measured a year later ($r = .45$). Furthermore, the conditions satisfying the assumption of the latter being caused by the former were met, i.e., the concurrent and reverse sequences produced lower correlations (between .21 and .28). The correlation between the amount of merit pay increase and peer-rated job performance was also significantly positive (above .40). However, the relationships did not clearly indicate whether either caused the other. Finally, it is of interest to note that the correlation between earlier job satisfaction and later rated performance was insigifnicant ($r = .17$), whereas that between earlier rated performance and subsequent satisfaction was markedly higher ($r = .49$). The evidence supported the notion that better performance causes higher job satisfaction (ostensibly because of associated higher merit pay). It did not support the view that people

_____

*These relations were analyzed by means of the cross-lagged correlation technique and FCP (frequency of change in product moment).

produce more because they are better satisfied with their jobs. However, although these correlational analyses are suggestive of causality, they do not prove it as firmly as would before-and-after assessments of experimental change.

In the following section, we will summarize our conclusions based on the foregoing discussions of amounts of pay and pay increments.

### Conclusions on Amounts of Pay and Increments

1. Absolute amount of pay is positively related to:
   a. overall job satisfaction
   b. satisfaction with pay
   c. life satisfaction
   d. mental health
   e. tension
2. Absolute amount of pay, in and of itself, is not related to performance.
3. Satisfaction with pay has the following relations to other outcomes:
   a. Turnover: slight inverse relation.
   b. Absenteeism: slight inverse relation.
   c. Performance: moderate positive relation, provided pay is tied to performance.
   d. Overall job satisfaction: moderate positive correlation.
   e. Strikes: positively related to pay dissatisfaction.

4.  Regarding relative pay (equity):

    a.  Overpaying in an hourly pay system may lead
to a greater quantity and/or quality of output.

    b.  Overpaying in a piece-rate or incentive system
may lead to restriction of quantity of and/or
to higher quality of output.

    c.  Underpaying in an hourly pay system may lead
to a lower quantity and/or lower quality of
output.

    d.  Underpaying in a piece-work or incentive pay
system may lead to a greater quantity of
output.

    e.  Underpaying in general leads to pay dissatis-
faction and/or job dissatisfaction; in real
work situations, this may be expressed as
grievances.

    f.  Overpaying may also lead to dissatisfaction or
discomfort, but to a lesser extent than
underpaying.

    g.  There are several ways of coping with inequity,
so that none of the above trends would apply to
all workers or all situations; to predict, one
must also know which modes of coping are least
"costly" to the workers.

    h.  These findings on relative pay level are based
on mostly laboratory or simulated situations,

and are therefore of uncertain applicability to actual work situations; however they do receive some support from field studies and everyday experience.

5. Regarding increments in pay:

    a. Satisfaction with future prospects (which partly represent pay increases) is moderately positively correlated with overall job satisfaction and inversely with turnover.

    b. Larger merit increases lead to greater job satisfaction, and are a factor in performance as well.

As mentioned earlier, when discussing the relationship between employee's pay and his performance and attitudes, it is useful to distinguish between two broad subtopics. One subtopic examines the effects of differing amounts of pay on worker response, while the second subtopic researches the effects of the way in which the pay, regardless of its absolute amount, is administered. The following discussion will deal with the latter of these two areas.

## Pay Plans

It is well recognized that the method for determining pay is a complex task, and the number and scope of differing plans reflect this complexity. It is not the purpose of this discussion to evaluate the numerous individual plans along all relevant criteria. We are here interested mainly in the effects

of differing forms of wage and salary plans on the performance
and attitudes of employees. In this regard, one of the dimensions of pay administration seems particularly relevant: the
degree to which pay is explicitly dependent upon worker performance. This particular dimension also happens to be one
for which there exists some theoretical or empirical research
to indicate its importance for worker motivation.

## Pay-for-Performance ("Incentive") Plans

The famous work of F. W. Taylor during the early part
of this century inspired many organizations to formulate pay
plans designed to increase worker motivation by having pay
depend upon performance. These plans have been devised at the
individual, group and total organization performance level.
Individual plans typically involve the comparison of an
individual's performance with some predetermined standard,
while group and organization-wide plans use indices of results
for units larger than the individual worker for pay determination.

a. Individual Incentive Plans. In his recent reviews
of the literature on the effectiveness of different pay plans,
Lawler (1971, 1973) concludes that the effectiveness of individual incentive plans for increasing worker productivity has
been well documented over the years. Although most of the
documentation consists of uncontrolled case studies, in
aggregate these cases provide strong support for the contention
that, all other things being equal, paying an individual for

what he produces will increase his productivity. Illustrative supporting literature includes a 1945 U.S. government survey of 145 companies indicating an average productivity increase of 39% when wage incentive plans were installed, and studies reported by Viteles (1953) and by Wyatt (1934) demonstrating productivity gains of 16% and 46% respectively when pay was changed from a fixed wage to an individual pay for performance plan. From these and other data, Lawler was able to conclude that "even the most conservative studies seem to suggest that individual incentive plans can increase productivity from 10 to 20 percent" (1971, p. 124). Viteles (1953) has cautioned, however, that it is usually impossible to isolate the specific effects of incentive plans from other changes that usually accompany their installation; for example, in the study he reported, changes were also made in work procedures, working hours, and union-management relations.

Further support for the effects of incentive plans appears in a study by Rothe (1970) showing that the removal of an already existing wage incentive plan can have an adverse impact on productivity. Rothe studied unionized welders who as a result of a new collective bargaining agreement had their financial incentive system removed. Immediately after the removal of the incentive, productivity dropped by 25 percent.

There are also numerous studies which indicate that the utility of an individual wage incentive plan is contingent upon a number of situational factors (moderater variables).

One such factor is the amount of worker cooperation or interdependence needed for effective performance. Lawler (1971) points out that individual incentive plans foster competitive behavior among workers. This increased competition can have a negative impact on worker effectiveness when tasks demand cooperation among them.

A second factor limiting the effectiveness of individual incentive plans is the degree to which relevant criteria of performance can be operationalized. A wage incentive system requires objectively quantifiable standards for pay determination. Even when this is done, it may often lead to worker neglect of equally important job behaviors which are not as easily quantifiable and therefore not part of the standard. A study by Babchuk & Goode (1951) well illustrates both of these problems. They examined the job behavior of salesmen who were under a plan whereby part of their pay was determined by their individual sales. This scheme produced a competition among the salesmen, which adversely affected total group functioning. In addition, it was found that the salesmen were neglecting other important aspects of the job, such as keeping stock records, in favor of selling. While such behavior may have short-term payoffs, it can have negative impact over the long run.

Aspects of the task other than the degree of necessary cooperation may also influence the effectiveness of an individual wage incentive system. A study by Bass, Hurder & Ellis

(1954) indicated that high task complexity may decrease the effectiveness of a wage incentive plan. Opsahl & Dunnette (1966) also suggested that liking for the task may increase the positive outcomes of incentive systems. Finally, it is well documented (Whyte, 1955; Lawler, 1971; Opsahl & Dunnette, 1966) that incentive systems can lead to worker restriction of output if the organizational climate is one of insecurity and mistrust.

     b.  <u>Group Incentive Plans</u>. Incentive plans can also be administered at the group level. In these systems, a bonus is divided among members of the group, the amount depending on some measure of the level of group effectiveness. Lawler (1971) concluded that although there are few studies which examine the effectiveness of group incentive plans, those which exist do indicate that productivity under such plans is higher than productivity under fixed-payment plans. In addition, group plans have the advantage of being better suited to situations where cooperation is important. As mentioned earlier, Babchuk & Goode found that too much competition existed among salesmen paid on an individual payment plan; however, when the pay system was changed to one of group bonus, cooperation increased.

     Although group plans seem to offer that advantage over individual plans, the limited existing evidence indicates that group plans do not generate as much productivity increase. Marriott (1949) has shown that as the size of the work group increased, the effectiveness of the incentive plan, as measured

by output rates, decreased. Further, those individuals paid
on an individual plan were, on the average, higher producers
than those paid under group plans. Thus, as an incentive
plan moves further away from tying a single individual's pay
to his own performance, worker productivity suffers. Similarly, plans that tie incentive pay more specifically to the
output of the face-to-face work group seem to have better
effects on productivity than those which are based on depart-
mental output (Roethlisberger & Dickson, 1939).

  c. <u>Organization-wide Incentive Plans</u>. Finally, a wage
incentive system can also be administered on the basis of some
measure of total organizational effectiveness (i.e., of a
company or a plant). This approach is most clearly illustrated
by profit-sharing plans (Metzger, 1966). Such plans have
become rather widely adopted in the U.S.A., a 1969 survey
showing that about one-third of companies used some type of
such plan (Research Institute of America, 1969). Most of
these plans deposit a portion of company profits to a fund for
later payouts to employees in the form of retirement and other
benefits. About 40% of the plans, however, involve cash
bonuses to employees tied to improvements in productivity and
profitability. Metzger (1966) reported that management generally considered the latter type of system as more effective
in terms of concerns for productivity.

  Healey (1965), Metzger (1966), and Fein (1971) have all
made the point that profit-sharing, if it is to work at all,
must be part of a total program of policies and practices

which lead to labor-management cooperation in operating pro-
fitably.  As part of such a program, most companies using
profit-sharing also employ other incentives (Metzger, 1966).

The idea that profit-sharing should be part of a broad
program leads to such strategies as the Lincoln Electric
system (Lincoln, 1951) and Scanlon Plan (Lesieur, 1958; Frost,
Wakeley & Ruh, 1974), which are better conceptionalized as
total-systems than just as incentive plans.  Considerable
factual data has been developed concerning the effects of the
latter, and it will therefore be discussed in detail in
Chapter IX.  Unfortunately, there are no scientific studies
of profit-sharing or related company-wide incentive plans
per se, so their evaluation depends on the accumulation of
managerial experience as was summarized above.  That experience would suggest that company-wide incentives are not in
themselves particularly effective in improving employee motivation and performance (at least among rank-and-file),
although they may be a useful ingredient in a broader program.

d.  Problems with Pay-for-Performance Plans.  Although
the preceding evidence has generally favored pay-for-
performance as compared to time-based plans, the former are
not an unalloyed boon.  Indeed, there have been a number of
reports of restriction of output by workers under them (e.g.,
Mathewson, 1931; Roethlisberger & Dickson, 1939; Dalton, 1948;
Roy, 1952; Whyte, 1955).  Although those studies were typically observational and lacking precise analysis of reasons,
they do attest to the prevalence of the phenomenon.

Hickson (1961) has analyzed the reasons for such output restriction as falling under the following rubrics:

    (1)   uncertainty that management will continue to
           live up to the bargain about rates;

    (2)   insecurity about possible layoffs;

    (3)   uncertainty regarding continuation of social
           relations on the job;

    (4)   social satisfactions derived from restriction,
           e.g., the "game" of outsmarting the system;

    (5)   desire to maintain control over one's own
           behavior.

In his analysis, Whyte (1955) has emphasized the
importance of conflict between the cues signalling reward and
those signalling punishment, as doled out by management and
by co-workers.

Viteles (1953), Gomberg (1948) and Fein (1971), among
others, have pointed out additional technical factors which
impair the effectiveness of incentive plans, including in-
ability to reliably define and measure standards of performance and criteria of results, lack of control by workers
over their own productivity, changes in technology and work
methods, and, most important perhaps, adversary relations
between management and labor.

To summarize thus far, sixty years of experience with
different forms of pay-for-performance plans leads to the
following general conclusions:

(1) All other factors held constant, tying at least part of a worker's pay to some measure of performance has a positive effect on productivity.

(2) The closer a system comes to tying individual pay to individual performance, the greater will be the productivity increase.

(3) Aspects of the task, such as complexity, necessity for cooperation and liking for it, can moderate the general effectiveness of incentive systems; in particular, conclusion 2 should be modified in the direction of group incentives where production requires team-work among group members.

(4) The effectiveness of wage incentive plans is neutralized by worker restriction of output when used in a climate of insecurity and mistrust, or in other ways characterized by divergence of the goals of workers and management.

e. Pay-for-Performance Plans and Work Motivation. Although the influence of paying for performance on productivity is well documented, the motivational dynamics of such increases are less well understood. Only in recent years have researchers attempted to go beyond the demonstration of a relationship between wage incentive plans and worker productivity. This change can be partially explained by the recent interest in more cognitive theories of worker motivation, particularly

the expectancy theories of March & Simon (1958). These theoretical positions are well suited for explaining the motivational basis of pay for performance plans. Generally these
theories hold that an important influence on worker motivation
is the extent to which the employee sees a connection between
his increased output and the rewards he receives.

In a large scale study of managerial behavior and attitudes, Porter & Lawler (1968b) found a relationship between
employees' perceptions about how their pay is determined and
their motivation and performance. Porter & Lawler questioned
a sample of 563 lower and middle management personnel from
seven different organizations. They asked these managers to
rate the extent to which their pay was based upon the job performance factors of quality, productivity, and effort expended.
The authors then split the sample into two groups. One group
contained those who had a strong belief that pay was dependent
upon job performance, while the second group did not believe
there was a pay-performance relationship. When these contrasted groups were compared on self and superior's ratings of
job performance, the group that believed their pay level to be
dependent upon their performance was rated consistently higher
than the other group. In two of the four comparisons reported,
the high belief group exhibited significantly higher performance, while in the other two comparisons the differences
were not significant, although in the same direction. In addition, Porter & Lawler were able to demonstrate that

325

perception of a pay-performance relationship affects the
mediating variable of worker motivation. They obtained
superior and self ratings of effort expended and compared
these criteria with beliefs about how pay is determined. In
all four comparisons made, those individuals who believed
their pay to be based upon job performance factors were rated
as expending more effort on their jobs.

This study therefore appears to show that the positive
effect of pay-for-performance plans operates first through a
belief that better performance leads to higher pay, and then
through increased motivation or effort on the part of the
worker to perform well. Thus, when workers perceive that
their pay is based upon their performance, they will increase
their work effort with a consequent increment in productivity.
However, the finding would be more persuasive had performance
been measured independently and objectively. Also, its
generalizability is limited by the fact that it is based only
on workers at the managerial level, who may be more strongly
motivated to succeed, less concerned with layoff due to over-
production, or in other ways different from lower-level
employees.

f. <u>Pay-for-Performance Plans and Workers' Perceptions</u>.
If the foregoing study by Porter & Lawler is to be applicable to understanding the dynamics of wage incentive plans,
it is necessary to demonstrate that such plans have an effect
on worker perceptions of a performance-pay relationship ("take"
variable). <u>Schwab</u> (1973) performed such a study on 273

production workers of a large midwestern consumer goods manufacturer.  This company assigned its workers to jobs under one
of three wage plans:  piece-rate, group incentive, or salary.
When Schwab questioned the workers about the role of their
performance in determining their pay level, he found that
workers paid under the piece-rate system were stronger in their
belief that pay was dependent upon performance than either the
group-incentive or the salaried workers.

A study by <u>Cammann & Lawler</u>  (1973)  bears  on
this same issue.  These authors endeavored to examine the
difference in effectiveness which existed between two seemingly similar group-incentive systems.  Workers under the two
systems were doing similar types of jobs, but productivity was
higher under one plan than under the other.  When the authors
examined the perceptions of the workers in the two groups,
they found that those workers under the less effective system
were less likely to subscribe to the statement "how much I
earn depends upon how hard I work."  The investigators concluded that the less effective system was not adequately com-
municating to employees the relationship between their performance and their pay, and was therefore not having as much
impact on motivation and productivity.

Taken together, the studies by Porter & Lawler, by Schwab,
and by Cammann  & Lawler  provide  insight  into  the
nature of effective wage incentive plans.  The wage incentive
plan communicates to workers the information that their pay is
based upon their performance.  This perception, in turn,

produces increased efforts in employees. When a wage incentive plan is administered poorly, and the pay-performance
relationship is not perceived or understood by workers, the
system will have little effect on motivation and productivity.

Lawler (1971) has used this theoretical position to
explain the difference between individual and group incentive
plans. As mentioned earlier, research seems to indicate that
the closer a plan comes to tying individual performance to
individual pay, the more effective it will be. Lawler be-
lieves that in group plans workers perceive less of a connection between their own performance and the pay they receive.
This perception of a weaker pay-performance relationship has
the effect of decreasing worker motivation and subsequent
productivity. The aforementioned study by Schwab (1973)
supports Lawler's contention. Schwab found that workers paid
under a group incentive plan were less likely than piece rate
workers to believe that their weekly pay depended upon their
performance. However, they were still more likely to subscribe to this belief than were salaried workers. Similarly,
Campbell (1952) found a negative relationship between size
of work group and worker understanding of the relationship
between their performance and their pay. However, the Schwab
study indicates that among group incentive workers, this relationship is still likely to be stronger than for salaried
workers. These results parallel the previously reviewed
literature on the productivity differences found among these
plans. Group plans are likely to produce smaller productivity

gains than individual plans, but will still increase productivity over non-incentive (time-based) systems. The qualification should be borne in mind that group plans may be superior when the work requires high degrees of cooperation among the workers, and the product is truly a group effort.

     g. <u>Pay-for-Performance Plans and Job Satisfaction</u>. While there is extensive literature on the effects of wage incentive plans on worker productivity, there has been little research relating pay system to worker satisfaction. A study by Penner (1966) indicates that employees who believe their pay to be contingent upon their performance are generally more satisfied with that pay. Lawler (1966) found similar results, but also demonstrated that this held true only for those who wanted their pay so determined.

     Relevant to the question of satisfaction with pay are studies examining worker preference for different pay plans. After reviewing that literature, Lawler (1971) concluded that managerial personnel generally prefer their pay to be based upon their performance. However, preferences among blue-collar workers are less clear. Opsahl & Dunnette (1966) reported that surveys of workers in four companies showed that a majority in only one of the companies favored incentive plans over time-based earnings. Overall, it seems that the preferences of blue-collar workers are not easily generalizable and are often dependent upon a number of contextual factors such as experience with the plan (Jones & Jeffrey, 1964), presence or absence of a union (Jones & Jeffrey, 1964), and the needs and goals of the employees (Beer & Gery, cited in Lawler, 1971).

In addition to these studies on satisfaction and prefer-
ence, there is some evidence to indicate that the relationship
between satisfaction and performance is stronger under performance payment systems than under time-based plans.
Schneider & Olson (1970) compared the behavior and attitudes
of 146 nurses from two different hospitals. In one hospital
nurses' pay was based explicitly on effort and performance,
with only minimal annual or biannual increases for tenure.
In the second hospital, pay was explicitly based upon tenure.
When Schneider & Olson compared the correlation between pay
satisfaction and nurse effort they found that correlation to
be much higher in the hospital where pay was based upon performance ($r = .24$) than in the hospital where pay was based
upon seniority ($r = -.30$). It should be noted that while
this result is interesting, it must be taken as tentative
since other differences, aside from pay plan, existed between
the hospitals (size, public vs. private).

Pritchard (1973) reports a study dealing with the same
question. Students were recruited to work on what they
thought was an actual job. When they reported for work they
were placed into either an hourly or individual incentive pay
system. His results, using two satisfaction measures and a
number of conditions, are mixed and do not provide clear indication as to the relationship between satisfaction and performance under different pay systems. It should be noted also
that the external validity of this study is suspect due to the

nature of the job and the sample (college students recruited
on a temporary basis to do a menial clerical task).

In summary, the relationship between incentive-type
plans and job satisfaction is not clearly established, but
appears to depend on the level of workers, their background,
and features of the work situation. There is evidence to
indicate that the correlation between pay satisfaction and
performance is greater where workers are under some form of
a pay-for-performance system. This makes sense in that under
such systems those who perform better will be paid more. In
such systems, higher performance leads to greater satisfaction.

## Miscellaneous Aspects of Pay Plans

Although most of the research relating pay plans to
worker productivity and attitudes pertains to the issue of
pay-for-performance, other aspects are also germaine to this
topic. In particular, within time-rate systems whether an
individual is paid on an hourly or salaried basis and whether
his pay level is secret or public may have an influence on
his motivation and attitudes. Unfortunately, little research
has been done on such questions, and certainly none that meet
the prototype standards described earlier.

Lawler (1967, 1971) has hypothesized that where an organization maintains a policy of secret pay levels, the aware-
ness of performance-pay contingency cannot exist, thus reducing the influence of pay on motivation. Unfortunately,

no research has been done which compares the motivation of workers under open vs. secret pay policies. However, a laboratory experiment by Leventhal et al. (1972) indicates that secrecy is conducive to pay in relation to performance, whereas public information favors equal allocation of rewards.

Lawler (1967) was able to show that managers paid under a secret policy generally underestimated the pay of their bosses and overestimated the pay of their peers or subordinates. Further, overestimation of peer salary was positively related to dissatisfaction with pay. However, incorrect estimation of superior or subordinate pay was not related to dissatisfaction. Of particular interest is the finding that managers underestimate the pay of superiors. Where this is true, promotion may become a weaker incentive, possibly decreasing worker motivation. In support of this contention, Lawler found that those who most seriously underestimated the pay of their superiors gave a lower importance rating to promotion.

Whether an individual is paid by the hour or by weekly salary may also be relevant to the question of employee motivation and satisfaction, partly because the mode of pay administration may carry certain status implications over and above the absolute amount paid. Related to this is whether or not a time clock is used. We were not able to find any controlled research which isolates answers to these questions. However, Weeks (1965) surveyed a number of companies which had switched at least part of their blue-collar workers from hourly to salaried pay. Of the 31 companies reporting before-after comparisons, 20 cited no change in absenteeism rates, while the rest were split approximately equally as to whether absence rates rose or fell. Since a belief that absence rates rise when hourly workers are converted to salary payment is one reason why some organizations are unwilling to attempt such a change, these data indicate that organizations may be unwisely ruling out a possible strategy for improved employee attitudes. However, it should be understood that the absence of negative effects is not evidence of positive effects. Research in this area is therefore needed.

## Conclusions About Compensation

Earlier in this chapter, conclusions were drawn on the implications of pay levels and increments. Below, we will summarize those implications in conjunction with those derived from the studies of various compensation systems.

1. Not surprisingly, the more workers are paid, the better they like it, the better they like their jobs, and the better their general state of mind. However, these benefits may not be due solely to the increased earnings but also to factors associated with pay (prestige, security, etc.).

2. Workers who are more satisfied with their pay are more likely to like their jobs better, and are less likely to quit, be absent, or strike.

3. Job performance is not appreciably better on the part of workers who are higher paid or those who are better satisfied with their pay (unless pay is linked to performance, as in 6 below).

4. Workers who are underpaid, relative to those with whom they compare themselves, are likely to be dissatisfied with their pay.

5. Workers who are overpaid, relative to their contributions, tend also to be less satisfied; those on piece or incentive rates are prone to restrict output.

6. Pay plans (incentives, bonuses, etc.) which are linked to performance usually generate higher levels of work motivation and higher levels of performance or productivity.

7. However, this is unlikely to be true unless the workers understand the relationship between their performance and their pay, and unless they are confident that increased production will not result in changes in the pay rates or standards.

8. Where the work requires close cooperation, group incentive plans generate better results in terms of productivity than individual incentives; however, in general, group plans do not appear to improve productivity as much as individual plans, particularly when the groups are large.

9. Satisfaction with pay seems to be greater if it is tied to performance; under this circumstance, the correlation between performance and satisfaction with pay is also likely

to be greater.

10. Pay-for-performance plans are not without their problems, particularly when there is job insecurity, when there are frequent changes in markets or methods, when not all important aspects of performance can be quantified, and when there is a climate of mistrust.

11. There is little firm evidence on the effects of other aspects of compensation systems, such as schedules of payment, secrecy, etc.

12. Some of the more recent issues in compensation policy include conversion of hourly to salaried basis, guaranteed annual wage, and payment on the basis of number of different tasks learned, but firm data as a guide to policy decisions are lacking.

# CHAPTER IX

## SYSTEM-WIDE STUDIES

In previous chapters, we have examined three major ways of restructuring work in order, it has been hoped, to improve both the job satisfaction and productivity of workers:  changes in the distribution of tasks, of control and of financial rewards.  There have also been experiments in which the changes in work have been so extensive that they have massively implicated more than one of the above structures, and even other kinds of changes.  These kinds of interventions essentially represent changes in the very socio-technical systems whereby productive work gets done.

A number of such system-wide changes have been described in the form of case studies.*  From these we have selected three examples on the grounds that (a) they were performed in the socio-economic culture of the U.S.A.; (b) they supply data of sufficient quantity, quality, and scope as to approximate our criteria for "prototypes"; and (c) they ostensibly differ from one another in philosophy, strategy, and methods, if not in objectives.  The three are Corning Glass (Medfield plant), Weldon Manufacturing Corp., and Scanlon Plan.  They are not offered as "models," either as to substance or methods of

---

*Many are described in Work in America (HEW, 1973), Glaser (1973), Walton (in Rosow, 1974), and Fein (1971, 1974).

inquiry, but rather as reasonably well-documented American illustrations of system-wide approaches.

Each will be described in some detail below, paying particular attention to findings pertaining to independent, "take," mediating, and dependent (outcome) variables. We will conclude with the inferences which we draw from them, as well as from the other case studies mentioned above.

## Weldon Manufacturing Company

This experiment was done in the period 1962-1964, and is reported in a book by Marrow, Bowers & Seashore (1967), and in a non-technical summary by the same authors (in Marrow, 1972). A 1969 follow-up was made by Seashore & Bowers (1970).

The title of the book is "Management by Participation," and that is the theme emphasized throughout the publications cited above. The concept of "participation" was sufficiently similar to that of Likert (1961) so that his scales were deemed appropriate to use in assessing change. However, it is clear that numerous other techniques were introduced, so that the authors also state that "the term 'sociotechnical system'... conveys much of our orientation to the Weldon case" (Marrow, Bowers & Seashore, 1967, p. 226). They used the term in the sense made popular by Trist and his associates (see for example, Emery & Trist, 1960) to refer to concern with the interdependencies of social and technical factors in organizational systems.

## Setting

The Harwood Manufacturing Company, a garment manufacturer, purchased its major competitor, the Weldon Company, in 1961. The two companies were similar in products, manufacturing methods, and size. However, whereas Harwood had a history of emphasizing participative management, Weldon's management was described as authoritarian. And although Weldon, like Harwood, had a profitable history, it was suffering from many signs of inefficiency at the time of the merger. The new owners therefore undertook to shape Weldon more on the Harwood model, with the effort being shared among local management at the Weldon plant, the new owners, and a variety of technical consultants and change agents.

Observations and measurements were made at Weldon by a research team from the University of Michigan at the inception of the change program in 1962 and again in 1964. Parallel data were gathered at the Harwood plant, which served as a comparison if not quite a control situation. A follow-up study was performed at Weldon in 1969 to check on the durability of changes.

Operators and some other production workers were paid on the basis of piece rates and other wage incentives. The Weldon plant was not unionized until January 1, 1964. It had about 1,000 employees at peak periods.

## Independent Variables

The changes carried out at various times between 1962 and 1964 may be conveniently grouped into those addressed to rank-and-file workers on the "shop floor" and those addressed to managers and supervisors.

Shop Floor Changes. The principal actions directed at operators and production workers may be listed as follows:

- Revised plant layout and organization of production lines.
- Attitude surveys of production employees in 1962, 1963, and 1964.
- Reorganization of the shipping room.
- Conversion of compensation system in cutting and shipping rooms from hourly to incentive basis.
- Training program for new operators (abandoned in less than a year as unsuccessful).
- Coaching of low-performing operators, helping also to improve incentive earnings.
- Program of vision and dexterity tests for selecting new workers.
- Tightening of termination policy for chronic absentees.
- Tightening of termination policy for low-performing operators.
- Vestibule training program for new operators and occasional retraining of experienced operators.

- Increase in pay rates of one of the production
  units to make up for decreased earnings due to
  increased complexity of work.
- Group problem-solving in sessions involving supervisors, assistant supervisors, and operators.
- Unionization and collective bargaining as of
  January 1, 1964.

Changes in Supervision and Management. The principal
changes directed to supervisors and managers appear to have
included:

- Increase in the number of supervisors, mainly by
  enlarging the supervisory role of assistant
  supervisors.
- Training and consultation with supervisors and
  assistant supervisors on work administration
  and human relations.
- Increasing the decision-making authority of
  supervisors and assistant supervisors.
- Sensitivity training of top executives and managers both from the New York headquarters and the
  Weldon plant.
- "Team building" of Weldon managers, mainly via
  meetings with and discussion of reports to the new
  owners, their representatives, and consultants.

Seashore & Bowers (1970) reported that there were further
improvements in the work system, production facilities, and

organizational activities between 1964 and 1969, at a "normal and permanent" rate.

## Take Variables

We now address ourselves to the evidence of whether the change efforts as outlined above in fact led to modifications in how workers, supervisors and managers experienced or described their work situations. Again, it is useful to divide this question into perceptions of the production workers, and those of supervisory and managerial personnel.

Production Workers. On two occasions, once in 1963 and again in 1964, workers were specifically asked by questionnaire about whether they perceived changes in their work situations as compared to a year earlier. Questions covered perceived changes in supervision, in job assignment, in equipment, in workplace, in product worked on, and in work group. The authors concluded from the data that: "The striking result... is that in both years -- periods of very extensive changes -- only a minority of employees recalled having personally experienced each of the possible changes. Furthermore, about half of those having any given change said that it made no significant difference for them, the remainder splitting about equally in saying the change was for the better or for the worse" (Marrow, Bowers & Seashore, 1967, p. 199).

Another kind of change data consists of the same measure obtained at different times. Such data exist with respect to workers' perceptions of the amount and gradient of control,

341

measured by means of the Michigan "control graph," in 1962, 1963, and 1964. Although the perceptions of production workers were not separated from those of supervisors, the former were much more numerous and would dominate the averages. Those averages showed very little shift from year to year either on total amount or in gradient of control at Weldon. A repetition of the assessment in 1969 showed some flattening in perceived control among the three echelons of management, but no appreciable change in the influence of workers; the overall amount of control also remained constant.

In brief, it would appear that Weldon production workers in general perceived little difference in the way things worked for them during the period of study, at least as regards the topics under investigation.

Supervisory and Managerial Workers. The main body of data here was derived by responses to Likert's "Profile of Organizational and Performance Characteristics" (Likert, 1961). That instrument is composed of 43 items in terms of which the respondent rates the "climate" of his organization; the 43 items are then scored in terms of the six dimensions of motivations, communications, interactions, decision making, goal setting, and control. The instrument was filled out by supervisors and managers retrospectively to describe the organization in 1962, and then again in 1964 and 1966; a gradual shift in these perceptions occurred from the "authoritarian" end of the pattern toward the region which

Likert calls "consultative" or "System 3." Ratings by
Michigan researchers approximated those of the managers in
1962; a repetition in 1969 showed that in the researchers'
judgment, the managerial system had mostly moved to the
region of "participative" or "System 4."

Another set of data on supervisory styles consisted of
the perceptions of their rank-and-file subordinates. The
latter reported no change in levels of support from their
superiors in 1964 as compared to 1962, but did report declines
in supervisors' emphasis on goal attainment, in facilitating
their subordinates' work, and in closeness of supervision. By
1969, perceptions in the last three respects showed gains to
levels above 1962. The temporary declines as of 1964 were
attributed by the investigators to shifts in responsibility
from supervisors to assistant supervisors.

## Mediating Variables

Among the numerous questionnaire items on worker attitudes were five which may be considered as direct expressions
of motivational states or effort. Their results for Weldon
workers at four different points in time are shown below:

| Item | % of Workers Agreeing | | | |
|---|---|---|---|---|
| | 1962 | 1963 | 1964 | 1969 |
| Produce what rate calls for | 44 | 50 | 67 | 53 |
| Work very hard | 47 | 53 | 67 | n.a.* |
| Expect own production to increase | 63 | 60 | 55 | 62 |
| Workers do not disapprove of high producers | 58 | 59 | 58 | 66 |
| Earnings reflect performance | 76 | 72 | 82 | n.a.* |

*(n.a. = not available.)

The mixed picture at Weldon is manifest. The results at the comparison Harwood plant in 1964 compared to 1962 showed stability for the first two items, and declines for the latter three.

Also included was an item covering motivation to remain with the company, which received affirmative response from 72% of Weldon workers in 1962, 87% in 1964, and 66% in 1969.

Similar information exists for Weldon employees' responses to four items reflecting the other major mediating construct, production capability. The following tabulation reports those findings:

| | % of Workers Agreeing | | | |
|---|---|---|---|---|
| Item | 1962 | 1963 | 1964 | 1969 |
| Company quick to improve methods | 18 | 30 | 24 | 31 |
| Company good at planning | 22 | 30 | 26 | 35 |
| Not delayed by poor service | 76 | 77 | 79 | 90 |
| Job gives good chance to do best | 71 | 60 | 78 | n.a. |

All items reflect increasing capability. The response at Harwood also improved on all four items between 1962 and 1964 (not measured in 1969).

All in all, the foregoing data do not clearly show changed levels of motivation among Weldon workers over the years, but there is some trend for an increase in the perceived capacity to perform their jobs.

Dependent Variables

These may be sub-divided into organization-wide data and data pertaining directly to production workers.

a. Organization-Wide. The data shown in Table VIII-A were reported for Weldon and for Harwood as of 1962 and 1964 (Marrow, Bowers & Seashore, 1967, p. 147).

Table IX-1

INDICATORS OF ORGANIZATION EFFECTIVENESS

| Area of Performance | Year | Weldon | Harwood |
|---|---|---|---|
| Return on invested capital (in per cent) | 1962 | -15* | 17 |
| | 1964 | 17 | 21 |
| Make-up pay (% of payroll) | 1962 | 12 | 2 |
| | 1964 | 4 | 2 |
| Production efficiency (% deviation from standard) | 1962 | -11 | 6 |
| | 1964 | 14 | 16 |
| Incentive earnings above base (% of actual pay) | 1962 | 0 | 17 |
| | 1964 | 16 | 22 |
| Operator turnover rate (monthly) | 1962 | 10 | 0.75 |
| | 1964 | 4 | 0.75 |
| Absenteeism rate (daily, for production workers) | 1962 | 6 | 3 |
| | 1964 | 3 | 3 |

*Loss.

It is apparent from those data that there were improvements in Weldon business performance between the two comparison years, and that Weldon was catching up to Harwood although the latter was continuing to improve.  Seashore & Bowers (1970) reported that Weldon continued to show improvement in return on

investment through 1968, the last year of record.  There were
also substantial gains in efficiency and volume; employee
earnings have been sustained at the level reached by 1964.  The
authors note that economic conditions during the 1962-1969
period were favorable, but that they were also favorable prior
to that when the firm was in trouble.

     b.  <u>Production Workers</u>.  The two main sets of dependent
variables for production workers were the quantity of production of machine operators at Weldon and job satisfaction questionnaire responses of samples of Weldon and Harwood non-
supervisory employees.

     1.  Production of Machine Operators.  With some ir-
regularities, production rose gradually over the 3-year period
of 1962-1964 inclusive, from a "stable low" of 89 percent of
standard to a "stable high" of about 114 percent.  There was a
trough during the middle part of 1962, and the curve appeared
to be nearing a plateau during 1964, so that the main rise
occurred between August 1962 and January 1964.  As to production since 1964, Seashore & Bowers (1970) estimated that it
had been stable, with a slight decline in 1969 because of the
recent addition of inexperienced workers.

     Although recognizing the impossibility of precisely
attributing fractions of the gain to particular ones of the
numerous changes made in independent variables, above, the
investigators nevertheless attempted to sort out causality by
analyzing the time relations between the introduction of
changes and alterations in production.  The investigators figure
that the main factors were the following (with the estimated

percentage of the total gain shown in parentheses):

| | |
|---|---|
| Coaching low-performing operators, plus earnings improvement | (37%) |
| Termination of chronic low performers | (17%) |
| Group problem-solving sessions | (10%) |
| Training of supervisory staff | (17%) |

The last of those estimates is admittedly "tenuous," a description we believe is apt, based on the evidence presented. All this leaves at least 20% of the gain not definitely attributable, but described by the investigators as probably due to a combination of the following remaining "main events": production changes; vestibule operator training; pay rate adjustment; and selection tests. The other independent variables were judged to have had negligible effects. Curiously, no effort was made to assess the impact of the changes in numbers and roles of direct supervisors which were taking place during 1963 and 1964; it seems probable that these changes had appreciable impact, too, given the general importance of supervision and the evidence that the changes had an impact on worker perceptions.

It is worth noting that the improvement in production was apparently due at least as much to factors that increased the capability of the workers as to motivational factors. This is consistent with the evidence mentioned earlier that the mediating variable of work motivation changed very little, whereas there was some increase in the measures of production capability.

2. Worker Job Satisfaction. Satisfaction items in the job attitude questionnaire administered to Weldon employees in 1962, 1963, and 1964, were grouped into five categories, with the following trends emerging:

Attitude toward company: slight improvement, but less than at Harwood.

Attitude toward job: slight improvement compared to none at Harwood.

Attitude toward fellow employees: no appreciable change either place.

Attitude toward supervisor: declined.

The changes in job satisfaction were therefore modest, at best, and it still remained mediocre both in absolute terms and relative to Harwood. Seashore & Bowers reported 1969 levels of response only for nine selected items; those either improved further or maintained 1964 levels. One exception was in the intention to remain with the company, which declined from 87% favorable in 1964 to 66% in 1969. The investigators attributed this decline in part to the presence of a larger proportion of short-service employees owing to recent expansion.

## Conclusions Regarding Weldon

The two-year intervention period served to improve the productive and economic performance of a previously mismanaged plant. However, its effects on the workers' attitudes and job satisfaction were neither marked nor consistent.

The results were associated with the following effects
on mediating variables:

- Negligible or mixed changes in worker reports
  of motivation.
- Reports of increased worker capability to produce.
- Self-reports of increased motivation of managers.

The factors which appear to have been mainly responsible
for these effects include a variety of shop-floor practices
such as improved operator selection, training, and coaching,
adjustments in production methods and in pay rates, and
changes in first-line supervision; at the managerial level, the
main changes included team training, training in supervisory
methods, and increased participation.

All in all, the experiment represented not so much an
integrated "system" as a pragmatic spectrum of changes
featuring standard improvements in production and personnel
management in the factory, coupled with team-building and
participation among managers. These steps served to improve
the efficiency and profitability of the plant, but without much
measurable improvement in the quality of the lives of workers,
save in the form of higher earnings.

Although the Weldon experience appears to be rather widely
applicable, two possibly limiting circumstances should be noted
about its onset: (1) the plant had been plagued by a host
of inefficiencies and had been "run into the ground" by an
entrepreneurial rather than professional management; (2) it

was not unionized until after the experiment was well under way.

## Corning Glass (Medfield, Mass. Plant)

This study, done in the latter 1960's, has been reported
in a set of papers by Michael Beer and Edgar F. Huse (Beer,
1969; Beer & Huse, 1970; Huse & Beer, 1971; Beer & Huse, 1972),
the 1971 paper providing the best over-all picture for the
non-technical reader. Beer & Huse refer to their work as
"organization development," but unlike many "OD" proponents, the
authors make a point of eclecticism, i.e., readiness "to
employ and integrate a wide variety of OD approaches in order
to improve the quality and profitability of operations"
(1971, p. 104).

### Setting

The work reported was done in a small plant of a large
multi-plant corporation. The plant manufactured a variety
of electronics instruments for laboratory use and, at the time
the program began in 1966, was organized in a conventional
fashion. It had at that time about 35 hourly employees, 15
technical and clerical personnel, and 8 professional and
managerial personnel.

### Independent Variables

Over time, numerous changes were made, the chief ones of
interest being summarized below:

a.  Job re-design, aimed at giving individual workers more opportunity to handle a whole job, entailing planning, doing, and controlling of their own work, with the objective of increasing employee job investment.

b.  Autonomous  work groups, aimed at creating integrated and cohesive  teams having total responsibility for a particular product or activity, with the objective of furthering identification with a particular group and/or product.

c.  Increased participation and influence by means of:

(1) direct involvement of  employees in problems of production, quality, layout, and methods;

(2) mutual goal-setting, coupled with feedback on performance;

(3) increased communication and group problem-solving among management.

d.  Changes in plant-wide organization structure, including:

(1) formation of a "matrix organization," to integrate more closely groups in different but related goals and missions;

(2) "flattening" the structure by eliminating a layer of supervision and reducing by one-third the number of first-line supervisors.

e.  Changes toward a more "merit-based" pay system for the salaried clerical and technical employees, "to reinforce and legitimize an escalating climate of  work involvement."

(However, the authors confess that in general, appropriate
revisions in compensation methods and levels were not worked
out to parallel the objective and subjective increases in
effort and performance, and that this later became a source
of problems.)

## Take and Mediating Variables

Although the  reports make frequent allusion to changes
in how people perceived their work and to increased job involvement and motivation, no detailed or systematic data are
furnished.  However, we believe that these claims warrant
greater acceptance than similar ones often made in case reports.
The latter are typically merely unsystematic retrospective
impressions on the part of managerial and staff people, usually themselves involved in effecting the changes, whereas
those in the Corning study were based, at least in part. on the
observations of a staff researcher whose job it was to gather
interview and other data on what was going on; the "change
agents" also kept detailed notes of their observations.

## Dependent Variables

The several publications cite a variety of changes in
performance, for different periods of time and in different
departments.  The data are not typically provided in precise
form, nor are the methods of measurement or the level of significance of the changes usually specified.  Because of the
aforementioned impossibility, in our judgment, of isolating

specific causes and effects, we are citing the changes below as evidence of the kinds of impact the "eclectic" approach produced, rather than as proof of the effects of any given technique.

a.  Hot Plate Department:

   (1)  In 6 months following change in job design vs. preceding 6 months -

   Productivity increased 84%.

   Controllable rejects decreased from 23% to 1%.

   Absenteeism declined from 8% to 1%.

   (2)  An inspector position was eliminated, thereby saving costs.

b.  Glass Shop:

   (1)  Productivity increase of 20% over unspecified period.

c.  Materials Control Department:

   (1)  Parts shortage list "showed a considerable net decrease."

d.  Instrument Department (Unspecified period):

   (1)  Productivity increase of 17% (worth $1,500 per year per worker).

   (2)  Quality improvement of 50%.

   (3)  Absenteeism reduced by "over 50%."

   (4)  Four new assemblies introduced, with only slight drop in productivity (previously had been appreciably greater).

e.  Plant-wide:

>    (1)  Elimination of position of manufacturing manager.
>
>    (2)  Elimination of 1/3 of first-line supervisor positions.
>
>    (3)  Incremental profit "one of best among 50 plants in corporation."
>
>    (4)  Turnover among female employees less than 1%, compared to area rate of 3.5%.
>
>    (N.B.: Baseline data for comparison not supplied for last two measures.)

Comments: The study is technically deficient in several respects, especially the absence of control or comparison data, the small numbers of workers or groups involved in most of the changes, the absence of assessments of statistical signifi- cance of changes, the lack of detail in reporting many of the results, and the absence of quantitative data on take and mediating variables. One would also like to see some assess- ment of the cost of making the changes, so that cost-benefit considerations could be weighed. Finally, there are some situational limitations on external validity, including the small size of the plant, the small-town, female cultural back- ground of the workers, and the absence of a union.

Nevertheless, it is apparent that some impressive im- provements have been made in plant economic performance and that the attitudes of workers have improved; those gains appear to have been due in large part to increased motivation and commitment on the part of employees at all levels of the organization, although it seems likely that capabilities to perform were also increased in some instances; and finally, the changes in operating policies and practices which were responsible for the above improvements appear to be due to a combination of the structural variables described in earlier chapters: enlargement of work roles, increasing the total amount and balance of authority, and (to a limited extent) redesign of the compensation scheme toward a pay-for-merit system. Additional factors which appeared to play a part were also of both the technical and social sorts.

## Scanlon Plan

Our third illustration will differ from the other two in that it will describe not a particular case study, but the distillation of a number of case studies supplemented by a set of survey data, all bearing on the system called the "Scanlon Plan." Readers interested in reviewing specific cases will find a number of them described and cited in the two major compendia on the Scanlon Plan (Lesieur, 1958; Frost, Wakeley & Ruh, 1974).

### Setting

The Scanlon Plan (SP) grew out of the experiences of Joseph N. Scanlon in a Pennsylvania steel mill in which he was a union officer. The mill was faced with the prospect of going

out of business during the Great Depression, and union demands
for higher wages and improved working conditions compounded
the problems. Scanlon induced the company president to agree
to a meeting with Clinton S. Golden at the Pittsburgh office
of the Steelworkers Union. Golden recommended that they
return to the mill and attempt to enlist the aid of every
employee in eliminating waste, improving efficiency, reducing
cost, and improving quality in order to help the company sur-
vive. Under Scanlon's leadership and with the cooperation of
management, this was done. The company not only survived,
but was soon able to grant wage increases and otherwise to
improve the conditions of employment.

Scanlon worked the next few years at the union headquarters and then accepted a position at M.I.T., where
Douglas McGregor had become interested in his ideas and
methods. These were then further formulated and refined by
Scanlon and his M.I.T. colleagues through implementation in a
number of companies, among the early ones being LaPointe
Machine Tool, Market Forge, Tubular Rivet, Towle Silver, Cox
Foundry, and Stromberg-Carlson. Some of those, and a number
of later ones, have been reported as cases for which summaries
and/or citations may be found in the references given above.
There is now an association of its practitioners, called the
Scanlon Plan Associates, but we have not been able to locate
a statistical picture of the use of the Plan.

## Independent Variables

One reason for our decision to report a distillation of various studies rather than a single case is that SP does not take identical forms in all companies. As observed in Frost, Wakely & Ruh (1974, p. 1):

"The Scanlon Plan is a philosophy, a theory of organization, and a set of management principles. As a philosophy, the Scanlon Plan rests on the assumptions that people prefer to express themselves fully in all situations including work situations and that, when they do express themselves, they can be constructive and supportive of other people and the groups to which they belong. The theory which follows from this position states that the basic philosophy is best served when all members of an organization participate as fully as they can in the activities of the organization and when they are equitably rewarded for their participation. All principles of management that encourage people to identify with their work group, that encourage people to participate as much as they can, and that continually focus on equitably rewarding all members of the organization are seen as ways of applying the Scanlon Plan philosophy."

Although the particulars of implementation are variable, two basic sets of independent variables are essential:

1. Increased opportunities to participate in improving productivity.

2. Sharing more widely and equitably in the financial

rewards of any productivity improvement.

Not infrequently, other elements deemed to be consistent
with the above are also incorporated. To illustrate, Donnelly
Mirrors, Inc., which has been using its version of SP for about
20 years, is characterized by the following features (Glaser,
1973):

1. Competitive basic wages.

2. Payment of productivity improvement bonuses which
   average 10% per month.

3. Payment of all workers on a salaried basis and
   elimination of time-clocks.

4. Organization of workers into teams of 15 to 20, each
   having responsibility for some aspect of the work,
   including setting goals and plans, determining production methods, hiring new members, handling disciplinary cases, and helping to select supervisors.

5. Organization of supervisors and managers according to
   Likert's "linking-pin" concept, and their participation in managerial decision-making.

## Take Variables

Although the case reports frequently cite instances of
increased participation and improved work methods, they are
anecdotal and qualitative in nature. The main body of systematic facts bearing on what are the perceived effects of SP
comes from a set of studies jointly sponsored by the Scanlon
Plan Associates and Michigan State University, and summarized
by Frost, Wakeley & Ruh (1974, pp. 156-191).

The data generated by those studies included questionnaires received from 2,636 employees from 27 plants of 6
companies, all of which had adopted SP at one time or another.
Several of the items  may be viewed as employee perceptions of
the impact of SP on them; thus, most respondents reported that
SP "increases their knowledge about the company" and "provides
the opportunity to learn more about their jobs," but not that
it "allows them to really influence decisions which affect
their jobs."

Thus, at least among these workers, those findings imply
that SP may be usually experienced by workers more as a mechanism for increasing their technical and cognitive competence
rather than their influence.  However, the findings are
based on only a few items.

## Mediating Variables

Some of the items of the same survey bear testimony as
to whether motivation and ability-related factors were perceived by employees to have been affected.  Thus most of them
report that SP:  "encourages hard work," and "helps them to do
a better job," and also that the "Committees improve company
efficiency."

These limited data suggest that SP increases both work
motivation and capability.  Some confirmation of this interpretation is furnished by comparing the ratings given to
subordinates by managers of 8 organizations which had tried

and later abandoned SP, and ratings given to subordinates in 10 companies in which SP was still in operation. The latter ratings were significantly higher on such motivational traits as Responsibility, Dependability, Pride in Performance, and Initiative, which appear to have motivational components. The scales did not cover aspects of capability which might be expected to be affected by SP, such as skill or workmanship, except perhaps for Judgment, which also improved, and Creativity, which did not. A cautionary note here is that since this is a correlational analysis, it is as plausible to believe that SP doesn't work as well when managers have less confidence in their subordinates as it is to believe that better SPs have more favorable effects on employees' motivation and ability than do poorer SPs.

Further confirmation of the potential motivational benefits from SP comes from certain other scales included in the same employee survey described above. Those scales covered Job Involvement, Work Motivation, and Identification with Organization. Employee perceptions of level of participation in SP correlated significantly with their motivational attitudes as follows:

| | Correlations | |
|---|---|---|
| Scale | For Individuals | For Plants |
| Job Involvement | .43 | .88 |
| Work Motivation | .30 | .56 |
| Identification | .40 | .73 |

The first column of coefficients represents the correlations among 2,488 individual employees, whereas the second is composed of the correlations for the average responses among 15 plants. The foregoing correlations between participation and motivation were not appreciably different for individuals of different occupational status, educational level, size of community, or personal values. In short, these data indicate that the more workers experienced participation under SP, the higher their motivation.

It should be noted that these data came from organizations that all employed SP. Hence, they are not relevant to the question of whether SP is more highly motivating than other plans. What they do indicate is that, to the degree that employees see themselves as having power and influence under SP, they are likely to be more highly motivated. Coupled with the earlier finding that most employees do not experience SP as really providing them with significant influence over job-related decisions, it implies that SP does not necessarily serve to increase employee influence and motivation, and that there are some SP implementations which are apparently more effective in these regards than others.

## Dependent Variables

Case reports of the Scanlon Plan have frequently cited increased productive efficiency and associated increased employee earnings; most of them are summarized in the previously cited references. As an example, the Donnelly Mirrors case previously cited reports that employee productivity bonuses average 10% of base rates, and that in 20 years the level of productivity per worker has doubled, tardiness has fallen from 6% to less than 1%, and absenteeism has decreased from 5% to 1.5%.

As a further illustration, Puckett (in Lesieur, 1958, p. 113) has reported the following results from 10 studies where productive efficiency was compared with a base period for two years following installation of SP:

PERCENTAGE INCREASES IN PRODUCTIVITY

| Company | First-Year Relative Efficiency (1) | Second-Year Relative Efficiency (2) | Two-Year Average-Relative Efficiency (Unweighted) (3) |
|---------|------|------|------|
| A | 14.9 | 10.9 | 12.9 |
| B | 21.9 | 12.7 | 17.3 |
| C | 16.7 | 13.2 | 15.0 |
| D | 36.7 | 29.3 | 33.0 |
| E | 28.9 | 49.4 | 39.2 |
| F | 32.9 | 42.9 | 37.9 |
| G | 38.7 | 25.1 | 31.9 |
| H | 14.1 | 16.5 | 15.3 |
| I | 12.9 | 23.2 | 18.1 |
| J | 6.8 | 13.7 | 10.3 |
| Average (Unweighted) | 22.5 | 23.7 | 23.1 |

As mentioned previously, however, such case reports have not furnished sufficient data to illuminate why the results are being achieved, nor whether the quality of working life is appreciably different.

The Michigan State studies reported by Frost, Wakeley & Ruh (1974) did suggest that in some instances SP does result in improved worker motivation and also increased capability to produce. However, when they compared work motivation measures with individual productivity measures, absenteeism, and turnover in two plants of a large company, only turnover was found to be significantly correlated with their measure of motivation and even that correlation was not high (-.17).

As to whether SP contributes to improved job satisfaction, firm evidence is lacking although the claim has been made. Frost, Wakeley & Ruh (1974) did report some questionnaire data that bear on the question, but it is both ambiguous and indirect. Most of the 2,636 respondents from 6 manufacturing companies having SP plans felt that SP "increases their knowledge about the company" and "increases their trust and confidence in management" and that it "has helped this company's financial position." However, as previously noted, most do not see their power appreciably increased, and they also say that "the Plan may be a way for management to get more out of the workers."

Finally, it should be noted that SP has not succeeded everywhere. We have already alluded to the fact that a number

of companies which tried it later discontinued it, although
the reasons have not been systematically explained. Frost,
Wakely & Ruh (1974, pp. 145-148) have summarized three case
reports in which SP failed to live up to expectations. Fein
(1971) analyzed the Kaiser Steel experience with a version of
SP, and concluded that it was not living up to expectations
for a variety of reasons, chief among them being that the productivity payouts were less than those earned by workers under
the former incentive plan, compounded by the large size of the
plant and the fact that earnings were based on plant-wide
rather than individual or group performance. Fein (1974) has
also criticized the usual SP productivity measures as being
too broad.

Strauss & Sayles (1957) have examined situational factors
which may be necessary to account for the success of SP.
These include:

- high interaction and cooperation among all
  parties involved;
- management's acceptance of criticism and suggestions; which in turn depends on
- the absence of threat;
- free flow of adequate information on production
  and costs;
- ability to expand sales so as to absorb increased production;

> - the larger the company, the more important for
> departments to have their own performance goals
> in conjunction with overall goals.

In addition, it has been pointed out that workers and management must feel the need for such a plan; financial difficulty is an example of, but not necessarily the only condition generating such a need.

## Conclusions Regarding Scanlon Plan

There is evidence from a number of companies that introduction of some version of the Scanlon Plan was followed by improved productive and economic performance. However, there is no convincing data on changes in workers' satisfaction.

Sparse data on mediating variables suggest that the productivity benefits of SP may come as much from improvements in capability generated by suggestions as from increased motivation. The key independent variables responsible for such changes include (1) a mechanism for worker participation in plans for improving productivity and (2) a method for sharing the economic rewards of those improvements.

However, SP has not been universally successful even in the economic domain, which has resulted in its discontinuation in a number of instances where it was tried. Failures seem to have been due to major flaws in the design or implementation of one or both of the above two key independent variables. It is probable that not all or even most organizations provide the circumstances required for a successful Scanlon Plan.

## Conclusions from System-Wide Studies

Although individually the cases are flawed, as we have noted, by lack of experimental controls, incompleteness of findings, and inadequacies in measurement and analysis, they collectively furnish convergent results which are distinctly suggestive. Moreover, in stating our specific conclusions below, we draw further support from other system-wide studies, as cited at the beginning of this chapter. The main implications we derive from all of those sources include:

1. Changes of the nature and magnitude of those represented in these studies can have major effects in raising the productivity and improving the economic performance of manufacturing plants.

2. Those kinds of changes may have beneficial effects on the job satisfaction of the workers, although this finding is not as well documented nor does its magnitude appear to be as great as the effect on productivity. In short, whereas such programs have not generated impressive proof of improvements in job satisfaction, it is clear that their productivity benefits have not been achieved at the expense of job satisfaction.

3. This is not to say that workers are not motivationally affected by such programs, for there is some evidence that they work harder and that their job involvement and commitment to work goals may be enhanced, although again this evidence is not strong or consistent.

4. The beneficial effects of system-wide programs on

employee productivity are also mediated by improvements in production capability, perhaps even more than by the motivational changes.

5. The system elements that appear usually to be responsible for the above effects include the following:

(a) mechanisms whereby employees participate more actively in proposing and making decisions affecting their work and their jobs;

(b) in addition to (a), further enlargements in the scope of duties and responsibilities of rank-and-file workers;

(c) increased participation also by managers and supervisors in decisions affecting their own and related operations;

(d) reduction in the number and length of channels of communication and authority, such as by "flattening" the organization or by "linking-pin" or "matrix" arrangements;

(e) increases in financial compensation commensurate with improved performance and increased responsibility;

(f) improvements in resources (supervision, methods, and technology) so as to facilitate greater effectiveness and reduce frustrations of workers.

However, it should be noted that each case is unique: not all involve all of the foregoing elements, and many have their

own special features in addition. Moreover, the particular
techniques and mechanisms whereby these elements are affected
are usually tailored to the "personality" of each organization.
In short, these elements should be regarded more as suggested
guidelines than as a road map.

REFERENCES

Adams, J.S.  Wage inequities, productivity and work quality.
Industrial Relations, 1963(a), 3 (6), 9-16.

Adams, J.S.  Toward an understanding of inequity.  Journal of Abnormal
and Social Psychology, 1963(b), 67, 422-436.

Adams, J.S.  Injustice in social exchange.  In L. Berkowitz (Ed.),
Advances in Experimental Social Psychology.  New York:  Academic
Press, 1965.

Adams, J.S. & Jacobsen, P.  Effects of wage inequities on work quality.
Journal of Abnormal and Social Psychology, 1964, 69, 19-25.

Adams, J.S. & Rosenbaum, W.B.  The relationship of worker productivity
to cognitive dissonance about wage inequities.  Journal of
Applied Psychology, 1962, 46, 161-164.

Andrews, I.R.  Wage inequity and job performance:  An experimental study.
Journal of Applied Psychology, 1967, 51, 39-45.

Andrews, I.R. & Henry, M.M.  Management attitudes toward pay.
Industrial Relations, 1963, 3 (6), 29-39.

Armstrong, T.B.  Occupational level as an indicator of "satisfiers" and
"dissatisfiers":  A test of the Herzberg et al. theory.  Paper
presented at I.B.M. Personnel Research Conference, 1968.

Arrowwood, A.J.  Some effects on productivity of justified and unjusti-
fied levels of reward under public and private conditions.
Unpublished doctoral dissertation, University of Minnesota, 1961.

Babchuk, N. & Goode, W.J.  Work incentives in a self-determined group.
American Sociological Review, 1951, 16, 679-687.

Bachman, J.G., Smith, C.G., & Slesinger, J.A.  Control performance and
satisfaction:  An analysis of structure and individual effects.
Journal of Personality and Social Psychology, 1966, 4, 127-136.

Bass, B.M., Hurder, W.P., & Ellis, N.  Assessing Human Performance under
Stress.  (Technical Report A.F. 33, 616, 134).  Baton Rouge, La.:
Louisiana State University, 1954.

Beach, D.N., & Mahler, W.R.  Management by objectives.  In A.J. Marrow
(Ed.), The Failure of Success, N.Y. AMACOM, 1972.

Beer, M. A systems approach to organizational development. Paper presented at the American Psychological Association Convention, Washington, D.C., 1969.

Beer, M., & Gery, G.J. Pay system preferences and their correlates. Paper presented at the American Psychological Association Convention, San Francisco, 1968.

Beer, M., & Huse, E. Improving Organizational Effectiveness Through Planned Change and Development. Corning, N.Y.: Corning Glass, 1970. (Mimeo.)

Beer, M., & Huse, E.F. A systems approach to organizational development. Journal of Applied Behavioral Science, 1972, 8, 79-109.

Belcher, D.W. Wage and Salary Administration (2nd ed.). Englewood, N.J.: Prentice-Hall, 1962.

Bishop, R.C., & Hill, J.W. Effects of job enlargement and job change on contiguous but non-manipulated jobs as a function of worker status. Journal of Applied Psychology, 1971, 55, 175-181.

Blauner, R. Alienation and Freedom. Chicago: University of Chicago Press, 1964.

Bluestone, I. Worker participation in decision making. Paper presented at Institute for Policy Studies, Washington, D.C., 1973.

Bowers, D.G. Organizational control in an insurance company. Sociometry, 1964, 27, 230-244.

Bracht, G.H., & Glass, G.V. The external validity of experiments. American Educational Research Journal, 1968, 5, 437-474.

Brayfield, A.H., & Crockett, W.H. Employee attitudes and employee performance. Psychological Bulletin, 1955, 52, 396-424.

Brogden, H. & Taylor, E.K. The dollar criterion -- Applying the cost accounting concept to criterion construction. Personnel Psychology, 1950, 3, 133-154.

Brown, M.E. Identification and some conditions of organizational involvement. Administrative Science Quarterly, 1969, 14, 346-355.

Buchsbaum, H.J., et al. From conflict to cooperation. Applied Anthropology, 1946, 5, (special issue No. 4), 1-31.

Bureau of Labor Statistics. Directory of National Unions and Employee Associations, Washington, D.C., 1972.

Burke, R.J. Are Herzberg's motivators and hygienes unidimensional? Journal of Applied Psychology, 1966, 50, 317-321.

Cammann, C., & Lawler, E.E. III. Employee reactions to a pay incentive plan. Journal of Applied Psychology, 1973, 58, 163-172.

Campbell, D.T. Factors relevant to the validity of experiments in social settings. Psychological Bulletin, 1957, 54, 297-312.

Campbell, H. Group incentives. Occupational Psychology, 1952, 26, 15-21.

Campbell, J.P., Dunnette, M.D., Lawler, E.E. III., & Weick, K.E. Jr. Managerial Behavior, Performance and Effectiveness. New York: McGraw-Hill, 1970.

Carpenter, H.H. Formal organizational structural factors and perceived job satisfaction of classroom teachers. Administrative Science Quarterly, 1971, 16, 460-465.

Carroll, S.J., Jr., & Tosi, H.L., Jr. The relationship of characteristics of the review process as moderated by personality and situational factors to the success of the management-by-objectives approach. Academy of Management Proceedings, 1969, 11, 139-143.

Carroll, S.J., Jr., & Tosi, H.L., Jr. Goal characteristics and personality factors in a management-by-objectives program. Administrative Science Quarterly, 1970, 15, 295-305.

Carroll, S.J., Jr., & Tosi, H.L., Jr. Management by Objectives: Applications and Research. New York: Macmillan, 1973.

Carzo, R., Jr., & Yanouzas, J.N. Effects of flat and tall organization structure. Administrative Science Quarterly, 1969, 14, 178-191.

Centers, R., & Bugental, D.E. Intrinsic and extrinsic job motivation among different segments of the working population. Journal of Applied Psychology, 1966, 50, 193-200.

Centers, R., & Cantril, H. Income satisfaction and income aspiration. Journal of Abnormal and Social Psychology, 1946, 41, 64-69.

Chamberlain, N.W. The Union Challenge to Management Control. New York: Harper, 1948.

Clark, J.V. A preliminary investigation of some unconscious assumptions affecting labor efficiency in eight supermarkets. Unpublished doctoral dissertation, Harvard University, 1958.

Coch, L., & French, J.R.P., Jr. Overcoming resistance to change. Human Relations, 1948, 1, 512-532.

Cureton, E.E., & Katzell, R.A. A further analysis of the relations among job performance and situational variables. Journal of Applied Psychology, 1962, 46, 230.

Dale, E. Greater Productivity through Labor-Management Cooperation. New York: American Management Association, 1949.

Dalton, G.W. Motivation and control in organizations. In G.W. Dalton, & P.R. Lawrence (Eds.). Motivation and Control in Organizations. Homewood, Ill.: Irwin/Dorsey, 1971

Dalton, G.W., Barnes, L.B., & Zaleznik, A. The Distribution of Authority in Formal Organizations. Boston: Division of Research, Graduate School of Business Administration, Harvard University, 1968.

Dalton, M. The industrial rate-buster: A characterization. Applied Anthropology, 1948, 7, 5-18.

Davis, L.E. Job design and productivity: A new approach. Personnel, 1957, 33, 418-430.

Davis, L.E. The design of jobs. Industrial Relations, 1966, 6 (1), 21-45.

Davis, L.E., & Valfer, E.S. Studies in supervisory job design. Human Relations, 1966, 19, 339-352.

Derber, M., et al. Labor-Management Relations in Illini City (2 vols.). Champaign, Ill.: Institute of Labor and Industrial Relations, University of Illinois, 1953 and 1954.

Dettleback, W., & Kraft, P. Organization change through job enrichment. Training and Development Journal, 1971, 25, 2-6.

Dubin, R., Homans, G.C., Mann, F.C., & Miller, D.C. Leadership and Productivity. San Francisco: Chandler, 1965.

Dunnette, M.D., Campbell, J.P., & Hakel, M.D. Factors contributing to job satisfaction and job dissatisfaction in six occupational groups. Organizational Behavior and Human Performance, 1967, 2, 143-174.

Emery, F.E., & Trist, E.L. Socio-technical systems. In C.W. Churchman, & M. Verhulst (Eds.), Management Sciences, Models and Techniques. New York: Pergamon, 1960.

Etzioni, E. Organizational control structure. In J.G. March (Ed.), Handbook of Organizations. Chicago: Rand McNally, 1965.

Evans, E.E., & Laseau, V.N. My job contest. Personnel Psychology, Monograph No. 1, 1950.

Ewen, R.B. Some determinants of job satisfaction: A study of the generalizability of Herzberg's theory. Journal of Applied Psychology, 1964, 48, 161-163.

Ewen, R.B., Smith, P.C., Hulin, C.L., & Locke, E.A. An empirical test of the Herzberg two-factor theory. Journal of Applied Psychology, 1966, 50, 544-550.

Farris, G. Organizational factors and individual performance: A longitudinal study. Journal of Applied Psychology, 1969, 53, 87-92.

Fein, M. Motivation for Work. New York: American Institute of Industrial Engineers, 1971.

Fein, M. The real needs and goals of blue collar workers. The Conference Board Record, 1973 (February), 26-33.

Fein, M. Rational Approaches to Raising Productivity. Norcross, Georgia: American Institute of Industrial Engineers, 1974.

Flamholtz, F. Toward a theory of human resource value in formal organizations. The Accounting Review, 1972, 47, 666-677.

Fleishman, E.A. Attitude versus skill factors in work group productivity. Personnel Psychology, 1965, 18, 253-266.

Fleishman, E.A., & Hunt, J.G. (Eds.). Current Developments in the Study of Leadership. Carbondale, Ill.: Southern Illinois University, 1973.

Ford, R.N. Motivation Through the Work Itself. New York: American Management Association, 1969.

Form, W. Auto workers and their machines: A study of work, factory, and job satisfaction in four countries. Social Forces, 1973, 52, 1-16.

Foulkes, F.K. Creating More Meaningful Work. New York: American Management Association, 1969.

Fox, J.B., & Scott, J.F. Absenteeism: Management's Problem. Boston: Harvard Graduate School of Business Administration, 1943.

Frederiksen, N., Jensen, O., & Beaton, A.E. Prediction of Organizational Behavior. New York: Pergamon, 1972.

French, J.R.P., Jr. Field experiments: Changing group productivity. In J.G. Miller (Ed.), Experiments in Social Process. New York: McGraw-Hill, 1950.

French, J.R.P., Jr., et al. Employee participation in a program of industrial change. Personnel, 1958, 35, 16-29.

French, J.R.P., Kay, E., & Meyer, H.H. Participation in the appraisal system. Human Relations, 1966, 19, 3-20.

Friedlander, F. Underlying sources of job satisfaction. Journal of Applied Psychology, 1963, 47, 246-250.

Friedlander, F. Job characteristics as satisfiers and dissatisfiers. Journal of Applied Psychology, 1964, 48, 388-392.

Friedlander, F. Relationships between the importance and the satisfaction of various environmental factors. Journal of Applied Psychology, 196 , 49, 160-164.

Friedlander, F., & Walton, E. Positive and negative motivations toward work. Administrative Science Quarterly, 1964, 9, 194-207.

Friedman, A., & Goodman, P.S. Wage inequity, self-qualifications, and productivity. Organizational Behavior and Human Performance, 1967, 2, 406-417.

Frost, C.F., Wakeley, J.H., & Ruh, R.A. The Scanlon Plan for Organization Development: Identity, Participation, and Equity. East Lansing, Michigan: Michigan State University Press, 1974.

Gay, E.G., et al. Manual for the Minnesota Importance Questionnaire. Minneapolis: Industrial Relations Center, University of Minnesota, 1971.

Gellerman, S.W. Motivation and Productivity. New York: American Management Association, 1963.

Gellerman, S. Motivating men with money. Fortune, 1968, 77 (3), 144 ff.

Giles, B.A., & Barrett, G.V. Utility of merit increases. Journal of Applied Psychology, 1971, 55, 103-109.

Glaser, E.M. Improving the Quality of Work Life...And in the Process, Improving Productivity. Los Angeles: Human Interaction Research Institute, 1973 (in preparation).

Gomberg, W. A Trade Union Analysis of Time Study. Chicago: Science Research Associates, 1948.

Gomberg, W. The trouble with democratic management. Trans-Action, 1966, 3 (5), 30-35.

Gottlieb, B., & Kerr, W.A. An experiment in industrial harmony. Personnel Psychology, 1950, 3, 445-453.

Greene, C.N. Causal connections among manager's merit pay, job satisfaction, and performance. Journal of Applied Psychology, 1973, 58, 95-100.

Guion, R.M. A note on organizational climate. Organizational Behavior and Human Performance, 1973, 9, 120-125.

Gurin, G., Veroff, J., & Feld, S. Americans View Their Mental Health. New York: Basic Books, 1960.

Hackman, J.R., & Lawler, E.E. III. Employee reactions to job characteristics. Journal of Applied Psychology, 1971, 55, 259-286.

Haire, M., Ghiselli, E.E., & Porter, L.W. Psychological research on pay: An overview. Industrial Relations, 1963, 3, 3-8.

Hall, D., & Lawler, E.E. Job characteristics and pressures and organizational integration of professionals. Administrative Science Quarterly, 1970, 15, 271-281.

Harbison, F.H., & Coleman, J.R. Goals and Strategy in Collective Bargaining. New York: Harper, 1951.

Healy, J.J. (Ed.) Creative Collective Bargaining: Meeting Today's Challenges to Labor-Management Relations. Englewood Cliffs, N.J.: Prentice-Hall, 1965.

Henle, P. Economic effects: Reviewing the evidence. In J. Rosow (Ed.), The Worker and the Job. Englewood Cliffs, N.J.: Prentice-Hall, 1974.

Herzberg, F. Work and the Nature of Man. Cleveland: World, 1966.

Herzberg, F. One more time: How do you motivate employees? Harvard Business Review, 1968, 46 (1), 53-62.

Herzberg, F., Mausner, B., Peterson, R.O., & Capwell, D.F. Job Attitudes: Review of Research and Opinion. Pittsburgh: Psychological Service of Pittsburgh, 1957.

Herzberg, F., Mausner, B., & Snyderman, B. The Motivation to Work. New York: Wiley, 1959.

Hickson, D.J. Motives of work people who restrict their output. Occupational Psychology, 1961, 35, 110-126.

Hill, A.S., & Thickett, J.M.B. Batch size, cycle time, and setting-time as determinants of productivity in skilled machinery work. Occupational Psychology, 1966, 40, 83-89.

Hinrichs, J.R. Correlates of employee evaluations of pay increases. Journal of Applied Psychology, 1969, 53, 481-489.

Hinrichs, J.R., & Mischkind, L.A. Empirical and theoretical limitations of the two-factor hypothesis of job satisfaction. Journal of Applied Psychology, 1967, 51, 191-200.

Homans, G.C. Status among clerical workers. Human Organization, 1953, 12, 5-10.

Homans, G.C. Social Behavior: Its Elementary Forms. New York: Harcourt, Brace, & World, 1961.

House, R.J., & Wigdor, L.A. Herzberg's dual factor theory of job satisfaction and motivation: A review of the evidence and a criticism. Personnel Psychology, 1967, 20, 369-390.

Hulin, C.L. Job satisfaction and turnover in a female clerical population. Journal of Applied Psychology, 1966, 50, 280-285.

Hulin, C.L. Effects of changes in job satisfaction levels on employee turnover. Journal of Applied Psychology, 1968, 52, 122-126.

Hulin, C.L. & Blood, M.R. Job enlargement, individual differences and worker responses. Psychological Bulletin, 1968, 69, 41-55.

Hulin, C.L., & Smith, P.C. An empirical investigation of two implications of the two-factor theory of job satisfaction. Journal of Applied Psychology, 1967, 51, 396-402.

Hunnius, G., Garson, G.D., & Case, J. (Eds.). Workers Control. New York: Random House, 1973.

Huse, E., & Beer, M. Eclectic approach to organizational development. Harvard Business Review, 1971, 49 (5), 103-112.

Indik, B. Organization size and member participation. Human Relations, 1965, 18, 339-350.

Ivancevich, J.M. An analysis of control, bases of control, and satisfaction in an organizational setting. Academy of Management Journal, 1970, 13, 427-436.

Ivancevich, J.M. A longitudinal assessment of management by objectives. Administrative Science Quarterly, 1972, 17, 126-138.

Ivancevich, J.M., Donnelly, J.H., & Lyon, H.L. A study of the impact of management by objectives on perceived need satisfaction. Personnel Psychology, 1970, 23, 139-151.

James, J. An experimental study of tensions in work behavior. University of California Publications in Culture and Society. 1951, 2, 203-242.

Janson, R. Job enrichment trial -- data processing department analysis and results in an insurance organization. Paper presented at the International Conference on the Quality of Working Life, Arden House, Harriman, N.Y., 1972.

Jaques, E. Equitable Compensation. New York: Wiley, 1961.

Jenkins, D.J. Job Power. Garden City, N.Y.: Doubleday, 1973.

Jones, L.V., & Jeffrey, T.E. A quantitative analysis of expressed preferences for compensation plans. Journal of Applied Psychology, 1964, 48, 201-210.

Kahn, R.L., Wolfe, D.M., Quinn, R.P., & Snoek, J.D. Organizational Stress. New York: Wiley, 1964.

Katz, D., & Kahn, R.L. Human organization and worker motivation. In L.R. Tripp (Ed.), Industrial Productivity. Madison, Wis.: Industrial Relations Research Association, 1951.

Katz, D., & Kahn, R.L. The Social Psychology of Organizations. New York: Wiley, 1966.

Katzell, R.A. Contrasting systems of work organization. American Psychologist, 1962, 17, 102-108.

Katzell, R.A. Personal values, job satisfaction, and job behavior. In H. Borow (Ed.), Man in a World at Work. Boston: Houghton, Mifflin, 1964.

Katzell, R.A., Barrett, R.S., & Parker, T.C. Job satisfaction, job per- formance, and situational characteristics. Journal of Applied Psychology, 1961, 45, 65-72.

Kay, E., Meyer, H.H., & French, J.R.P., Jr. The effect of threat in a performance appraisal interview. Journal of Applied Psychology, 1965, 49, 311-317.

Kennedy, J.E., & O'Neill, H.E. Job content and workers' opinions. Journal of Applied Psychology, 1958, 42, 372-375.

Kerr, W.A. Dual allegiance and emotional acceptance-rejection in industry. Personnel Psychology, 1954, 7, 59-66.

Kornhauser, A. Mental Health of the Industrial Worker. New York: Wiley, 1965.

Kraft, W.P., Jr. Job enrichment for production typists: A case study. In J.R. Maher (Ed.), New Perspectives in Job Enrichment. New York: Van Nostrand,Reinhold, 1971.

Lawler, E.E., III. Managers' perceptions of their subordinates' pay and of their superiors' pay. Personnel Psychology, 1965, 18, 413-422.

Lawler, E.E., III. Managers' attitudes toward how their pay is and should be determined. Journal of Applied Psychology, 1966, 50, 273-279.

Lawler, E.E., III. Secrecy about management compensation: Are there hidden costs? Organizational Behavior and Human Performance, 1967, 2, 182-189.

Lawler, E.E., III. Pay and Organizational Effectiveness. New York: McGraw-Hill, 1971.

Lawler, E.E., III. Motivation in Work Organizations. Monterey, Calif.: Brooks/Cole, 1973.

Lawler, E.E., III., & Hackman, J.R. The impact of employee participation in the development of pay incentive plans. Journal of Applied Psychology, 1969, 53, 467-471.

Lawler, E.E., III., Hackman, J.R., & Kaufman, S. Effects of job redesign: A field experiment. Journal of Applied Social Psychology, 1973, 3, 39-48.

Lawler, E.E., III., Koplin, C.A., Young, T.F., & Faden, J.A. Inequity reduction over time in an induced overpayment situation. Organizational Behavior and Human Performance, 1968, 3, 253-268.

Lawler, E.E., III., & O'Gara, P.W. The effects of inequity produced by underpayment on work output, work quality, and attitudes toward the work. Journal of Applied Psychology, 1967, 51, 403-410.

Lawrence, L., & Smith, P.C. Group decision and employee participation. Journal of Applied Psychology, 1955, 39, 334-337.

Lesieur, F.G. (Ed.). The Scanlon Plan. Cambridge: Technology Press, 1958.

Leventhal, G.S.,et al. Inequity and interpersonal conflict: Reward allocation and secrecy about reward as methods of preventing conflict. Journal of Personality and Social Psychology, 1972, 23, 88-102.

Levine, E.L. Problems of organizational control in microcosm. Journal of Applied Psychology, 1973, 58, 186-196.

Levine, E.L., & Katzell, R.A. Effects of variations in control structure on group performance and satisfaction: A laboratory study. Proceedings, 79th Annual Convention, American Psychological Association, 1971.

Lichtman, C.M., & Hunt, R.G. Personality and organizational theory: A review of some conceptual literature. Psychological Bulletin, 1971, 76, 271-294.

Likert, R. New Patterns of Management. New York: McGraw-Hill, 1961.

Likert, R. The Human Organization. New York: McGraw-Hill, 1967.

Likert, R. Human resource accounting: Building and assessing productive organizations. Personnel, 1973 (May-June), 8-24.

Lincoln, J.F. Incentive Management. Cleveland: Lincoln Electric Company, 1951.

Locke, E.A. Toward a theory of task motivation and incentives. Organizational Behavior and Human Performance, 1968, 3, 157-189.

Lodahl, T.M., & Kejner, M. The definition and measurement of job involvement. Journal of Applied Psychology, 1965, 49, 24-33.

Lowin, A. Participative decision making: A model, literature critique and prescription for research. Organizational Behavior and Human Performance, 1968, 3, 68-106.

Macy, B.A., & Mirvis, P.H. Measuring Quality of Work and Organizational Effectiveness in Behavioral-Economic Terms. Columbus, O.: College of Administrative Science, Ohio State University, 1974. (Mimeo)

Maher, J.R. (Ed.). New Perspectives in Job Enrichment. New York: Van Nostrand,Reinhold, 1971.

March, J.G., & Simon, H.A. Organizations. New York: Wiley, 1958.

Marriott, R. Size of working groups and output. Occupational Psychology, 1949, 23, 47-57.

Marrow, A.J. (Ed.). The Failure of Success. New York: AMACOM, 1972.

Marrow, A.J., Bowers, D.G., & Seashore, S.E. Management by Participation. New York: Harper & Row, 1967.

Mathewson, S.B. Restriction of Output among Unorganized Workers. New York: Viking, 1931.

McCormick, C.P. The Power of People. New York: Harper & Brothers, 1949.

Merrihue, W.F., & Katzell, R.A. ERI -- Yardstick of employee relations. Harvard Business Review, 1955, 33 (6), 91-99.

Merton, R.K. Social Theory and Social Structure. New York: Free Press, 1962.

Metzger, B.L. Profit Sharing in Perspective. Chicago: Profit Sharing Research Foundation, 1966.

Metzner, H., & Mann, F. Employee attitudes and absences. Personnel Psychology, 1953, 6, 467-485.

Meyer, H.H. Feedback that spurs performance. In A.J. Marrow (Ed.), The Failure of Success. New York: AMACOM, 1972.

Meyer, H.H., Kay, E., & French, J.R.P. Split roles in performance appraisal. Harvard Business Review, 1965, 43 (1), 123-129.

Morse, N.C., & Reimer, E. The experimental change of a major organizational variable. Journal of Abnormal and Social Psychology, 1956, 52, 120-129.

Morse, N.C., & Weiss, R.S. The function and meaning of work and the job. American Sociological Review, 1955, 20, 191-198.

Myers, M.S. Every Employee a Manager. New York: McGraw-Hill, 1970.

National Industrial Conference Board. Factors Affecting Employee Morale. Studies in Personnel Policy No. 85. New York, 1947.

Opsahl, R.L., & Dunnette, M.D. The role of financial compensation in industrial motivation. Psychological Bulletin, 1966, 63, 94-118.

Oster, A. Attitudes as mediators of the effects of participation in an industrial setting. Unpublished doctoral dissertation, Wayne State University, 1970.

Otis, J.L., & Leukart, R.H. Job Evaluation (2nd ed.). Englewood Cliffs, N.J.: Prentice-Hall, 1954.

Patchen, M. The Choice of Wage Comparisons. Englewood Cliffs, N.J.: Prentice-Hall, 1961.

Patchen, M. Participation, Achievement, and Involvement on the Job. Englewood Cliffs, N.J.: Prentice-Hall, 1970.

Penner, D.D. A study of the causes and consequences of salary satisfaction. Crotonville, N.Y.: General Electric Behavioral Research Service, 1966. (Mimeo)

Porter, L.W. A study of perceived need satisfactions in bottom and middle management jobs. Journal of Applied Psychology, 1961, 45, 1-10.

Porter, L.W., & Lawler, E.E., III. The effects of "tall" versus "flat" organization structures on managerial satisfaction. Personnel Psychology, 1964, 17, 135-148.

Porter, L.W., & Lawler, E.E., III. Properties of organization structure in relation to job attitudes and job behavior. Psychological Bulletin, 1965, 64, 23-51.

Porter, L.W., & Lawler, E.E., III. Managerial Attitudes and Performance. Homewood, Ill.: Irwin/Dorsey, 1968(a).

Porter, L.W., & Lawler, E.E., III. What job attitudes tell about motivations. Harvard Business Review, 1968(b), 46 (1), 118-126.

Powell, R.M., & Schlacter, I. Participative management: A panacea? Academy of Management Journal, 1971, 14, 165-173.

Powers, J.E. Job enrichment: How one company overcame the obstacles. Personnel, 1972, 49, 18-22.

Pritchard, R.D. Equity theory: A review and critique. Organizational Behavior and Human Performance, 1969, 4, 176-211.

Pritchard, R.D. Effects of varying performance-pay instrumentalities on the relationship between performance and satisfaction. Journal of Applied Psychology, 1973, 58, 122-125.

Pritchard, R.D., Dunnette, M.D., & Jorgenson, D.O. Effects of perceptions of equity and inequity on worker performance and satisfaction. Journal of Applied Psychology, 1972, 56, 75-94.

Pritchard, R.D., & Karasick, B. The effects of organizational climate on managerial job performance and job satisfaction. Organizational Behavior and Human Performance, 1973, 9, 126-146.

Purcell, T.V. The Worker Speaks His Mind on Company and Union. Cambridge, Mass.: Harvard University Press, 1953.

Purcell, T.V. Blue Collar Man. Cambridge, Mass.: Harvard University Press, 1960.

Quinn, R.P., Staines, G.L., & McCullogh, M.R. Job Satisfaction: Is There a Trend? Washington, D.C.: U.S. Government Printing Office, 1974.

Raia, A.P. Goal setting and self control. Journal of Management Studies, 1965, 2, 34-53.

Raia, A.P. A second look at goals and controls. California Management Review, 1966, 8, 49-58.

Research Institute of America. Fringe Benefits for Rank-and-File Employees. New York, 1969.

Ritchie, J.R., & Miles, R.E. An analysis of quantity and quality of participation as mediating variables in the participative decision making process. Personnel Psychology, 1970, 23, 347-359.

Roach, J.M. Worker Participation: New Voices in Management. New York: The Conference Board, 1973.

Robinson, J.P., Athanasiou, R., & Head, K.B. Measures of Occupational Attitudes and Occupational Characteristics. Ann Arbor, Mich.: Institute for Social Research, University of Michigan, 1969.

Roethlisberger, F.J., & Dickson, W.J. Management and the Worker. Cambridge, Mass.: Harvard University Press, 1939.

Rosen, H. Dual allegiance: A critique and a proposed approach. Personnel Psychology, 1954, 7, 67-80.

Rosow, J.M. (Ed.). The Worker and the Job. Englewood Cliffs, N.J.: Prentice-Hall, 1974.

Rothe, H. Output rates among welders: Productivity and consistency following removal of a financial incentive system. Journal of Applied Psychology, 1970, 54, 549-551.

Roy, D. Quota restrictions and goldbricking in a machine shop. American Journal of Sociology, 1952, 57, 427-442.

Rush, H.M.F. Behavioral Science Concepts and Management Application. New York: National Industrial Conference Board, 1969.

Rush, H.M.F. Job Design for Motivation. New York: The Conference Board, 1971.

Rush, H.M.F. Organization Development: A Reconnaissance. New York: The Conference Board, 1973.

Salpukas, A. Unions: A new role? In J. Rosow (Ed.), The Worker and the Job. Englewood Cliffs, N.J.: Prentice-Hall, 1974.

Sayles, L.R. Behavior of Industrial Work Groups. New York: Wiley, 1958.

Scheflen, K., Lawler, E.E., III., & Hackman, J.R. Long term participation in the development of pay incentive plans: A field experiment revisited. Journal of Applied Psychology, 1971, 55, 182-186.

Schneider, B., & Olson, L.K. Effort as a correlate of an organizational reward system and individual values. Personnel Psychology, 1970, 23, 313-326.

Schwab, D.P. Impact of alternative compensation systems on pay valence and instrumentality perceptions. Journal of Applied Psychology, 1973, 58, 308-312.

Schwab, D.P., & Cummings, L.L. Theories of performance and satisfaction: A review. Industrial Relations, 1970, 9, 408-430.

Seashore, S.E., & Bowers, D. Changing the Structure and Functioning of an Organization. Ann Arbor, Mich.: Institute for Social Research, University of Michigan, 1963.

Seashore, S.E., & Bowers, D.G. Durability of organizational change. American Psychologist, 1970, 25, 227-233.

Shepard, J.M. Functional specialization, alienation, and job satisfaction. Industrial and Labor Relations Review, 1970, 23, 207-219.

Shepard, J.M. Automation and Alienation: A Study of Office and Factory Workers. Cambridge: M.I.T. Press, 1971.

Sheppard, H.L., & Herrick, N.Q. Where Have all the Robots Gone? New York: Free Press, 1972.

Sibson, R.F. Wages and Salaries: A Handbook for Managers (Rev. ed.). New York: American Management Association, 1967.

Siegel, A., & Ruh, R. Job involvement, participation in decision making, personal background and job behavior. Organizational Behavior and Human Performance, 1973, 9, 318-327.

Slichter, S.J., Healy, J.J., & Livernash, R.E. The Impact of Collective Bargaining on Management. Washington, D.C.: The Brookings Institution, 1960.

Smith, C.G. A comparative analysis of some conditions and consequences of intraorganizational conflict. Administrative Science Quarterly, 1966, 10, 504-529.

Smith, C.G. Consultation and decision processes in a research and development laboratory. Administrative Science Quarterly, 1970, 15, 203-215.

Smith, C.G., & Jones, G. The role of the interaction-influence system in a planned organizational change. In A.S. Tannenbaum (Ed.), Control in Organizations. New York: McGraw-Hill, 1968.

Smith, C.G., & Tannenbaum, A.S. Organizational control structure: A comparative analysis. Human Relations, 1963, 16, 299-316.

Smith, P.C., & Kendall, L.M. Cornell studies of Job Satisfaction: VI. Implications for the Future. Unpublished Manuscripts, Cornell University, 1963.

Smith, P.C., Kendall, L.M., & Hulin, C.L. The Measurement of Satisfaction in Work and Retirement. Chicago: Rand McNally, 1969.

Sorcher, M. Motivation on the assembly line. Personnel Administration, 1969, 32, 40-48.

Stagner, R. Working on the railroad: A study of job satisfaction. Personnel Psychology, 1952, 5, 293-306.

Stagner, R., et al. Dual allegiance to union and management (A symposium). Personnel Psychology, 1954, 7, 41-80.

Stefflre, B. Concurrent validity of the Vocational Values Inventory. Journal of Educational Research, 1959, 52, 339-351.

Stogdill, R.M. Handbook of Leadership Research. New York: Free Press, 1974.

Strauss, G.P., & Rosenstein, E. Workers' participation: A critical view. Industrial Relations, 1970, 9, 197-214.

Strauss, G.P., & Sayles, L.R. The Scanlon Plan: Some organizational problems. Human Organization, 1957, 16, 15-22.

Sturmthal, A. Workers Councils. Cambridge, Mass.: Harvard University Press, 1964.

Sturmthal, A. Workers' participation in management: A review of the U.S. experience. International Institute for Labor Studies Bulletin, 1969, 6, 149-186.

Survey Research Center. Survey of Working Conditions. Ann Arbor, Mich.: University of Michigan, 1970.

Tannenbaum, A.S. Control in organizations: Independent adjustment and organizational performance. Administrative Science Quarterly, 1962, 7, 236-257.

Tannenbaum, A.S. Unions. In J.G. March (Ed.), Handbook of Organizations. Chicago: Rand McNally, 1965.

Tannenbaum, A.S., & Allport, F.H. Personality structure and group structure: An interpretative study of their relationship through an event-structure hypothesis. Journal of Abnormal and Social Psychology, 1956, 53, 272-280.

Tannenbaum, A.S., et al. Hierarchy in Organizations: A Cross-Cultural Comparison. San Francisco: Jossey-Bass, 1974.

Taylor, F.W. The Principles of Scientific Management. New York: Harper, 1911.

Turner, A.N., & Lawrence, P.R. Industrial Jobs and the Worker: An Investigation of Responses to Task Attributes. Boston: Graduate School of Business Administration, Harvard University, 1965.

U.S. Department of Health, Education and Welfare. Work in America. Cambridge, Mass.: M.I.T. Press, 1973.

Van Zelst, R.H., & Kerr, W.A. Workers' attitudes toward merit ratings. Personnel Psychology, 1953, 6, 159-172.

Viteles, M.S. Motivation and Morale in Industry. New York: Norton, 1953.

Vroom, V.H. Some Personality Determinants of the Effects of Participation. Englewood Cliffs, N.J.: Prentice-Hall, 1960.

Vroom, V.H. Work and Motivation. New York: Wiley, 1964.

Walker, C.R., & Guest, R.H. The Man on the Assembly Line. Cambridge, Mass.: Harvard University Press, 1952.

Walsh, W.B. Theories of Person-Environment Interaction. Iowa City: A.C.T. Publications, 1973.

Walters, R.E. Paper delivered before Metropolitan New York Association for Applied Psychology, New York, 1973.

Wass, D.L. The relationship between attitudes toward union and management. Dissertation Abstracts, 1962, 23, 696-697.

Waters, K., & Roach, D. Job attitudes as predictors of termination and absenteeism: Consistency over time and across organizational units. Journal of Applied Psychology, 1973, 57, 341-342.

Weeks, D.A. Salaries for blue collar workers. Conference Board Record, Nov., 1965, 2, 15-25.

Weick, K.E. Laboratory experimentation with organizations. In J.G. March (Ed.), Handbook of Organizations. Chicago: Rand McNally, 1965.

Weiss, D.J. A study of the relationship of participation in decision making, selected personality variables and job satisfaction of the educational research and development council of elementary school principals. Dissertation Abstracts, 1969, 29, 3404.

Wernimont, P.F. Intrinsic and extrinsic factors in job satisfaction. Journal of Applied Psychology, 1966, 50, 41-50.

Wernimont, P.F., & Fitzpatrick, S. The meaning of money. Journal of Applied Psychology, 1972, 56, 218-226.

Whyte, W.F. Money and Motivation. New York: Harper, 1955.

Wikstrom, W.S. Managing By-And With-Objectives. New York: National Industrial Conference Board, 1968.

Wild, R. Job needs, job satisfaction and job behavior of women manual workers. Journal of Applied Psychology, 1970, 54, 157-162.

Wollack, S., Goodale,J.G., Wijting, J.P., & Smith, P.C. Development of the survey of work values. Journal of Applied Psychology, 1971, 55, 331-338.

Worthy, J.C. Organization structure and employee morale. American Sociological Review, 1950, 15, 169-179.

Wyatt, S. Incentives in Repetitive Work: A Practical Experiment in a Factory. Industrial Health Research Board, Report No. 69. London: H.M. Stationery Office, 1934.

Yankelovich, D. Changing Values on Campus. Philadelphia: Washington Square Press, 1972.

Yankelovich, D. Turbulence in the working world: Angry workers, happy grads. Psychology Today, 1974, 8 (7), 81-87.

Zaleznik, A., Christensen, C.R., & Roethlisberger, F.J. The Motivation, Productivity, and Satisfaction of Workers: A Prediction Study. Boston: Harvard University, Graduate School of Business Administration, 1958.

Zedeck, S. Problems with the use of 'moderator' variables. Psychological Bulletin, 1971, 76, 295-310.

ADDITIONAL BIBLIOGRAPHY

Literature listed below was examined but not specifically cited in the text.

Aiken, W.J., & Hage, J. Organizational alienation: A comparative analysis. American Sociological Review, 1966, 31, 497-507.

Aiken, W.J., Smits, S.J., & Lollar, D.J. Leadership behavior and job satisfaction in state rehabilitation agencies. Personnel Psychology, 1972, 25, 65-73.

Alderfer, C.P. An organizational syndrome. Administrative Science Quarterly, 1967, 12, 440-460.

Alderfer, C.P. An empirical test of a new theory of human needs. Organizational Behavior and Human Performance, 1969, 4, 142-175.

Alderfer, C.P. Job enlargement and the organizational context. Personnel Psychology, 1969, 22, 418-426.

Alderfer, C.P. Existence, Relatedness and Growth: Human Needs in Organizational Settings. New York: The Free Press, 1972.

Alutto, J., & Belasco, J. A typology for participation in organizational decision making. Administrative Science Quarterly, 1972, 17, 117-125.

American Institute for Research. Project Talent: Progress in Education, a Sample Survey. New York, 1971.

American Management Association. Manager Unions. New York, 1972.

Anderson, J.W. The impact of technology on job enrichment. Personnel, 1970, 47, 29-37.

Andrews, K.R. Can the best corporations be made moral? Harvard Business Review, 1973, 51, 57-64.

Aram, J.D., Morgan, C.P., & Esbeck, E.S. Relations of collaborative interpersonal relationships to individual satisfaction and organizational performance. Administrative Science Quarterly, 1971, 16, 289-297.

Argyle, M., Gardner, G., & Cioffi, F. Supervisory methods related to productivity, absenteeism and labor turnover. Human Relations, 1958, 11, 23-40.

Argyris, C. The individual and the organization: An empirical test. Administrative Science Quarterly, 1959, 4, 145-167.

Argyris, C. Management and Organizational Development. New York: McGraw-Hill, 1971.

Atchinson, T., & French, W. Pay systems for scientists and engineers. Industrial Relations, 1967, 7, 44-56.

Atkinson, J.W. Towards experimental analysis of human motivation in terms of motives, expectancies, and incentives. In J.W. Atkinson (Ed.), Motives in Fantasy, Action, and Society. Princeton: Van Nostrand, 1958.

Atkinson, J.W., & Ritman, N.R. Performance as a function of motive strength and expectancy of goal attainment. Journal of Abnormal and Social Psychology, 1956, 53, 361-366.

Bachman, J.G. Faculty satisfaction and the dean's influence: An organizational study of 12 liberal arts colleges. Journal of Applied Psychology, 1968, 52, 55-61.

Back, K.W. Power, influence and pattern of communication. In Petrullo, L. & Bass, B. (Eds.) Leadership and Interpersonal Behavior. New York: Holt, Rinehart, and Winston, 1961.

Barkin, S. Job redesign: A technique for an era of full employment. In W. Harber, et al., (Eds.), Manpower in the United States. New York: Harper & Brothers, 1954.

Barnett, R.C., & Tagiuri, R. What young people think about managers. Harvard Business Review, 1973, 51 (3), 106-118.

Barrett, G.V. Motivation in Industry. Cleveland: Allen, 1966.

Barrett, J.H. Integrating individual goals and organizational objectives. Dissertation Abstracts, 1971, 31 (7-B), 4377.

Bass, A.R., Rosen, H., & Hill, J.W. The prediction of complex organizational behavior: A comparison of decision theory with more traditional techniques. Organizational Behavior and Human Performance, 1970, 5, 449-462.

Bassitt, G.A., & Meyer, H.H. Performance appraisal based on self review. Personnel Psychology, 1968, 21, 421-430.

Baum, B.H., Sounser, P.F., & Place, W.S. The effects of managerial training and organizational control: An experimental study. Organizational Behavior and Human Performance, 1970, 5, 170-182.

Bavelas, A., & Strauss, G. Group dynamics and intergroup relations. In Bennis, W.G., Benne, K.W., & Chin, R. (Eds.). The Planning of Change. New York: Holt, 1961.

Beer, M. Needsand need satisfaction among clerical workers in complex and routine jobs. Personnel Psychology, 1968, 21, 209-222.

Bell, D. Work in the life of an American. In W. Harber, et al., (Eds.), Manpower in the United States. New York: Harper Brothers, 1954.

Bennis, W.G. When democracy works. Trans-Action, 1966, 3, 35-36.

Beynon, H., & Blackburn, R. Perceptions of work variations within a factory. Cambridge Papers in Sociology, 3, London: Cambridge University Press, 1972.

Bishop, T.S. Factors affecting job satisfaction and job dissatisfaction among Iowa public school teachers. Dissertation Abstracts, 1970, 30 (9-A), 3661.

Blain, I., & Keohane, J. One company's management structure before and after a change. Occupational Psychology, 1969, 43, 23-38.

Blood, M.L., & Hulin, C.L. Alienation, environmental characteristics and workers' responses. Journal of Applied Psychology, 1967, 51, 284-290.

Bloom, R., & Barry, J.R. Determinants of work attitudes among negroes. Journal of Applied Psychology, 1967, 51, 291-294.

Blough, R.M. Business can satisfy the young intellectual. Harvard Business Review, 1966, 44, 49-57.

Bluestone, I. The next step toward industrial democracy. Paper presented to the National Industrial Conference Board, New York, 1972.

Bockman, V.M. The Herzberg controversy. Personnel Psychology, 1971, 24, 155-189.

Bohr, R., & Swertloff, A. Workshift, occupational status and the perception of a job prestige. Journal of Applied Psychology, 1969, 53, 227-229.

Bonjean, C.M., & Grimes, M.A. Bureaucracy and alienation: A dimensional approach. Social Forces, 1970, 48, 365-373.

Borgatta, E., Ford, R., & Bohstedt, G. Work orientation as hygienic orientation: A bipolar approach to the study of work motivation. Journal of Vocational Behavior, 1973, 3, 253-268.

Bouchard, T. Training, motivation and personality as determinants of the effectiveness of brainstorming groups and individuals. Journal of Applied Psychology, 1972, 56, 324-331.

Braustein, D. Interpersonal behavior in a changing organization. Journal of Applied Psychology, 1970, 54, 184-191.

Bray, D.W., Grant, D.L., & Campbell, R.J.  Studying careers and assessing ability.  In Marrow, A.J. (Ed.), The Failure of Success.  New York: AMACOM, 1972.

Bregard, A., & Gulowsen, J., et al.,  Norsk Hydro Experiment in the Fertilizer Factories.  Work Research Institute, 1968.

Brody, M.  The relationship between efficiency and job satisfaction. Unpublished master's thesis.  New York:  New York University, 1945.

Buch, V.E.  Working Under Pressure.  New York:  Crane, Russak, 1972.

Buchlowe, M.  A new role for the work group.  Administrative Science Quarterly, 1966, 11, 59-78.

Bureau of Labor Statistics,  U. S. Department  of  Labor.  Improving Productivity:  Labor and Management Approaches.  Bulletin 1715, Washington, D.C., 1973.

Bureau of Labor Statistics, U.S. Department of Labor.  Productivity:  A Selected, Annotated Bibliography, 1965-1971.  Bulletin 1776, Washington, D.C., 1973.

Campbell, J.P., & Dunnette, M.D.  Effectiveness of T-group experiences in managerial training and development.  Psychology Bulletin, 1968, 70, 73-104.

Carlson, R.E.  Degree of job fit as a moderator of the relationship between job performance and job satisfaction.  Personnal Psychology, 1969, 22, 159-170.

Carlson, R.E., Dawis, R.V., & Weiss, D.J.  Satisfaction as a moderator of the relationship between abilities and satisfactoriness. Minneapolis:  Industrial Relations Center, University of Minnesota, 1968.

Carroll, B.  Job Satisfaction:  A Review of the Literature.  New York: Cornell University, 1973.

Chaney, F.B.  Employee participation in manufacturing job design. Human Factors, 1969, 11, 101-106.

Chaney, F.B., & Kenneth, S.T.  Participative management:  A practical experience.  Personnel, 1972, 49, 8-19.

Cherrington, D.J., Reitz, H.J., & Scott, W.E.  Effects of contingent and noncontingent reward on the relationship between satisfaction and task performance.  Journal of Applied Psychology, 1971, 55, 531-536.

Chung, K.H.  Incentive theory and research.  Personnel Administration, 1972, 35, 31-44.

Clark, A., & McCabe, J. The motivation and satisfaction of Australian managers. Personnel Psychology, 1972, 25, 625-638.

Collins, B.E. An experimental study of satisfaction, productivity, turnover, and comparison levels. Unpublished doctoral dissertation. Northwestern University, 1963.

Conant, E.H., & Kilbridge, M.D. An interdisciplinary analysis of job enlargement: Technology, costs and behavioral implications. Industrial and Labor Relations Review, 1965, 18, 377-395.

Crystal, G.S. Financial Motivation for Executives. New York: American Management Association, 1970.

Cummings, L.L., & El Salmi, A.M. Empirical research on the basis and correlates of managerial motivation: A review of the literature. Psychological Bulletin, 1968, 70, 127-144.

Cummings, L.L., Schwab, D.P., & Rosen, W. Performance and knowledge of results as determinants of goal setting. Journal of Applied Psychology, 1971, 55, 526-530.

Dachler, H.P., & Hulin, C.C. A reconsideration of the relationship between satisfaction and judged importance of environmental and job characteristics. Organizational Behavior and Human Performance, 1969, 4, 252-266.

Dachler, H.P., & Mobley, W.H. An interorganizational study of the relationship between attitudes, motivation, and production behavior. University of Maryland Technical Report, 1971, 71 (1).

Davis, L.E. Job satisfaction research: The post-industrial view. Industrial Relations, 1971, 10, 176-193.

Davis, L.E., & Valfer, E.S. Intervening responses to changes in supervisor job designs. Occupational Psychology, 1965, 39, 171-189.

Davis., L.E., & Werling, R. Job design factors. Occupational Psychology, 1960, 34, 109-132.

Dawis, R.V., England, G.E., & Lofquist, L.H. A Theory of Work Adjustment. Minneapolis: Industrial Relations Center, 1964.

Dawis, R.V., Lofquist, L.H., & Weiss, D.J. A Theory of Work Adjustment (A Revision). Minneapolis: Industrial Relations Center, University of Minneapolis, 1968.

Dawis, R.V., Weiss, D.J., Lofquist, L.H., & Betz, E. Satisfaction as a moderator in the prediction of satisfactoriness. _Proceedings, 75th Annual Convention_, American Psychological Association, 1967, 2, 269-270.

De Salvia, D.N., & Gemmill, G.R. An exploratory study of the personal value systems of college students and managers. _Academy of Management Journal_, 1971, June, 227-238.

Deci, E.L., & Vroom, V.H. The stability of post-decision dissonance: A follow-up of business school graduates. _Organizational Behavior and Human Performance_, 1971, 6, 36-49.

Denhardt, R.B. Leadership style, worker involvement and deference to authority. _Sociology and Social Research_, 1970, 54, 170-180.

Derber, M. _The American Idea of Industrial Democracy, 1865-1965_. Chicago: University of Illinois Press, 1970.

Dichter, E. _Motivating Human Behavior_. New York: McGraw-Hill, 1971.

Doll, R.E., & Gunderson, E.K.E. Occupational group as a moderator of the job satisfaction - job performance relationship. _Journal of Applied Psychology_, 1969, 53, 359-361.

Donnelly, J.F. Increasing productivity by involving the people in the total job. _Personnel Administration_, 1971, 34, 8-13.

Dowling, W.F., & Sayles, L.R. _How Managers Motivate: The Imperatives of Supervision_. New York: McGraw-Hill, 1971.

Dunbar, R.L.M. Budgeting for control. _Administrative Science Quarterly_, 1971, 16, 88-96.

Dunn, J.D., & Rachel, F.M. _Wage and Salary Administration: Total Compensation Systems_. New York: McGraw-Hill, 1971.

Educational Testing Service. _Motivation of Managers_. Princeton, N.J., 1967.

Ekval, G. _Creativity at the Work Place_. Stockholm, The Swedish Council for Personnel Administration, 1971.

Evans, G.E. The effects of supervisory behavior upon workers' perceptions of their path-goal relationships. Unpublished doctoral dissertation, Yale University, New Haven, Conn., 1968.

Evans, M.G., & McKee, D. Some effects of internal versus external orientations upon the relationships between various aspects of job satisfaction. _Journal of Business Administration_, 1970, 2, 17-29.

Farris, G.F. A predictive study of turnover. Personnel Psychology, 1971, 24, 311-328.

Fein, M. Job enrichment: A reevaluation. Sloan Management Review, 1974, 15 (2), 69-88.

Fiedler, F. Personality, motivational systems and behavior of high and low LPC persons. Industrial Relations, 1972(a), 25, 391-412.

Fiedler, F. Predicting the effects of leadership training and experience from the contingency model. Journal of Applied Psychology, 1972(b), 56, 114-117.

Fielden, J.S. The right young people for business. Harvard Business Review, 1966, 44, 76-83.

Filey, A.C., & House, R.J. Managerial Process and Organizational Behavior. Glenview, Ill.: Scott, Foresman, 1969.

Fitzgerald, T. Why motivation theory does not work. Harvard Business Review, 1971, 49 (3), 37-44.

Fleishman, E.A. A relationship between incentive motivation and ability level in psychomotor performance. Journal of Experimental Psychology, 1958, 15, 30-40.

Fleishman, E.A., Harris, E.F., & Burtt, H.E. Leadership and Supervision in Industry. Columbus: Ohio State University, Bureau of Educational Research, 1955.

Ford, R.N. Job enrichment lessons from A T & T. Harvard Business Review, 1973, 51, 96-106.

Ford, R.N., & Borgatta, E.F. Satisfaction with the work itself. Journal of Applied Psychology, 1970, 54, 128-134.

Fried, J., Weitman, M., & Davis, M. Man-machine interaction and absenteeism. Journal of Applied Psychology, 1972, 56, 428-429.

Friedman, E.H., & Hellestein, H.K. Occupational stress, law school hierarchy, and coronary artery disease in Cleveland attorneys. Psychosomatic Medicine, 1968, 30, 72-86.

Fuchs, V.R. Productivity Trends in the Goods and Service Sectors, 1929-61. A Preliminary Survey. N.Y.: National Bureau of Economic Research, 1954.

Fuchs, V.R. The Growing Importance of the Service Industries. N.Y.: National Bureau of Economic Research, 1965.

Fuchs, V.R., & Wilburn, J.A. Productivity Differences within the Service Sector. N.Y.: National Bureau of Economic Research, 1967.

Fucigna, J.T. The ergonomics of offices. Ergonomics, 1967, 10, 589-604.

Galbraith, J.R. Motivational determinants of job performance. Unpublished doctoral dissertation, Indiana University, 1966.

Galbraith, J., & Cummings, L.L. An empirical investigation of the motivational determinants of task performance: Interactive effects between instrumentality and motivation-ability. Organizational Behavior and Human Performance, 1967, 2, 237-257.

Gallup, G., Jr. Job dissatisfaction growing. Speech given before the American Management Association, 1972.

Gannon, M., & Hendrickson, H. Career orientation and job satisfaction among working wives. Journal of Applied Psychology, 1973, 58, 339-340.

Garson, B. Luddites in Lordstown. Harpers Magazine, 1972, 244 (6), 68-73.

Gavin, J.F. Self-esteem as a moderator of the relationship between expectancies and job performance. Journal of Applied Psychology, 1973, 58, 83-88.

Gellerman, S.W. Management by Motivation. New York: American Management Association, 1968.

Ghiselli, E.E. Some motivational factors in the success of managers. Personnel Psychology, 1968, 21, 431-440.

Ghiselli, E.E., & Gordon, M.E. A psychological study of pay. Journal of Applied Psychology, Monograph Supplement, 1967, 51, 1-24.

Ghiselli, E.E., & Johnson, D.A. Need satisfaction, managerial success, and organizational structure. Personnel Psychology, 1970, 23, 569-576.

Ghiselli, E.E., & Wyatt, T. Need satisfaction, managerial success, and attitudes toward leadership. Personnel Psychology, 1972, 25 (3), 413-420.

Golden, R.R., & Weiss, D.J. Relationship of Vocational Satisfaction to the Correspondence of Job Reinforcement and Vocational Needs. Minneapolis: Industrial Relations Center, University of Minnesota, 1968.

Goldner, F.H. Success versus failure: Prior managerial perspectives. Industrial Relations, 1970, 9, 453-474.

Goldthorpe, J.H., Lockwood, D., Beckhofer, F., & Platt, J. The Affluent Worker: Industrial Attitudes and Behavior. Cambridge, England: Cambridge University Press, 1968.

Golembiewski, R.T. Organization,Men and Power. Chicago: Rand McNally, 1967.

Gomberg, W. Job satisfaction: Sorting out the nonsense. AFL-CIO American Federationist, 1973, 80.

Gooding, J. It pays to wake up the blue-collar worker. Fortune, 1970(a), 79, 133-135.

Gooding, J. The fraying white collar. Fortune, 1970(b), 82 (12), 78-82.

Gooding, J. The accelerated generation moves into management. Fortune, 1971, 83 (3), 101-104.

Goodman, P.S. The Scanlon Plan: A Need for Conceptual and Empirical Models. Paper presented at the American Psychological Association Convention, 1973.

Goodman, P.S., & Friedman, A. An examination of Adams' theory of inequity. Administrative Science Quarterly, 1971, 10, 271-286.

Goodman, P.S., Rose, J.H., & Furcon, J.E. Comparison of motivational antecedents of the work performance of scientists and engineers. Journal of Applied Psychology, 1970, 54, 491-495.

Goodspeed, J. GM zeroes in on employee discontent. Business Week, 1973, May 12, 140-148.

Goodstadt, B., & Kipnis, D. Situational influences on the use of power. Journal of Applied Psychology, 1970, 54, 201-207.

Graen, G.B. Instrumentality theory of work motivation; some experimental results and suggested modifications. Journal of Applied Psychology, Monograph Supplement, 1969, 53, 1-25.

Greenhaus, J., & Gavin, J.F. The relationship between expectancy and job behavior for white and black employees. Personnel Psychology, 1972, 25, 449-456.

Gruenfeld, L.W., & Foltman, F.F. Relationship among supervisors' integration, satisfaction and acceptance of technological change. Journal of Applied Psychology, 1967, 51, 74-77.

Hackman, J.R., & Porter, L.W. Expectancy theory predictions of work effectiveness. Organizational Behavior and Human Performance, 1968, 3, 417-426.

Hackman, R.C. The Motivated Working Adult. New York: American Management Association, 1969.

Hall, D.T., & Nongaim, K.E. An examination of Maslow's need hierarchy in an organizational setting. Organization Behavior and Human Performance, 1968, 3, 12-35.

Hall, D., Schneider, B., & Nygren, H. Personal factors in organizational identification. Administrative Science Quarterly, 1970, 15, 176-190.

Hansen, J. Job satisfaction and effective performance of school counselors. Personnel and Guidance Journal, 1968, 46, 864-869.

Harding, F.D., & Bottenberg, R.A. Effect of personal characteristics on relationship between attitudes and job performance. Journal of Applied Psychology, 1961, 45, 428-430.

Hedges, J.N. Absence from work - a look at some national data. Monthly Labor Review, 1973, (7), 24-30.

Heller, F., & Yukl, G. Participation, managerial decision making, and situational variables. Organizational Behavior and Human Performance, 1969, 4, 227-241.

Heneman, H.III.Impact of performance on managerial pay levels and pay changes. Journal of Applied Psychology, 1973, 58, 128-130.

Heneman, H.G., III., & Schwab, D.P. An evaluation of research on expectancy value theory predictions of employee performance. Psychological Bulletin, 1972, 78, 1-9.

Heron, A. Satisfaction and satisfactoriness. Occupational Psychology, 1954, 28, 140-153.

Herrick, N., & Quinn, R.P. The working conditions as a source of social indicators. Monthly Labor Review, 1971, April, 15-24.

Heslin, R., & Blake, B. Performance as a function of payment, commitment, and task interest. Psychonomic Science, 1969, 15, 323-324.

Heyel, C. (Ed.). Handbook of Modern Office Management and Administrative Services. New York: McGraw-Hill, 1972.

Hill, R. Two income maintenance plans: Work incentives and the closure of poverty gap. Industrial and Labor Relations Review, 1972, 25, 545-554.

Hill, W.W., & French, W.L. Perceptions of the power of department chairmen by professors. Administrative Science Quarterly, 1967, 11, 548-574.

Hinkle, L., et al. Occupation, education and coronary heart disease. Science, 1968, 161, 238-245.

Hoeur, H.J., & Stevenson, W.W. The effects of on-the-job counseling on employer's ratings and job satisfaction of persons training in selected Oklahoma MDTA classes during 1967-1968. Stillwater: Research Foundation, Oklahoma State University, 1968, ERIC Document # Ed. 023930.

Hollander, S. The Sources of Increased Efficiency. Cambridge, Mass.: M.I.T. Press, 1965.

Holtes, H. Attitudes toward employee participation in company decision making processes. Human Relations, 1965, 18, 297-322.

Horsfall, A.B., & Arensberg, C.M. Team work and productivity in a shoe factory. Human Organization, 1949, 8, 13-25.

House, R. A path-goal theory of leader effectiveness. Administrative Science Quarterly, 1971, 16, 321-328.

House, R.J., Filey, A.C., & Gujardti, D.N. Leadership style, hierarchical influence, and the satisfaction of subordinate sale expectations. Journal of Applied Psychology, 1971, 55, 422-432.

Howell, M.A. Time off as a reward for productivity. Personnel Administration, 1971, 34, 48-51.

Hulin, C.L. Effects of community characteristics on measures of job satisfaction. Journal of Applied Psychology, 1966, 50, 280-285.

Hundal, P.S. Knowledge of performance as an incentive in repetitive industrial work. Journal of Applied Psychology, 1969, 53, 224-226.

Hunt, J.G., & Hill, J.W. The new look in motivational theory for organizational research. Human Organization, 1969, 28, 100-109.

Huskey, R. Effects of anticipated job loss on employee behavior. Journal of Applied Psychology, 1972, 56, 273-274.

Ilgen, D.R. Satisfaction with performance as a function of the initial level of expected performance and deviations from expectations. Organizational Behavior and Human Performance, 1961, 6, 354-361.

Ilgen, D.R., & Humstra, B.W. Performance satisfaction as a function of differences between expected and reported performance at five levels of reported performance. Organizational Behavior and Human Performance, 1972, 7, 359-378.

Ingham, G.K. Size of Industrial Organization and Worker Behavior. London: Cambridge University Press, 1970.

Inkson, K., Payne, R., & Pugh, D. Extending the occupational environment: The measurement of organizations. Occupational Psychology, 1967, 41, 33-47.

Iris, B., & Barrett, G. Some relations between job and life satisfaction and job importance. Journal of Applied Psychology, 1972, 50, 101-304.

Ivancevich, J.M., & Donnelly, J.H. Job satisfaction research: A management guide for practitioners, Personnel Journal, 1968, 47, 172-177.

Ivancevich, J.M., & Donnelly, J.H. Leader influence and performance. Personnel Psychology, 1970, 23, 539-549.

Johnson, D.W., & Allen, S. Deviation from organizational norms concerning the relationship between status and power: Equity versus self interest theory. Sociological Quarterly, 1972, 13, 174-182.

Johnston, W.A., & Buggs, G.E. Team performance as a factor of team arrangement and work load. Journal of Applied Psychology, 1968, 52, 89-93.

Joint Economic Committee Congress of the U.S. Reducing Unemployment to 2 Percent. Washington, D.C.: U.S. Government Printing Office, 1972.

Jones, S.C., & Vroom, V.H. Division of labor and performance under co-operative and competitive conditions. Journal of Abnormal and Social Psychology, 1964, 68, 313-320.

Jorgensen, D., Dunnette, M., & Pritchard, R. Effects of manipulation of a performance-reward contingency on behavior in a simulated work setting. Journal of Applied Psychology, 1973, 57, 271-280.

Kaffa, V.W. A motivation system that works both ways. Personnel, 1971, 48, 19-25.

Kahn, D.G., Slocum, J.W., & Chase, R.B. Does job performance affect employee satisfaction? Personnel Journal, 1971, 50, 455-459.

Kahn, R.L. Productivity and job satisfaction. Personnel Psychology, 1960, 13, 275-287.

Kahn, R.L. The meaning of work: Interpretation and proposals for measurement. In Campbell, A.A., & Converse, E. (Eds.), The Human Meaning of Social Change. New York: Russell Sage Foundation, 1972.

Kahn, R.L., & Katz, D. Leadership practices in relation to productivity and morale. In Cartwright, D., & Zander, A. (Eds.), Group Dynamics (2nd ed.). Evanston, I..l: Row-Peterson, 1960.

Kapar, S. Authority patterns and subordinate behavior in Indian organizations. Administrative Science Quarterly, 1971, 16, 298-307.

Karpik, L. Expectations and satisfaction in work. Human Relations, 1968, 21, 327-350.

Katzell, R., Barrett, R.S., Vann, D.H., & Hogan, J.M. Organizational correlates of executive roles. Journal of Applied Psychology, 1968, 52, 22-28.

Kavcic, B., Veljko, R., & Tannenbaum, A. Control, participation, and effectiveness in four Yugoslav industrial organizations. Administrative Science Quarterly, 1971, 16, 74-87.

Kerr, W.A., Koppelmeir, G., & Sullivan, J.J. Absenteeism, turnover and morale in a metals fabrication factory. Occupational Psychology, 1951, 25, 50-55.

King, N. Characteristics and evaluation of the two-factor theory of job satisfaction. Psychological Bulletin, 1970, 74, 18-31.

Kipnis, D., & Cosentino, J. Use of leadership power in industry. Journal of Applied Psychology, 1969, 53, 460-466.

Kirshner, W.K. Job attitudes and performance. Personnel Administration, 1967, 30, 42-45.

Kirton, M.J., & Mulligan, G. Correlates of managers' attitudes toward change. Journal of Applied Psychology, 1973, 58, 101-107.

Klaus, D., & Glaser, R. Reinforcement determinants of team proficiency. Organizational Behavior and Human Performance, 1970, 5, 33-67.

Klein, S.M., & Maher, J.R. Education level, attitudes and future expectations among first level management. Personnel Psychology, 1968, 21, 43-53.

Klein, S.M., & Maher, J.R. Decision making, autonomy and personnel conflict among first-line management. Personnel Psychology, 1970, 23, 481-492.

Kobayshi, S. Creative Management. New York: American Management Association, 1971.

Korman, A.K. Task success, task popularity, and self-esteem as influences on task liking. Journal of Applied Psychology, 1968, 52, 484-490.

Korman, A.K. Toward an hypothesis of work behavior. Journal of Applied Psychology, 1970, 54, 31-41.

Korman, A.K. Organizational achievement, aggression and creativity: Some suggestions toward an integrated theory. Organizational Behavior and Human Performance, 1971, 6, 593-613.

Krulee, G.K. Company wide incentive systems. Journal of Business, 1955, 28, 37-47.

Kubiloff, A.H. An experiment in management: Putting theory Y to the test. Personnel, 1963, 40, 8-17.

Landsberger, H.A. The behavioral sciences in industry. Industrial Relations, 1967, 7 (1), 1-19.

Lawler, E.E., III. Attitude surveys and job performance. Personnel Administration, 1967, 30, 222-227.

Lawler, E.E., III. A correlational-causal analysis of the relationship between expectancy attitudes and job performance. Journal of Applied Psychology, 1968(a), 52, 462-468.

Lawler, E.E., III. Effects of hourly overpayment on productivity and work quality. Journal of Personality and Social Psychology, 1968(b), 10, 306-313.

Lawler, E.E., III. Equity theory as a predictor of productivity and work quality. Psychological Bulletin, 1968(c), 70, 596-610.

Lawler, E.E., III. Motivation and the design of jobs. A.S.T.M.E. Vectors, 1968(d).

Lawler, E.E., III. Job design and employee motivation. Personnel Psychology, 1969, 426-435.

Lawler, E.E., III. Job attitudes and employee motivation: Theory, research, and practice. Personnel Psychology, 1970, 23, 223-237.

Lawler, E.E., III. Compensating the new life-style worker. Personnel, 1971, 48, 19-25.

Lawler, E.E., III., & Hall, D.T. The relationship of job characteristics to job involvement, satisfaction and intrinsic motivation. Journal of Applied Psychology, 1970, 54, 305-312.

Lawler, E.E., III., & Porter, L.W. Perceptions regarding management compensation. Industrial Relations, 1963, 3, 41-49.

Lawler, E.E., III., & Porter, L.W. Antecedent attitudes of effective managerial performance. Organizational Behavior and Human Performance, 1967(a), 2, 122-142.

Lawler, E.E., III., & Porter, L.W. The effect of performance on job satisfaction. Industrial Relations, 1967(b), 7, 20-28.

Lawler, E.E., III., & Suttle, L. Expectancy theory and job behavior. Organizational Behavior and Human Performance, 1973, 9, 482-503.

Lawrence, A.C. Individual differences in work motivation. Human Relations, 1972, 25, 327-335.

Lawshe, C.H., & Nagle, B.F. Productivity and attitude toward supervision. Journal of Applied Psychology, 1953, 37, 159-162.

Lederman, T et al. A Review of the Relationship between Research and Development and Economic Growth Productivity. Washington, D.C.: National Science Foundation, 1971.

Lee, H.C. Do workers really want flexibility on the job? Personnel, 1965, 42, 74-77.

Lehman, E., Schulman, J., & Hinkle, L.E. Coronary deaths and organizational mobility: The 30 years experience of 1,160 men. Archives of Environmental Health, 1967, 15, 455-461.

Lesieur, F., & Puckett, E.S. The Scanlon Plan has proved itself. Harvard Business Review, 1969, 47 (5), 109-118.

Levine, J., & Butler, J. Lecture versus group decision in changing behavior. Journal of Applied Psychology, 1952, 36, 29-33.

Levinson, H. The Great Jackass Fallacy. Boston: Harvard Graduate School of Business Administration, 1973.

Levitan, S.A., & Garth, L.M. U.S. manpower programs: Retreat or reform? Conference Board Record, 1973, July, 17-31

Levitan, S.A., & Johnston, W.B. Work Is Here to Stay, Alas. Salt Lake City: Olympus, 1973.

Lewin, K. The Conceptual Representation and the Measurement of Psychological Forces. Durham, N.C.: Duke University Press, 1938.

Lewin, K. Group decision and social change. In Newcomb, T.M., & Hartley, E.L. (Eds.), Readings in Social Psychology. New York: Holt, 1947.

Lifter, M.L., Bass, A.R., & Nassbaum, H. Effort expenditure and job performance of line and staff personnel. Organizational Behavior and Human Performance, 1971, 6, 501-515.

Likert, R., & Seashore, S. Increasing utilization through better management. In W. Harber, et al., (Eds.), Manpower in the United States. New York: Harper & Brothers, 1954.

Lippitt, R., & White, R. An experimental study of leadership and group life. In Newcomb, T.W., & Hartley, E.L., (Eds.), Readings in Social Psychology. New York: Holt, 1947.

Litwin, G.H., & Stringer, R.A. Motivation and Organizational Climate. Boston: Harvard Graduate School of Business Administration, 1968.

Locke, E.A. The relationship of task success to task liking and satisfaction. Journal of Applied Psychology, 1965, 49, 379-383.

Locke, E.A. Further data on the relationship of task success to liking and satisfaction. Psychological Reports, 1967(a), 20, 246-249.

Locke, E.A. Relationship of success and expectation to affect on goal seeking tasks. Journal of Personnel and Social Psychology, 1967(b), 7, 125-134.

Locke, E.A. What is job satisfaction? Organizational Behavior and Human Performance, 1969, 4, 309-336.

Locke, E.A. Job satisfaction and job performance: A theoretical analysis. Organizational Behavior and Human Performance, 1970, 5, 484-500.

Locke, E.A. Satisfiers and dissatisfiers among white-collar and blue-collar employees. Journal of Applied Psychology, 1973, 58, 67-76.

Locke, E.A., & Bryan, J.F. Goals and Intensions as Determinants of Performance Level, Task Choice, and Attitudes. American Institutes for Research, Washington, 1967(a).

Locke, E.A., & Bryan, J.F. Performance goals as determinants of level of performance and boredom. Journal of Applied Psychology, 1967 (b), 51, 120-130.

Locke, E.A., & Bryan, J.F. The directing function of goals in task performance. Organizational Behavior and Human Performance, 1969 (a), 4, 35-42.

Locke, E.A., & Bryan, J.F. Knowledge of score and goal level as determinants of work rate. Journal of Applied Psychology, 1969(b), 53, 59-65.

Locke, E.A., Cartledge, N., & Knerr, C.S. Studies of the relationship between satisfaction, goal setting, and performance. Organizational Behavior and Human Performance, 1970, 5, 135-158.

Locke, E.A., Cartledge, N., & Koeppel, J. Motivational effects of knowledge of results: A goal setting phenomenon. Psychological Bulletin, 1968, 70, 474-485.

Lofquist, L.H., & Dawis, R.V. Adjustment to Work. New York: Appleton, Century, Crofts, 1969.

Lowin, A., & Craig, J.R. The influence of level of performance on managerial style: An experimental object lesson in the ambiguity of correlational data. Organizational Behavior and Human Performance, 1968, 3, 440-458.

Lyons, T., & Dickinson, T. A comparison of perceived and computed change measures over a three year period. Journal of Applied Psychology, 1973, 58, 318-321.

Macarov, D. Incentive to Work. San Francisco: Jossey-Bass, 1970.

Manpower Administration, U.S. Department of Labor. Suggestions for Control of Turnover and Absenteeism. Washington, D.C.: Government Printing Office, 1972.

Margolies, B., & Kroes, W. Work and the Health of Man. 1972.

Marriott, R. Incentive Payment Systems: A Review of Research and Opinion. London: Staples, 1957.

Maurer, J.G. Work Role Involvement of Industrial Supervisors. W. Lansing: Bureau of Business and Economic Research, Graduate School of Business Administration, Michigan State University, 1969.

McBain, W. Arousal, monotony, and accidents in line driving. Journal of Applied Psychology, 1970, 54, 509-519.

McCarrey, M., & Edwards, S. Hierarchies of goal objectives. Individual characteristics and performance. Journal of Applied Psychology, 1972, 56, 271-272.

McCarty, J.J., & Shull, F.A. Productivity as a Function of Job Design. Athens: University of Georgia, 1974. (Mimeo)

McClelland, D.C., & Winter, D.G., et al. Motivating Economic Achievement. New York: The Free Press, 1969.

Meir, E.I., Camon, A., & Sardi, Z. Prediction of presistence at work of women dentists. Personnel and Guidance Journal, 1967, 46, 247-251.

Meltzer, H., & Ludwig, D. Memory dynamics and work motivation. Journal of Applied Psychology, 1968, 52, 184-187.

Metzger, B. Socio-economic Participation: Key to a Better World in the Future. Profit Sharing Research. Evanston, Illinois, 1969.

Milkavich, G., & Campbell, K. A study of Jaques' norms of equitable payment. Industrial Relations, 1972, 11, 267-271.

Miller, G.A. Professionals in bureaucracy: Alienation among industrial scientists and engineers. American Sociological Review, 1967, 32, 755-768.

Miner, J.B. Management Theory. New York: MacMillan, 1971.

Miner, J.B., & Dachler, P.H. Personnel attitudes and motivation. Annual Review of Psychology, 1973, 24, 379-402.

Mire, J. European workers' participation in management. Monthly Labor Review, 1973, February, 9-15.

Missauk, M.J. An investigation into supervisory skill mix among hetero-geneous operative employee groups and effectiveness in determining satisfaction and productivity of employees. Unpublished doctoral dissertation, Ohio State University, 1968.

Misumi, J., & Siki, F. Effects of achievement motivation on the effectiveness of leadership patterns. Administrative Science Quarterly, 1971, 16, 51-59.

Mitchell, T.R., & Beglan, A. Instrumentality theories: Current uses in psychology. Psychological Bulletin, 1971, 76, 432-454.

Mitchell, V.F. Expectancy theories of managerial motivation. Academy of Management Proceedings, 1972, 31, 210-220.

Mobley, W.H., & Locke, E.A. The relationship of value importance to satisfaction. Organizational Behavior and Human Performance, 1970, 5, 463-483.

Moore, L.M. Effects of wage inequities on work attitudes and performance. Unpublished master's thesis, Wayne State University, 1968.

Moore, E., Hybels, J., et al. Technological Advance in an Expanding Economy: Its Impact on a Cross-Section of the Labor Force. Ann Arbor: University of Michigan, Institute of Social Research, 1969.

Mulder, M., & Wilke, H. Participation and power equalization. Organizational Behavior and Human Performance, 1970, 5, 430-438.

Muller, P.H. Relationship between time span of discretion, leadership behavior, and Fiedler's LPC scores. Journal of Applied Psychology, 1970, 54, 140-144.

Myers, M.S.  Who are your motivated employees?  _Harvard Business Review_, 1964, _42_ (1), 73-88.

Myers, M.S.  Increasing manager motivation.  In Rush, H.M. (Ed.), _Managing Change_.  New York:  National Industrial Conference Board, 1970.

Myers, M.S.  Overcoming union opposition to job enrichment.  _Harvard Business Review_, 1971, _49_, 37-49.

Nagi, S., & Hadley, L.  Disability behavior:  Income change and motivation to work.  _Industrial and Labor Relations Review_, 1972, _25_, 223-233.

Nathanson, C., & Becker, M.  Job satisfaction and job performance:  An empirical test of some theoretical propositions.  _Organizational Behavior and Human Performance_, 1973, _9_, 267-279.

National Commission on Productivity, First Annual Report.  Washington, D.C.: U.S. Government Printing Office, 1972.

Nealy, S.  Pay and benefit preferences.  _Industrial Relations_, 1963, _3_, 17-28.

Negandhi, A., & Reiman, B.  Task environment, decentralization and organizational effectiveness.  _Human Relations_, 1973, _26_, 203-214.

Noble, G.  A study of the relationship between ability, performance, attitudes, inclinations, and speed of progress using intrinsic programmed instruction.  _Programmed Learning Educational Technology_, 1969, _6_, 109-121.

Nord, W.R.  Beyond the teaching machine:  The neglected area of operant conditioning in the theory and practice of management. _Organizational Behavior and Human Performance_, 1969, _4_, 375-401.

Nord, W.R., & Costigan, R.  Worker adjustment to the four-day week:  A longitudinal study.  _Journal of Applied Psychology_, 1973, _58_, 60-66.

O'Brien, G.E., & Owens, A.G.  Effects of organizational structure on correlations between members' abilities and group productivity. _Journal of Applied Psychology_, 1969, _53_, 525-530.

O'Reilly, C., & Roberts, K.  Job satisfaction among white and nonwhites:  A cross cultural approach.  _Journal of Applied Psychology_, 1973, _57_, 295-299.

Paul, W., Robertson, K., & Herzberg, F.  Job enrichment pays off. _Harvard Business Review_, 1969, _47_ (2), 61-78.

Pelz, D.C., & Andrews, F.M.  _Scientists in Organizations_.  New York: Wiley, 1966.

Penzer, W.N. Managing motivated employees. Personnel Journal, 1971, 50, 367-372.

Pervin, L.A. Performance and satisfaction as a function of individual-environment fit. Psychological Bulletin, 1968, 69, 56-68.

Peterson, P.G. The U.S. in the changing world economy. Address given before the National Association of Food Chains, Florida, 1972.

Peterson, R.A., & Rath, M.J. Structural determinants of peicework rates. Industrial Relations, 1964, 4 (1), 92-103.

Poulton, E.C. Environment and Human Efficiency. Springfield, Ill.: Thomas, 1970.

Price, J.L. Organizational Effectiveness. Homewood, Ill.: Irwin/Dorsey, 1968.

Pritchard, R, & De Leo, P. Experimental test of the valence-instrumentality in job performance. Journal of Applied Psychology, 1973, 57, 267-270.

Pritchard, R., & Sanders, M. The influence of valence, instrumentality and expectancy on effort and performance. Journal of Applied Psychology, 1973, 57, 61-67.

Pruden, H.O., & Peterson, R.A. Personality, and performance - satisfaction of industrial salesmen. Journal of Marketing Research, 1971, 8, 501-504.

Prybil, L.D. Job satisfaction in relation to job performance and occupational level. Personnel Journal, 1973, 52, 94-100.

Quinn, R. Linking in as a Moderator of the Relationships between Job Satisfaction and Mental Health. Ann Arbor, Mich.: Survey Research Center, University of Michigan, 1972.

Ramser, C.D. Performance, satisfaction, effort. Personnel Administration and Public Personnel Review, 1972. 1, 4-8.

Raynor, J.O., & Rubin, I.S. Effects of achievement motivation and future orientation on level of performance. Journal of Personality and Social Psychology, 1971, 17, 36-41.

Reddin, W.J. Managerial Effectiveness. New York: McGraw-Hill, 1970.

Regan, J.F. The relationship between dogmatism and productivity, accuracy and satisfaction in telephone operators: An investigation. Unpublished Doctoral Dissertation, George Washington University, 1968.

Richardson, R. Fair Pay and Work. Carbondale, Ill.: Southern Illinois University Press, 1971.

Roche, W.J., & MacKinnon, M.L. Motivating people with meaningful work. Harvard Business Review, 1970, 48, 97ff.

Rogow, R. Member participation and centralized control. Industrial Relations, 1968, 7, 132-145.

Ronan, W.W. Individual and situational variables relating to job satisfaction. Journal of Applied Psychology, 1970, 54, 1-28.

Ronan, W., Latham, G., & Kinne, S., III. Effects of goal setting and supervision on worker behavior in an industrial situation. Journal of Applied Psychology, 1973, 58, 302-307.

Rosen, N.A. Leadership Change and Work Group Dynamics. Ithaca, N.Y.: Cornell University Press, 1969.

Rosen, S.M. Two parts of the working class: Nixon, pro and con. Social Policy, 1973, July-August, 2-15.

Rosen, S.M., et al. Training Incentive Payments Program. A Report to the U.S. Department of Labor from the Institute of Public Administration, 1973.

Rosenbaum, L.L., & Rosenbaum, W.B. Morale and productivity consequences of group leadership styles, stress, and type of task. Journal of Applied Psychology, 1971, 55, 343-348.

Rosenblatt, O., & Suchman, E.A. Blue-collar attitudes and information toward health and illness. In A.B. Shostak & W. Gomberg, (Eds.), Blue-Collar World: Studies of the American Worker. Englewood Cliffs, N.J.: Prentice-Hall, Inc., 1964.

Rosow, J.M. Now is the time for productivity bargaining. Harvard Business Review, 1972, 50, 78-89.

Rush, H.M.F., & McGrath, P.S. Transactional analysis moves into corporate training. Conference Board Record, 1973, July, 38-44.

Ryan, T.A. Intentional Behavior: An Approach to Human Motivation. New York: Ronald, 1970.

Sales, S.M. Organizational role as a risk factor in coronary disease. Administrative Science Quarterly, 1969, 14, 325-336.

Sales, S.M., & House, J. Job dissatisfaction as a possible risk factor in coronary heart disease. Journal of Chronic Diseases, 1971, 23.

Salomone, R., & Muthard, J.. Canonical correlations of vocational needs and vocational style. Journal of Vocational Behavior, 1972, 2, 167-171.

Salter, M. What is fair pay for the executives? Harvard Business Review, 1972, 50 (3), 6-13.

Sayles, L.R. Managing human resources for higher productivity. Conference Board Record, 1973, 57-58.

Schachter, S., Willerman, B., Festinger, L., & Hyman, R. Emotional disruption and industrial productivity. Journal of Applied Psychology, 1961, 45, 201-215.

Schmitt, D. Punitive supervision and productivity. Journal of Applied Psychology, 1969, 53, 118-123.

Schneider, B., & Alderfer, C. Three studies of measures of need satisfaction in organizations. Administrative Science Quarterly, 1973, 18, 489-505.

Schneider, B., Hall, D., & Nygren, H. Self image and job characteristics as correlates of changing organizational identification. Human Relations, 1971, 24, 397-416.

Schoderbek, P.O., & Reif, W.E. Job Enlargement: Key to Improved Performance. Ann Arbor: Graduate School of Administration, University of Michigan, 1969.

Schultz, G.P. Worker participation in production problems. Personnel, 1951, 28, 201-210.

Schwab, D.P., & Dyer, L.D. The motivational impact of a compensation system on employee performance. Organizational Behavior and Human Performance, 1972, 9, 215-225.

Schwyhart, W.R., & Smith, P.C. Factors in the job involvement of middle managers. Journal of Applied Psychology, 1972, 56, 227-233.

Sewall, D.O. Training the Poor: A Benefit-Cost Analysis of Manpower Programs in the U.S. Antipoverty Program. Kingston, Ont.: Industrial Relations Center, Queen's University, 1971.

Shepard, J.M. Functional specialization and work attitudes. Industrial Relations Research, 1969, 8, 185-194.

Sheppard, H.L. A Simple Simon's partial list of issues about the current controversies surrounding the quality of working life. Paper presented at the 25th meeting of the Industrial Research Association, Toronto, 1972.

Sirota, D., & Wolfson, A.D. Job enrichment: What are the obstacles? Personnel, 1972(a) (May-June), 8-17.

Sirota, D., & Wolfson, A.D. Job enrichment: Surmounting the obstacles. Personnel, 1972(b) (July-August), 8-19.

Slezak, L. Effects of changes in payment system on productivity in Sweden. Monthly Labor Review, 1973, 96 (3), 51-52.

Slocum, J.W., Jr. Performance and satisfaction: An analysis. Industrial Relations, 1970, 9, 431-436.

Slocum, J.W.  Motivation in managerial levels:  Relationships of need satisfaction to job performance.  Journal of Applied Psychology, 1971, 55, 312-316.

Slocum, J.W., & Missauk, M.J.  Job satisfaction and productivity. Personnel Administration, 1970, 33, 52-58.

Slocum, J.W., & Topichak, P.M.  Do cultural differences affect job satisfaction?  Journal of Applied Psychology, 1972, 56, 177-178.

Smith, C.G., & Brown, M.  Communication structure and control structure in a voluntary organization.  Sociometry, 1964, 27, 449-468.

Smith, C.G., & Tannenbaum, A.S.  Some implications of a leadership and control for effectiveness in a voluntary association. Human Relations, 1965, 18, 265-272.

Smith, E.A., & Gude, G.F.  Reevaluation of the Scanlon Plan as a motivational technique.  Personnel Journal, 1971, 50, 916-919.

Smith, P.C., & Lem, C.  Positive aspects of motivation in repetitive work:  Effects of lot size upon spacing of voluntary work stoppages.  Journal of Applied Psychology, 1955, 39, 330-333.

Smith, R.C., Cobb, B.B., & Collin, W.E.  Attitudes and motivations of air traffic controllers in terminal areas.  Aerospace Medicine, 1972, 43, 1-5.

Sobel, R.S.  Tests of pre-performance and post-performance models of satisfaction with outcomes.  Journal of Social Psychology, 1944, 19, 213-221.

Starcevich, M.  Job factor importance for job satisfaction and dissatisfaction across different occupational levels.  Journal of Applied Psychology, 1972, 56, 467-471.

Steinberg, E.  Upward mobility of low-income workers.  A report to the U.S. Department of Labor from the Institute of Public Administration, New York, 1973.

Stern, G.G.  People in Context:  Measuring Person-Environment Congruence in Education and Industry.  New York:  Wiley, 1970.

Stetson, D.  For many concerns:  An inadvertent 4 day week.  New York Times, May 14, 1972.

Stoner, A., Dram, J., & Rubin, I.  Factors associated  with effective performance in overseas work assignments.  Personnel Psychology, 1972, 25, 303-138.

Strauss, P.J. Job satisfaction and productivity of engineers and scientists. Perceptual and Motor Skills, 1966, 23, 471-476.

Stroh, T.F. Managing the New Generation in Business. New York: McGraw-Hill, 1971.

Student, K.R. Supervisory influence and work-group performance. Journal of Applied Psychology, 1968, 52, 188-194.

Susman, G. The impact of automation on work-group autonomy and task specialization. Human Relations, 1970, 26, 567-577.

Susman, G. Process design, automation, and worker alienation. Industrial Relations, 1972, 12, 34-45.

Swadas, H. On the Line. Washington, D.C.: United States Department of Labor's Manpower Division, 1966.

Tannenbaum, A.S. (Ed.). Control in Organizations. New York: McGraw-Hill, 1968.

Tannenbaum, A.S., & Smith, C.G. Effects of member influence on organization. Journal of Abnormal and Social Psychology, 1964, 69, 401-410.

Taub, R.P. Bureaucrats Under Stress. Berkeley: University of California Press, 1969.

Taylor, J.C. Some effects of technology in organizational change. Human Relations, 1971(a), 24, 104-123.

Taylor, J.C. Technology and Planned Organizational Change. Ann Arbor, Mich.: Institute for Social Research, University of Michigan, 1971(b).

Taylor, J.C., et al. The Quality of Working Life: An Annotated Bibliography. Los Angeles: Graduate School of Management, U.C.L.A., undated. (Mimeo)

Taylor, L.K. Not for Bread Alone: An Appreciation of Job Enrichment. London: Business Books, 1972.

Terkel, S. Working. New York: Pantheon, 1974.

Torin, N. The bus driver: A study in role analysis. Human Relations, 1973, 26, 101-112.

Tornow, W.W. The development and applications of an input-outcome moderator test on the perception and reduction of equity. Organizational Behavior and Human Performance, 1972, 6, 614-638.

Tosi, H. Effect of the interaction of leader behavior and subordinate authoritarianism. Proceedings of the American Psychological Association Convention, 1971, 6, 473.

Tripp, L. (Ed.). Productivity: A Social and Economic Analysis. Industrial Relations Research Association, 1951.

Tseng, M.S. Need for achievement as a determinant of job proficiency, employability, and training satisfaction of vocational rehabilitation clients. Journal of Vocational Behavior, 1972, 2, 301-309.

Uhlaner, J. Human performance, effectiveness, and the systems measurement bed. Journal of Applied Psychology, 1972, 56, 202-210.

Ullrich, R.A. A Theoretical Model of Human Behavior in Organizations: An Eclectic Approach. Morristown: General Loaning Corporation, 1972.

Van Beck, H.G. The influence of assembly line organization on output, quality, and morale. Occupational Psychology, 1964, 38, 161-172.

Van Zelst, R.H. Sociometrically selected work teams increase production. Personnel Psychology, 1952, 5, 175-185.

Veen, P. Effects of participative decision making in field hockey training: A field experiment. Organizational Behavior and Human Performance, 1972, 7, 288-307.

Veroff, J., & Feld, S. Marriage and Work in America: A Study of Motives and Roles. New York: Van Nostrand, Reinhold, Co., 1970.

Viteles, M.S. The two faces of applied psychology. International Review of Applied Psychology, 1969, 18, 5-10.

Vroom, V.H. Ego-involvement, job satisfaction and job performance. Personnel Psychology, 1962, 15, 159-177.

Vroom, V., Grant, L., & Cotton, T. The consequences of social interaction in group problem solving. Organizational Behavior and Human Performance, 1969, 4, 77-95.

Waener, H.A., & Rubin, I.M. Motivation of research and development of entrepreneurs. Journal of Applied Psychology, 1969, 53, 178-184.

Wall, T. Ego defensiveness as a determinant of reported differences in sources of job satisfaction and job dissatisfaction. Journal of Applied Psychology, 1973, 58, 125-128.

Walton, R. How to counter alienation in the plant. Harvard Business Review, 1972, 50 (6), 70-81.

Wanous, J. Occupational preferences, perceptions of valences and instrumentality, and objective data. Journal of Applied Psychology, 1972, 56, 152-155.

Waters, L.K., & Waters, C.W. An empirical test of 5 versions of the two-factor theory of job satisfaction. Organizational Behavior and Human Performance, 1972, 7, 18-24.

Wedderburn, D., & Crompton, R. Workers' Attitudes and Technology. London: Cambridge University Press, 1972.

Weick, K.E. The concept of equity in the perception of pay. Administrative Science Quarterly, 1966, 11, 414-439.

Weiner, B., & Krekla, A. An attributional analysis of achievement motivation. Journal of Personality and Social Psychology, 1970, 15, 1-20.

Weinstein, A., & Holzbach, R. Impact of individual differences, reward distribution, and task structure on productivity in a simulated work environment. Journal of Applied Psychology, 1973, 58, 296-301.

Weiss, H., & Sherman, J. Internal-external control as a predictor of task effort and satisfaction subsequent to failure. Journal of Applied Psychology, 1973, 57 (2), 132-137.

Weiss, R.S., & Kahn, R.L. Definitions of Work and Occupations. Social Problems, 1960, 8 (2), 143-151.

Wendt, H.W. Motivation, effort and performance. In McClelland, D.C., (Ed.), Studies in Motivation. New York: Appleton-Century-Crofts, 1955.

Wernimont, P. A systems view of job satisfaction. Journal of Applied Psychology, 1972, 56, 173-176.

White, K.J. Recent research on the Scanlon Plan. Presented at the Annual Convention of the American Psychological Association, Montreal, 1973.

Wiener, Y. The effects of task and ego-oriented performance on two kinds of overcompensation inequity. Organizational Behavior and Human Performance, 1970, 5, 191-208.

Wild, R., & Kampner, T. Influence of community and plant characteristics on job attitudes of manual workers. Journal of Applied Psychology, 1972, 56, 106-113.

Wilensky, H.L. Syllabus of Industrial Relations. Chicago: University of Chicago Press, 1954.

Wilensky, H. Work as a social problem. In H.S. Becker (Ed.), Social Problems: A Modern Approach. New York: Wiley, 1966.

Williams, W., & Seiler, D. Relationship between measures of effort and job performance. Journal of Applied Psychology, 1973, 51, 49-54.

Wilson, G., Turnstall, O., & Eysenck, H. Measurement of motivation in predicting industrial performance: A study of apprentice gas fitters. Occupational Psychology, 1972, 46, 15-24.

Wofford, J.C. Managerial behavior, situational factors, and productivity and morale. Administrative Science Quarterly, 1971(a), 16, 10-18.

Wofford, J.C. The motivational basis of job satisfaction and job performance. Personnel Psychology, 1971(b), 24, 501-518.

Wolf, M.G. Need gratification theory: A theoretical reformulation of job satisfaction/dissatisfaction and job motivation. Journal of Applied Psychology, 1970, 54, 87-94.

Wood, D.A. Background characteristics and work values distinguishing satisfaction levels among engineers. Journal of Applied Psychology, 1971, 55, 537-547.

Wood, I., & Lawler, E.E. The effect of piece rate overpayment on productivity. Journal of Applied Psychology, 1970, 54, 234-238.

Yukl, G., Wexley, K.N., & Seymore, J.D. Effectiveness of pay incentives under variable ratio and continuous reinforcement schedules. Journal of Applied Psychology, 1972, 56, 19-23.

Zander, A. Motives and Goals in Groups. New York: Academic Press, 1971.

Zander, A., & Armstrong, W. Working for group pride in a slipper factory. Journal of Applied Social Psychology, 1972, 2, 293-307.

Zdep, S. Intra-group reinforcement and its effects on leadership behavior. Organizational Behavior and Human Performance, 1969, 4, 284-298.

# GLOSSARY

(Terms marked * are cross-referenced elsewhere in the Glossary.)

ATTITUDE.  A concept which a person has of something (such as a job), embodying in addition to a belief about its nature the elements of how much it is liked, or disliked and whether one is disposed to approach or avoid it.

AUTONOMOUS WORK GROUPS.  A practice in which work groups* are given relatively high responsibility for determining production methods and the jobs and tasks to be carried out by group members.  It combines elements of job enrichment,* participation,* and often group incentives.*

AVOIDANCE.  Same as withdrawal.*

COMPENSATION.  Monetary rewards provided by organizations in exchange for employees' services.  Also called pay.

CONTROL.  The degree to which the views or behavior of one person or group shape the views or behavior of another person or group.  As used here, the term is equivalent to influence.

CONTROL GRAPH.  A technique for charting the level and distribution of control* among various segments or levels of an organization.

CORRELATION.  A statistical term referring to the extent to which two variables or measures parallel each other, i.e., whether the scores which individuals or groups obtain on one measure (e.g., job satisfaction) are indicative of how high or low they perform in terms of some other variable (e.g., absenteeism).  The correlation coefficient is an index of the closeness and direction of correlation, and ranges from +1.00 (perfect positive relationship), through 0.00 (no relationship), to -1.00 (perfect inverse relationship).

EMPLOYEE.  Same as worker.*

EXTERNAL VALIDITY.  See validity.*

GOAL.  That object or condition with respect to which the behavior of individuals or groups is directed.  The terms reward* and incentive* are sometimes considered as equivalent.  However, in connection with organizations, the term goal is usually applied to a prescribed objective of work, whereas rewards and incentives are need-fulfilling things or conditions, received or attained by the person through working.  Ideally, the attainment of goals should result also in reward for the individual.

INCENTIVE. See reward.* Also, sometimes used loosely to mean incentive plan,* or the compensation* received from such a plan.

INCENTIVE PLAN. A system of financial compensation* in which workers' earnings are proportional to quantity of production.* There are a number of such plans varying in specifics, but they can be classified under two broad headings: individual and group, i.e., where earnings are proportional either to the worker's own output or that of some group of which he is a member.

INFLUENCE. Same as control.*

INTERNAL VALIDITY. See validity.*

JOB ENLARGEMENT. An increase in the variety or diversity of activities of a job, with the object of making it more satisfying and motivating to the worker. Distinguished by some from job enrichment,* in that the latter emphasizes challenge more than diversity.

JOB ENRICHMENT. The change in the content or activities of a job in a manner that increases its level of responsibility, challenge, meaningfulness, etc., with the object of making it intrinsically more satisfying and motivating to the worker. Distinguished by some from job enlargement,* in that the latter emphasized diversity more than challenge.

JOB INVOLVEMENT. How salient or important a person's job is to him, including the importance of performing it well. This is an aspect of work motivation.*

JOB REDESIGN. Change in the nature or scope of activities comprised by a job, with the object of making it more satisfying and motivating to the worker. Includes either or both job enlargement* and job enrichment.* Distinguished from methods or time study and from work rationalization in that those processes are addressed primarily to facilitating the ability of workers to perform their jobs rather than their motivation or satisfaction.

JOB SATISFACTION. How a person feels about his job, in terms of how much he likes or dislikes it. It is the evaluative component of one's job attitude,* and is usually measured by a questionnaire or interview.

MANAGEMENT BY OBJECTIVES. A form of participation* in which a worker and his supervisor collaborate periodically in setting objectives to be attained in his work, in evaluating his attainment of objectives set previously, and in considering what can be done to assist his goal attainment. The method has typically been employed with managerial rather than rank-and-file employees.

MOTIVATION. The processes determining what a person will try to do and
how hard he will try to do it. These processes partly depend on
characteristics of the person, of the situation, and on the
relation between the two. Successful efforts are those which
attain rewards,* at least in a humane system. In this sense,
motivation is a key both to high performance* and job satisfaction* at work.

OPINION. The verbal expression of an attitude.*

OUTPUT. Same as production.*

PARTICIPATION. A loosely used term referring to a number of related
practices, the common denominator being a relatively high level
of mutual influence among organization members. In essence, workers at all levels have a voice in plans and decision relating to
their work. Other terms employed to refer to this type of control*
pattern are participative management, participative decision-making,
industrial democracy, and similar phrases.

PAY. Same as compensation.*

PERFORMANCE. The behavior of workers, groups, or organizations, especially with respect to some standard or goal.* In addition to output or
production,* the performance of workers might be considered in
terms of absenteeism, turnover, or the like.

POWER. Potential control* or influence. A person or group may have
power to affect other persons or groups, but unless the power is
exercised no control or influence occurs.

PRODUCTION. A measure of the goods or services generated by work. It
includes both quantitative and qualitative aspects, such as number
of clients served or percentage of units produced which are defective
Less tangible aspects of production would include customer satisfaction or ratings of workmanship. Also called output.

PRODUCTIVITY. Technically, the ratio of output to input. Output (or
production) may be expressed in various ways, such as in dollars of
sales or number of units produced. Input may also refer to any one
of various investments required to produce the output, such as man-
hours of work or dollars of capital investment. In this report, the
focus is usually on labor productivity, i.e., amount of production
per man-hour.
The term productivity is often employed non-technically as meaning
production* or performance.*

QUALITY OF WORKING LIFE. A combination of job satisfaction,* job involvement* and motivation,* and the experience of balance between work
and other aspects of a person's life. A person may be said to experience high quality of working life when he (i) has positive feelings toward his job; (ii) is motivated to stay on it and do it well;
and (iii) feels that it fits with the other requirements that life
makes of him, i.e., as a family member, citizen, etc.

REWARD. An object or condition which meets a need or fulfills a desire.
Subjectively, its attainment is accompanied by feelings of pleasure.
Objectively, its attainment serves to elicit in the future the same
behavior which was rewarded; in this sense, behavior can be said to
be directed toward obtaining rewards or pleasure. In a technical
psychological sense, the term incentive* or positive incentive is
often regarded as meaning the same as reward. However, in organizational settings, incentive has come to connote officially bestowed
rewards, especially financial ones.

SOCIO-TECHNICAL SYSTEM. An integrated arrangement of material and human
resources developed to produce goods or services, with special attention to facilitating smooth and effective relations among workers*
and technology.* In a system, parts are inter-related, so that
something affecting one has repercussions in other parts.

STATISTICAL SIGNIFICANCE. A mathematical assessment of the dependability
or reliability of an obtained result or finding. Conventionally, a
finding (e.g., a correlation coefficient* of a given size) is considered to be statistically significant if the odds are less than 1
in 20 that it could have occurred by chance.

TECHNOLOGY. The system of procedures, equipment, and resources used to
produce goods or services.

VALIDITY OF A STUDY. Refers to the credibility of the results of a study,
i.e., the extent to which they are likely to be true or accurate.
Validity has two aspects, internal and external. Internal validity
depends on whether the design of the study took adequate precautions
against error or distortion, including the use of dependable data,
control groups, etc. External validity refers to whether the findings are applicable to other situations, or whether the conditions
under which they were obtained restrict their meaning to the kind of
situation studied.

WITHDRAWAL. Behavior by which a worker dissociates himself from his job
temporarily or permanently. Absenteeism and turnover are the most
frequently studied forms. Also sometimes called avoidance.*

WORK GROUP. A set of workers who have one or more common goals* to accomplish in their work and are therefore to some degree interdependent.
Ordinarily, they have the same supervisor and are in direct communication with him and with one another.

WORKER. A person employed by an organization to perform specified activities. As used in this report, the term embraces organization members at both managerial and non-managerial levels, at various skill levels, and performing either manual or intellectual activities. Same as employee.*

# AUTHOR INDEX

Adams, J.S., 299, 301, 303, 304.

Allport, F.H., 228, 252.

Andrews, I.R., 304, 308-309.

Armstrong, T.B., 297.

Arrowwood, A.J., 304.

Athanasiou, R., 124, 150.

Babchuk, N. 318, 319.

Bachman, J.G., 240-241, 258.

Barnes, L.B., 253-256, 258.

Barrett, G.V., 310-311.

Barrett, R.S., 143, 271-273.

Bass, B.M., 318-319.

Beach, D.N. 210.

Beer, M., 329, 350-355.

Belcher, D.W., 291.

Bishop, R.C., 162-164, 179, 181.

Blauner, R., 148.

Blood, M.R., 143, 174.

Bluestone, I., 268.

Bowers, D.G., 224-225, 234,
    239-240, 258, 272-273,
    336-350.

Bracht, G.H., 164.

Brayfield, A.H., 124, 150.

Brogden, H., 63.

Brown, M.E., 266-267.

Buchsbaum, H.J., 274-275.

Bugental, D.E., 176.

Burke, R.J., 141.

Cammann, C., 326-327.

Campbell, D.T., 132.

Campbell, H., 327.

Campbell, J.P., 141, 300.

Cantril, H., 295.

Capwell, D.F., 124, 150.

Carpenter, H.H., 247-248.

Carroll, S.J., Jr., 210, 215-217,
    218-219.

Carzo, R., 248.

Case, J., 199, 209, 262.

Centers, R., 176, 295.

Chamberlain, N.W., 274.

Christensen, C.R., 300.

Clark, J.V., 306.

Coch, L., 221-222, 230, 231, 234,
    253.

Coleman, J.R., 262.

Conference Board, The, 331.

Crockett, W.H., 124, 150.

Cummings, L.L., 124, 125.

Cureton, E.E.,  271-272.

Dale, E.,  262-266.

Dalton, G.W.,  249, 253-256, 258.

Dalton, M.,  321.

Davis, L.E.,  135-136, 168-170, 178, 179, 185.

Dettleback, W., 165, 167.

Dickson, W.J., 320, 321.

Donnelly, J.H., 218.

Dubin, R., 204.

Dunnette, M.D., 141, 288, 290, 291-293, 294, 300, 302-303, 304, 305, 319, 328.

Ellis, N.,  318-319.

Emery, F.E., 336.

Etzioni, E., 202.

Evans, E.E.,  297.

Ewen, R.B.,  141.

Faden, J.A.,  304.

Farris, G.,  243-244, 258.

Fein, M.,  149, 174, 183, 186, 320, 322, 335, 364.

Feld, S.,  150.

Fitzpatrick, S., 141, 293-294.

Flamholtz, E.,  63.

Fleishman, E.A.,  204, 230-231, 234.

Ford, R.N.,  158-161, 179, 181.

Form, W.  148.

Foulkes, F.K.,  185.

Fox, J.B.,  265.

Frederiksen, N., 164.

French, J.R.P., Jr., 211-214, 221-222, 229-230, 231, 234, 253.

Friedlander, F., 141, 176.

Friedman, A., 304.

Frost, C.F., 244, 252, 258, 321, 355, 357-361, 363-364.

Gay, E.G.,  175.

Gellerman, S.W.,  292-293.

Gery, G.J.,  320.

Ghiselli, E.E.,  290.

Giles, B.A.,  310-311.

Glaser, E.M.,  153, 166, 170, 185, 190, 194, 335, 358, 361-362.

Glass, G.V.,  164.

Gomberg, W.,  235, 322.

Goodale, J.G., 176.

Goode, W.J.,  318, 319.

Goodman, P.S.,  304.

Gottlieb, B.,  274-275, 276.

Greene, C.N.,  311-313.

Guest, R.H.,  148, 270-271, 297.

Guion, R.M.,  252.

Gurin, G.,  150.

Hackman, J.R., 136-137, 144, 146-147, 155-158, 174, 175, 179, 180, 181, 232-233, 234, 253.

Haire, M., 290.

Hakel, M.D., 141.

Hall, D., 145-146, 179, 181.

Harbison, F.H., 262.

Head, K.B., 124, 150.

Healy, J.J., 267, 320.

Henle, P., 274.

Henry, M.M., 308-309.

Herrick, N.Q., 148-149, 176, 198.

Herzberg, F., 124, 136, 140-142, 150, 152, 179, 180, 185-186, 226, 291-292, 297.

Hickson, D.J., 322.

Hill, A.S., 151.

Hill, J.W., 162-164, 179, 181.

Hinrichs, J.R., 141, 311.

Homans, G.C., 204, 299, 305.

House, R.J., 297.

Hulin, C.L., 141, 143, 174, 227, 297.

Hunnius, G., 199, 209, 262.

Hunt, J.G., 204.

Hunt, R.G., 249.

Hurder, W.P., 318-319.

Huse, E.F., 350-355.

Indik, B., 245-246.

Ivancevich, J.M., 218, 219, 241.

Jacobsen, P., 304.

Jaques, E., 300.

James, J., 299.

Janson, R., 166-168, 179, 180, 181.

Jeffrey, T.E., 328-329.

Jenkins, O.J., 199, 207, 209, 262, 269.

Jones, G., 224-225.

Jones, L.V., 328-329.

Jorgenson, D.O., 302-303, 304, 305.

Kahn, R.L., 129, 150, 202, 222-223, 248-249.

Karasick, B., 251-253, 258.

Katz, D., 129, 202, 222-223, 248-249.

Katzell, R.A., 124, 143, 150, 248-249, 260, 271-272, 303.

Kaufman, S., 155-158, 175, 179, 180, 181.

Kay, E., 211-214.

Kejner, M., 147, 228.

Kendall, L.M., 227, 295.

Kennedy, J.E., 143.

Kerr, W.A., 268, 274-275, 276, 298.

Koplin, C.A., 304.

Kornhauser, A., 148.

Kraft, W.P., Jr., 165-166, 167, 179.

Laseau, V.N., 297.

Lawler, E.E., 136-137, 144, 145-146, 146-147, 155-158, 174, 175, 179, 180, 232-233, 234, 246, 253, 388, 290, 295-299, 300, 304, 316-317, 318, 319, 324-325, 326-327, 328, 329, 330, 331.

Lawrence, L., 230, 234, 253.

Lawrence, P.R., 142-143, 174, 175, 179, 180.

Lesieur, F.G., 321, 355, 362-363.

Leukart, R.H., 291.

Leventhal, G.S., 331.

Levine, E.L., 260.

Lichtman, C.M., 249.

Likert, R., 63, 224, 225, 261, 336, 341-342.

Lincoln, J.F., 321.

Livernash, R.E., 267.

Locke, E.A., 141, 220.

Lodahl, T.M., 147, 228.

Lowin, A., 207, 235-236, 249, 260.

Lyon, H.L., 218.

Macy, B.A., 63.

Maher, J.R., 164, 179, 181.

Mahler, W.R., 210.

Mann, F., 204, 298.

March, J.G., 124, 324.

Marriott, R., 319.

Marrow, A.J., 221, 231-232, 253, 272-273, 336-350.

Mathewson, S.B., 321.

Mausner, B., 124, 140-142, 150, 152, 179, 180, 291-292, 297.

McCormick, C.P., 261.

McCullogh, M.R., 9, 124.

Merrihue, W.V., 150.

Merton, R.K., 76-77.

Metzger, B.L., 320, 321.

Metzner, H., 298.

Meyer, H.H., 211-214.

Miles, R.E., 249-250, 258.

Miller, D.C., 204.

Mirvis, P.H., 63.

Mischkind, L.A., 141.

Morse, N.C., 175, 222-224, 225, 234, 253.

Myers, M.S., 185.

National Industrial Conference Board, 269, 270.

O'Gara, P.W., 304.

Olson, L.K., 298, 229.

O'Neil, H.E., 143.

Opsahl, R.L., 288, 290, 291-293, 294, 319, 328.

Oster, A., 226-228, 234.

Otis, J.L., 291.

Parker, T.C., 143, 271-272.

Patchen, M., 143-145, 179, 180, 300, 306-308, 309.

Penner, D.D., 297, 328.

Peterson, R.O., 124, 150.

Porter, L.W., 246, 248, 290, 296, 298-299, 324-325, 326-327.

Powell, R.M., 225-226, 234.

Powers, J.E., 195.

Pritchard, R.D., 251-253, 258, 302-303, 304, 305, 329-330.

Purcell, T.V., 9, 275-277.

Quinn, R.P., 124, 150.

Raia, A.P., 214-215.

Reimer, E., 222-224, 225, 234, 253.

Research Institute of America, 320.

Ritchie, J.R., 249-250, 258.

Roach, D., 151.

Roach, J.M., 261.

Robinson, J.P., 124, 150.

Roethlisberger, F.J., 300, 320, 321.

Rosen, H., 277.

Rosenbaum, W.B., 304.

Rosenstein, E., 260, 268-269.

Rosow, J.M., 268, 274, 335.

Rothe, H., 317.

Roy, D., 321.

Ruh, R., 228-229, 234, 244, 252, 258, 321, 355, 357-361, 363-364.

Rush, H.M.F., 153, 161-162, 170-173, 179, 181, 186, 189, 191, 192, 193, 196, 197, 206, 261.

Salpukas, A., 268.

Sayles, L.R., 300, 364.

Schlacter, I., 225-226, 234.

Scheflen, K., 233.

Schneider, B., 298, 329.

Schwab, D.P., 124, 125, 325-327.

Scott, J.F., 265.

Seashore, S.E., 224-225, 234, 272-273, 336-350.

Shepard, J.M., 148, 174.

Sheppard, H.L., 148-149, 176, 198.

Sibson, R.F., 291.

Siegel, A., 228-229, 234.

Simon, H.A., 124, 324.

Slesinger, J.A., 240-241, 258.

Smith, C.G., 205, 224-225, 237-238, 240-241, 242-243, 246-247, 258.

Smith, P.C., 141, 176, 227, 230, 234, 295, 297.

Snoek, J.D., 150.

Snyderman, B., 140-142, 152, 179, 180, 291-292, 297.

Sorcher, M., 230, 234, 252.

Slichter, S.J., 267.

Stagner, R., 275.

Staines, G.L., 9, 124.

Stefflre, B., 175.

Stogdill, R.M., 204.

Strauss, G., 260, 268-269, 364.

Sturmthal, A., 262, 267.

Survey Research Center, 3, 149-150, 271, 295-297.

Tannenbaum, A.S., 203-204, 205, 228, 237-239, 241-242, 244, 246, 252, 258, 266, 267-268.

Taylor, E.K., 63.

Taylor, F.W., 316.

Thickett, J.M.B., 151.

Tosi, H.L., 210, 215-217, 218-219.

Trist, E.L., 336.

Turner, A.N., 142-143, 174, 175, 179, 180.

U.S. Department of Health, Education and Welfare, 3, 150, 153, 170, 199, 209, 335.

U.S. Department of Labor, Bureau of Labor Statistics, 84.

Valfer, E.S., 168-170, 178, 179.

Van Zelst, R.H., 298.

Veroff, J., 150.

Viteles, M.S., 317, 322.

Vroom, V.H., 124, 150, 227, 228, 252, 299.

Wakeley, J.H., 244, 252, 258, 321, 355, 357-361, 363-364.

Walker, C.R., 148, 270-271, 297.

Walsh, W.B., 249.

Walters, R.E., 185.

Walton, E., 141.

Wass, D.L., 281-282.

Waters, K., 151.

Weeks, D.A., 331.

Weick, K.E., 164, 300.

Weiss, D.J., 250-251, 252, 258.

Weiss, R.S., 175.

Wernimont, P.F., 141, 293-294, 297.

Whyte, W.F., 290, 319, 321, 322.

Wigdor, L.A., 297.

Wijting, J.P., 176.

Wikstrom, W.S., 210, 218.

Wild, R., 151.

Wolfe, D.M., 150.

Wollock, S., 176.

Worthy, J.C., 248.

Wyatt, S., 317.

Yankelovich, D., 176.

Yanouzas, J.W., 248.

Young, T.F., 304.

Zaleznik, A., 253-256, 258, 300.

Zedeck, S., 251.

425

## SUBJECT INDEX

✓ Absenteeism, 142-43, 144, 145, 146, 147, 150-51, 153, 157, 161, 166, 167, 169, 172, 178, 227, 298, 313, 353, 363

Absolute pay level, 295-299, 313

Action research, 60-61

Administrative management theory, 198

Advancement, 140, 144, 147, 151-52, 174, 175, 176

Age, and work trends, 176-77

Alienation, 174

American work ethic, erosion of, 91-92

Authoritarian work organization, 59-60

Authority, 158, 176, 367

   definition, 202, 204

Automation, and "Second Industrial Revolution," 3

Autonomous work groups, 12, 31, 34-35, 61, 101, 165, 208, 351

Autonomy  See under Worker

Avoidance  See Withdrawal

Benefits, shared, principle of, 26-27, 28, 29-30, 56, 57, 68

Blue-collar worker, 8, 174-77, 182

"Bread-and-butter" rewards  See "Hygiene" Factors

Capability, worker, 38, 128, 135, 363

Career structures, 39

Careers  See Advancement

Co-determination, 32

✓ Collective bargaining, 263, 267-82

Compensation, patterns of, 6, 7, 26-27, 36, 38, 127, 129, 177, 186, 288-335

   absolute pay level and job satisfaction, 295-299, 313

   conclusions, 332-35

   pay increases, 309-13

   pay plans, 315-32

   psychological meaning of money, 291-94

   relative pay levels, 299-309, 314

Control

   definition, 201, 204

   distribution of, 6, 7, 204-5

   domain of, 206-7

   scope of, 206

   worker, 136, 144, 145, 146, 149-50, 151, 156, 160, 161, 164, 165, 166, 168, 176, 177, 185
   See also Worker, autonomy

Control graph, defined, 205-06

Control, patterns of, 31-36, 127, 129, 300-87

    conclusions, 285-87

    in individual job, 33-34

    Management by Objectives, 209-21

    theory of organizational control, 200-09

    in work groups, 34-35, 221-36

    in work organization, 35-36, 236-85

Core dimensions, of jobs, 136-37, 144, 146, 147, 177

Corning Glass study, of system-wide changes, 350-55

"Critical Mass" Principle, and productivity/job satisfaction link, 24-25, 28-29


Decision-making, participation in, 17, 39, 68, 90, 92, 93, 177, 185, 186, 351, 358, 367 See also Control, patterns of

Democratization See Control, patterns of; Decision-making

Disincentives, undoing, as legislative goal, 50-51, 53

Diversity, in jobs, 136, 144, 146, 151, 156, 158, 162, 164, 166, 177, 184, 185


Economic security, as legislative goal, 50, 52

Education, post secondary school, 51-52, 53

Employee relations, 39 See also Labor-management relations

Equity See Relative pay


Feedback, in jobs, 136, 144, 145, 146, 147, 156, 166, 167, 171, 173, 177, 185, 351

Financial compensation See Compensation, pattern of; Pay

Fringe benefits, 36, 39, 98 See also "Hygiene" factors

Full Employment Act of 1946, 47-48

Funding, government, 48-50


Government, role of, in system-wide changes, 46-53

    funding, 48-50

    legislation, 50-53

    setting directions and goals, 46

✓ Grievances, employee, 16, 169, 171, 173

Group incentive plans, 319-20

Growth opportunity, 140, 144, 147, 151-52, 174, 175, 176


Health, worker, 149-50

Horizontal loading, 136 See also Diversity

Human relations, 18, 93, 140, 186

"Hygiene" Factors, 39, 55-56, 68, 136, 141, 162, 182, 183, 185

"I Am" plan, 170-73

Identity, in jobs, 136, 137, 144, 145, 146, 151, 156, 162, 164, 166, 177, 185, 360-61

Industrial Revolution, 3

Incentive programs, 52, 53, 92, 93, 94, 351, 358

group, 319-20

individual, 316-19

organization-wide, 320-21

See also Compensation, Pay plans

Influence See Control

Institutes, free-standing, role of, in system-wide changes, 64-77

accelerating consensus, 65-66

applications research, 72-74

demonstration projects, 74-75

expertise as resource, 75-76

as information clearing-houses, 71-72

measurement tools, developing, 66-71

Interaction, 146, 147, 156, 177, 184

Job challenge, 145, 151, 152, 158, 166, 177, 184

Job content, 140, 153, 163, 165, 176, 184, 186

Job design, 6, 7, 27-31, 36, 61, 127, 351

case reports, 187-97

general conclusions, 177-86

studies of, 137-40

correlational, 140-52

intervention, 152-73

theory of, 134-37

and worker characteristics, 174-77

Job difficulty See Job challenge

Job enlargement, 27, 31, 136, 153, 162, 163, 165-66, 177, 178, 17 80, 181, 182, 367 See also Jc design

Job enrichment, 12, 18, 27, 32, 95 136, 153, 162, 164, 166, 170-7 177, 181, 183, 185, 186 See also Job design

Job involvement, 360-61

Job performance, 128-29 See also Worker performance

Job satisfaction, 3, 5-9, 11-14, 1 20, 23-24, 37, 128

assumptions of management and union officials, 15-22, 81-

distinction between motivation and, 25-26, 69, 94

effective systems, 38-40

job design and, 27-31, 134-97

methods of improving, beliefs about, 97-99, 100, 113

Job satisfaction (continued)

and patterns of compensation, 36, 295-299, 313, 328-30

and patterns of control, 31, 36, 200-87

-productivity link, 17, 23-25, 124-34

study and theories of, 124-34

and system-wide studies, 335-68

Job security, 14, 29, 36, 39, 98

Job specialization, 148-49, 174
See also Diversity

Labor-management committees, 262-67, 284

Labor-management relations, 29, 32, 35-36, 40, 68, 98

bearing on productivity, 95-97, 102, 117-23

cooperation, in changing work system, 55, 61, 62, 66

See also Management; Unions

Leadership, definition, 202-3

Legislation, 50-53

Management, 24, 171, 173, 367

adversary relations between workers and, 14, 96, 98

Management (continued)

assumptions regarding worker productivity and job satisfaction, 15-22, 81-123

conclusions, 99-102

factors influencing productivity, 92-112

management-labor relations, 95-97, 114-23

meaning of productivity, 88-89, 103

motivation/job satisfaction/ productivity relationship, 94, 114-16

sample description, 83-86

value of work/productivity, 89-92, 104-8

participative, 12, 31, 209, 260ff., 336, 337

and patterns of control, 203ff.

in system-wide studies, 336ff., 341-42

-union relations, 19, 36  See also  Labor-management relations

Management by Objectives (MBO), 34, 61, 208, 209-21

conclusions, 219-21

miscellaneous studies, 217-19

prototype studies, 211-17

Manpower training, 51, 52

Money, psychological meaning of, 291-94

Motivation, 18-19, 27, 31, 58, 69-71, 101, 113, 128, 360-61, 363

    distinction between work satisfaction and, 25, 69, 94

    and job design, 136

    and patterns of compensation, 288-335

    and patterns of control, 200ff.

    productivity/job satisfaction relationship, 94, 114-16

Non-urban workers, 143, 174-75

Organization-wide incentive plans, 320-21

Organizational structure, definition, 6 _See also_ Work organization

Participative management, 12, 31, 209, 260ff. 336, 337 _See also_ Control, in work organizations

Pay, increased, 17, 27, 29-30, 36, 39, 90, 98, 101, 173, 175, 178, 185, 309-13, 315

Pay levels, 295-314

    absolute, 295-99, 313

    relative, 299-309, 314

Pay plans, 315-32

    miscellaneous aspects of, 330-3

    for performance, 316-30

Performance _See under_ Worker

Personnel management, 4

Power, definition and types of, 201-2 _See also_ Control

Production capability _See_ Capability

Production engineering, 4 _See also_ Work methods

Productivity, 3-9, 11-14, 15-22, 37-38, 46, 124

    definition, 128-29

    and effective systems, 38-40

    factors influencing, 92-93, 101 109-12

    general values and beliefs regarding, 89-92, 99-100, 104-

    and job design, 28, 134-97

    job satisfaction link, 17, 23-2 124-34

    and management/labor relations, 95-97, 102, 117-23

    meaning of, 19-20, 88-89, 99, 1

    motivation/job satisfaction/ productivity relationship, 94, 100, 114-16

    and patterns of compensation, 3 288-335

    and patterns of control, 31-36, 200-87

    and system-wide studies, 335-68

Profit-sharing, 320-21

Promotion  See Advancement

Prototype studies, defined, 131-33


Relative pay levels, 299-309,
    314-15

    field studies, 305-9

    laboratory research, 301-4


Scanlon Plan, 61, 355-65

Scientific management, 3, 124

Social relations, 36  See also
    Human relations

Stewardship, 185

Strikes, and pay satisfaction,
    299, 313

Studies, boundaries of sample
    reviewed, 131-34

Supervision, 39, 98, 140, 168-69,
    339ff., 351

System-wide changes, 36-40

    and labor-management coopera-
        tion, 55, 61, 62

    role of employing organization,
        53-64

    role of free-standing insti-
        tutes, 63-77

    role of government, 46-53

System-wide studies, 335-68

    conclusions, 366-68

    Corning Glass, 350-55

    Scanlon Plan, 355-65

    Weldon Manufacturing, 336-50


Tardiness, 158, 169, 172

Time, revised use of, 39

Turnover, 129, 136, 150-51, 152,
    153, 157, 161, 167, 178, 297-98
    313, 354, 363

Two-Factor theory, 141


Unemployment insurance, 51

Union officials

    assumptions regarding worker
        productivity and job satis-
        faction, 15-22, 81-123

    conclusions, 99-102

        factors influencing produc-
            tivity, 92-93, 109-10,
            111-12

        on management/labor relations,
            95-97, 117-23

        on meaning of productivity,
            88-89, 103

        on motivation/job satisfaction/
            productivity relationship,
            94, 114-16

        sample description, 83-84, 87

        on value of work/productivity,
            89-92, 104-8

Union officials (continued)

attitudes to change, 43-44

participation in changing
work organization, 59

Unions

collective bargaining with,
267-82

company relationships, 274-82

effects of presence or absence
of, 269-74

See also Labor-management relations

Urban workers, 143, 174-75


Validity, of studies, defined, 131

Variables, panels or types of, 127-
30

Vertical loading, 136   See also
Job enrichment


Weldon study, of system-wide change,
336-50

Welfare legislation, 50-51

White-collar worker, 8, 174-77

Withdrawal, 129, 136, 150-51, 152,
153,   See also Absenteeism,
Tardiness, Turnover

Work, general values and beliefs
regarding, 89-92, 104-8   See
also Job

Work cycle time, 151, 177, 184

Work group, patterns of control in
221-36

conclusions, 233-36

miscellaneous studies, 229-33

prototype studies, 221-29

See also Autonomous work groups

Work methods, 38, 39, 135, 159,
163, 168, 186, 367

Work organization, 127, 129

distribution of control in, 35,
208-09, 236-85

formal participation, 260-85

as open system, 129

role of, in increasing productivity and job satisfaction,
53-64

Work rationalization, 135

Work systems, 37

ingredients of effective, 38-40
See also System-wide changes
System-wide studies

Worker

adversary relationship between
management and, 14, 96, 98,

alienation, 174

autonomy, 31, 32, 33-34, 125, 12
136, 144, 145, 146, 149-50,
151, 156, 160, 161, 164, 165
166, 168, 176, 177, 185, 207

characteristics, and job redesign, 174-77

dissatisfaction, 17, 91, 100

performance, 26, 28, 37, 38, 92,
126, 298-99, 367, 313

Worker (continued)

retraining, 51

in system-wide studies, 340-41, 346-48

and work, matching, 38-39, 127, 135

Worker-task system, 126

Working conditions, 18, 29, 39, 93, 98, 140, 175

Working life, quality of, 3, 4, 11, 14, 16, 18, 20, 21, 46, 64, 93, 95, 100, 363

definition, 70

measuring, 69-71

*16*

16